Republicanism and Political Theory

To Anna Hewitson Laborde and Kaja Bakken Maynor
who were born as this book was being prepared
and Elias Bakken Maynor
who was there from the start

Republicanism and Political Theory

edited by

Cécile Laborde and John Maynor

Blackwell
Publishing

BLACKWELL PUBLISHING
350 Main Street, Malden, MA 02148-5020, USA
9600 Garsington Road, Oxford OX4 2DQ, UK
550 Swanston Street, Carlton, Victoria 3053, Australia

First published 2008 by Blackwell Publishing Ltd

1   2008

Library of Congress Cataloging-in-Publication Data

Republicanism and political theory / edited by Cécile Laborde and John Maynor.
    p. cm.
    Includes bibliographical references and index.
    ISBN 978-1-4051-5579-3 (hardcover : alk. paper) — ISBN 978-1-4051-5580-9 (pbk. : alk.
paper) 1. Republicanism. 2. Political science—Philosophy. I. Laborde, Cécile.
II. Maynor, John W.

JC423.R4255 2008
321.8′6—dc22

2007010447

A catalogue record for this title is available from the British Library.

Set in 11/13.5pt Bembo
by Graphicraft Limited, Hong Kong

For further information on
Blackwell Publishing, visit our website:
www.blackwellpublishing.com

Contents

Contents

Part III: Republicanism, Rights, and Domination

Notes on Contributors

Richard Bellamy is Professor of Political Science and Director of the School of Public Policy, University College London (UCL), University of London. His many publications include *Liberalism and Pluralism: Towards a Politics of Compromise* (1999), *Rethinking Liberalism* (2000) and (as co-editor) *The Cambridge History of Twentieth Century Political Thought* (2003), *Lineages of European Citizenship* (2004), *Making European Citizens* (2006), and *Political Constitutionalism: A Republican Defence of the Constitutionality of Democracy* (2007).

James Bohman is Professor of International Studies in the Department of Philosophy at St. Louis University. His areas of interest are political philosophy (deliberative democracy cosmopolitanism), philosophy of social science (explanation, interpretation and critical social science), and German philosophy (German Idealism and Critical Theory). His books include *Democracy Across Borders: From Demos to Demoi* (2007), *Public Deliberation: Pluralism, Complexity, and Democracy* (1996). His edited books include *Pluralism and the Pragmatic Turn*, edited with William Rehg (2001), *Deliberative Democracy: Essays on Reason and Politics*, edited with William Rehg (1997), and *Perpetual Peace: Essays on Kant's Cosmopolitan Ideal*. Cambridge: MIT Press, 1997.

Ian Carter is Associate Professor of Political Philosophy at the University of Pavia (Italy). His main research interests include the concepts of freedom, rights and equality in contemporary political philosophy. He is the author of *A Measure of Freedom* (1999) and *La libertà eguale* (2005), and the editor of *Freedom, Power and Political Morality* (with Mario Ricciardi) (2001), *L'idea di eguaglianza* (2001) and *Freedom: A Philosophical Anthology* (with Matthew H. Kramer and Hillel Steiner) (2007).

Richard Dagger is Professor of Political Science and Philosophy at Arizona State University, where he also directs the Philosophy, Politics, and Law Program for the Barrett Honors College. His many publications in political and legal philosophy include *Political Ideologies and the Democratic Ideal* (co-authored with Terence Ball) and *Civic Virtues: Rights, Citizenship, and Republican Liberalism*, which won the Spitz Prize of the Conference for the Study of Political Thought in 1999. In 2005–6 he was a fellow of the Center for Ethics and Public Affairs at the Murphy Institute for Political Economy, Tulane University.

Marilyn Friedman is Professor of Philosophy at Washington University, St. Louis, and at the Centre for Applied Philosophy and Public Ethics, Charles Sturt and the Australian National Universities in Australia. She works in social and political philosophy, ethics, and feminist theory. Her articles have appeared in *The Journal of Philosophy*, *Ethics*, and elsewhere. She is the author of three books: *What Are Friends For? Feminist Perspectives on Personal Relationships and Moral Theory* (1993); *Political Correctness: For and Against* (co-authored, 1995); and *Autonomy, Gender, Politics* (2003). She has also edited or co-edited four books, including *Women and Citizenship* (2005).

Matthew H. Kramer is Professor of Legal and Political Philosophy at Cambridge University; Fellow of Churchill College, Cambridge; and Director of the Cambridge Forum for Legal and Political Philosophy. His three most recently published books are *The Quality of Freedom* (2003), *Where Law and Morality Meet* (2004), and *Objectivity and the Rule of Law* (2007). With Ian Carter and Hillel Steiner, he has edited *Freedom: A Philosophical Anthology* (Blackwell, 2006).

Cécile Laborde is Reader in Political Theory at University College London. She is the author of *La Confrérie Layenne et les Lébous du Sénégal* (1995), *Pluralist Thought and the State in Britain and France* (2000) and *Critical Republicanism, The Hiiab Controversy Republican Theory and the Left* (2008). Her work on secularism, multiculturalism, patriotism, and republicanism has recently been published in *Journal of Political Philosophy*, *Political Theory*, *British Journal of Political Science*, *Political Studies* and *Constellations*. Current projects include republicanism and global justice, and the political philosophy of religion.

John Maynor is an Associate Professor in Political Philosophy at Middle Tennessee State University. He is the author of *Republicanism in the Modern World* (2003) and has published a number of articles on republican theory. His current research focuses on how new media is affecting political engagement and on republican responses to the forces of globalization.

David Miller is Professor of Political Theory at the University of Oxford and an Official Fellow of Nuffield College. Among his books are *On Nationality* (1995), *Principles of Social Justice* (1999), *Citizenship and National Identity* (2000) and *Political Philosophy: A Very Short Introduction* (2003). His main research interests are in contemporary political theory and philosophy, especially theories of justice and equality, democratic theory, the concepts of nationality and citizenship, multiculturalism and immigration, and global justice. He is currently finishing a book on National Responsibility and Global Justice.

Philip Pettit has taught political theory and philosophy at Princeton University since 2002, where he is L. S. Rockefeller University Professor of Politics and Human Values. Irish by background and training, he taught at University College, Dublin, Trinity Hall, Cambridge and the University of Bradford, before moving in 1983 to the Australian National University, Canberra, where he still retains a base. He works in moral and political theory and on background issues in philosophical psychology and social ontology. His books include *The Common Mind* (1996), *Republicanism* (1997), *A Theory of Freedom* (2001), *Rules, Reasons and Norms* (2002) and *Penser en Société* (2004). He is the co-author of *Economy of Esteem* (2004), with Geoffrey Brennan; and *Mind, Morality and Explanation* (2004), a selection of papers with Frank Jackson and Michael Smith. A new book, *Made with Words: Hobbes on Language, Mind and Politics* appears in 2007, and he is currently working on a book on group agents with Christian List (LSE).

Quentin Skinner is the Regius Professor of Modern History at the University of Cambridge and a Fellow of Christ's College. His principal publications include *The Foundations of Modern Political Thought* (2 vols., 1978); *Machiavelli* (1981); *Reason and Rhetoric in the Philosophy of Hobbes* (1996); *Liberty Before Liberalism* (1998); and *Visions of Politics* (3 vols., 2002).

Chapter 1
The Republican Contribution to Contemporary Political Theory

Cécile Laborde and John Maynor

A thorough assessment of the republican contribution to contemporary political theory is long overdue. Republican themes have been deployed by political theorists, with increasing theoretical sophistication and political acumen, for the last three decades or so. Yet the general feeling among professional political theorists has been, in the words of Bob Goodin, that "we were right to have a look, and we were right to reject" republicanism (Goodin 2003). The present volume purports to convince critics such as Goodin that republicanism is worth a second look and that, if there are good reasons to reject it, they need to be comprehensively articulated by critics of republicanism. It is our belief that republicanism has not been taken as seriously as it deserves in Anglo-American political philosophy because of the wrong-headed claim, attributed to some of its defenders, that – like conservatism or socialism before it – it is able to provide a comprehensive alternative philosophy to the dominant philosophy of liberalism. This claim is wrong-headed in two important ways. First, by judging republicanism exclusively in terms of its wholesale compatibility or incompatibility with liberalism, it denies the *sui generis* specificity of the conceptual connections and normative proposals of the former. Second, by focusing on the pre-liberal origins of republicanism, it obscures the fact that most contemporary republicans take seriously what we may call the circumstances of liberal modernity – moral individualism, ethical pluralism, and an instrumental view of political life – and seek to adapt old republican insights to them. In this (limited) sense, they may indeed be called liberal republicans.

The thought behind this volume is that, because such categorizations are often uninformative, the current terms of engagement set by the liberal-republican controversy should be avoided altogether, as they have too often resulted in mutual caricature. For example, our first section critically assesses the republican contribution to the understanding of the concept of liberty, asking whether interference or domination should be considered as its antonym. Yet it does not take a stance on whether liberalism *per se* is committed to the "pure negative" conception of freedom as non-interference, nor does it say anything about the centrality of negative liberty to contemporary liberalism. Side-stepping fruitless ideological controversies in this way allows us to go to the heart of the conceptual and normative disagreements between republicans and their critics. We hope that the pieces assembled in this volume will allow republican ideas to be looked at in their own terms, and judged accordingly. Put together, they point toward a distinctive theory of *citizenship* organized around the ideal of *non-domination*. This theory is sketched in Philip Pettit's seminal *Republicanism: A Theory of Freedom and Government* (1997a), whose influence on republican thought over the last 10 years is amply testified by the contributions in this volume. Pettit's ideal of non-domination (which the historian Quentin Skinner prefers to call independence) is central to contemporary republicanism. To be free, on the republican view, is to be free from arbitrary power: thus the republican concept of freedom offers a parsimonious conceptual basis for the defense of a normative ideal of political citizenship as non-subjection to arbitrary rule. This has led to distinctive republican contributions to debates about the geographical scope, institutional mechanisms, and motivational foundations of political democracy. The ideal of citizenship as an intersubjectively validated status of non-domination has also stimulated original contributions about the nature of republican community, the relationship between rights and power, and struggles about racial, gender, cultural, and socio-economic exclusion in the contemporary world. In the rest of this introduction, we develop these points and, in the process, offer a summary of each contribution to the present volume.

1. Conceptualizing Liberty

The republican revival began as a work of historical retrieval of a forgotten tradition of Western thought. Challenging the conventional view that liberal modernity in the Anglo-American world emerged out of Lockean natural-rights ideology, revisionist historians showed that there was a coherent republican tradition, running from the neo-classical civic humanism of Renaissance Italy powerfully exhibited in Niccolò Machiavelli, through to the works of James Harrington and the "Commonwealthmen," and later to Jean-Jacques Rousseau and James Madison, which deeply influenced English thought up to the late eighteenth century, and was a powerful inspirational force during the American Revolution (Baron 1955; Bailyn 1967; Fink 1962; Pocock 1975; Skinner 1978, 1997; Wood 1969). While the tradition as a whole was centrally concerned with the themes of freedom, political participation, civic virtue, and corruption, it was also (perhaps retrospectively) seen as exhibiting two distinct strands. The first, magisterially brought to life by J. G. A. Pocock, endorsed the Aristotelian concern for the good life and argued that human beings could only realize their nature as "political animals" through participation in self-governing communities. More recently, this reading of republicanism has become closely linked with certain writers such as Michael Sandel (1996: 24–5) and Charles Taylor (1995: 192), who favor a strong civic humanist neo-Athenian reading of republicanism. Alongside this tradition of republicanism could be discerned a neo-Roman tradition whose central concern was *libertas* – the powerful ideal of freedom under the rule of law passionately defended by Roman orators such as Cicero.

In a series of erudite historical writings, Quentin Skinner has demonstrated that neo-Roman thinkers held a distinctive conception of liberty. On the one hand, they did not endorse the Aristotelian view that real freedom consists in self-mastery or self-realization in a community with others. In particular, by contrast to followers of the neo-Athenian tradition, they believed that liberty is not definitionally linked to popular participation. The people, neo-Roman writers from Machiavelli through Harrington assured us, did not want to rule: instead, they wanted not to be ruled, or at least not to be ruled in a particular way. On the other hand, the only guarantee of not being so ruled is to live in what they called a free state. A free state is a state where citizens are not subjected to the arbitrary power of a ruler. It does not need to have the institutional form of a republic (English neo-Roman writers favored a mixed government with a limited monarchy), but it needs to be a republic in the sense that only if rulers are forced to uphold the *res publica*, instead of following their own whim or interests, can citizens enjoy *libertas*. In thus excavating the conceptual foundations of an old ideal – that of the *vivere libero* – Skinner believes that he has identified a coherent way of speaking about liberty which significantly departs from prevailing assumptions. These are that liberty and political participation can be only conceptually connected on the basis of controversial Aristotelian views about the good life. Not so, according to Skinner: liberty can have a "negative" content *and* only be present if certain "positive" conditions (citizen virtue, non-arbitrary rule, public service) obtain. To be free, on the neo-Roman (or republican for short) view, meant living in a free state. Thus republicans claimed that they had successfully rebutted Hobbes's denial of the relevance of political forms to liberty, according to which if liberty is seen as absence of interference, then it is the extent and reach of power, not its source, that matters. As Hobbes wryly put it, "Whether a Common-wealth be Monarchical, or Popular, the Freedome is still the same." Republicans disagreed: in Joseph Priestley's words, "the more political liberty a people have, the safer their civil liberty." By 2001, Skinner claimed that he had isolated a "Third Concept of Liberty" (as the title of his British Academy lecture indicated) which opposed "the key assumption of classical liberalism to the effect that force or the coercive threat of it constitute the only forms of constraint that interfere with individual liberty" (Skinner 1997: 84). For republican thinkers, living in subjection to the will of others *in itself* limits liberty (Skinner 2002a: 262).

Meanwhile, these republican insights had been deepened and formalized in Pettit's *Republicanism* – the book which more than any other has inspired the current revival in republican political theory. Like Skinner, Pettit believes that republican freedom represents a distinct conception of freedom, which he describes as non-domination. Also using Isaiah Berlin's equation of positive liberty with self-mastery and negative liberty with the absence of interference by others as his starting point, Pettit argues that republican liberty is a third conception of liberty. Pettit's argument centers on the claim that freedom consists not in the non-interference of others as in negative liberty, nor is it equated with self-mastery as in positive liberty. Instead, Pettit argues that agents are free when they are not subject to the possibility of arbitrary interference, or domination, by others. Importantly, in contrast to traditional liberal approaches, interference, or the absence of it, is not the primary measure of freedom. There are two ways in which domination importantly differs from interference. Firstly, you can be dominated without being interfered with. Consider the classical republican paradigm of unfreedom: slavery. Even if your master is of a benign disposition, and does not interfere with your actions, you are dependent upon his will and vulnerable to his interference: this is what makes you unfree. As Trenchard and Gordon put it in *Cato's Letters*, "Liberty is, to live upon one's own Terms; Slavery is, to live at the mere Mercy of another." To live at the mercy of another is to suffer unending anxiety about one's fate, to have permanently to anticipate the other's reactions, and to have to curry favor by behaving in a self-abasing, servile manner. Negative liberty theorists are, according to Pettit, unable to see that there is unfreedom when "some people hav[e] dominating power over others, provided they do not exercise that power and are not likely to exercise it" (Pettit 1997a: 9). Thus domination is a function of the relationship of unequal power between persons, groups of persons, or agencies of the state: the ideal of republican freedom is that "no one is able to interfere on an arbitrary basis – at their pleasure – in the choices of the free person." This raises the possibility, secondly and conversely, that you can be interfered with without being dominated. This happens when interference is not arbitrary, for example when it tracks what Pettit has recently called your "avowed interests." For example, while the state interferes in people's lives, levying taxes and imposing coercive laws, it may do so in a non-arbitrary way, if it only seeks ends, or employs only means, that are derived from the public good (the common, recognizable interests of the citizenry).

Pettit and Skinner's conceptualizations of republican freedom have not gone unchallenged. The first section of this volume ("Republican Freedom and its Critics") presents a series of completely new debates between them and defenders of "pure negative" liberty. The four chapters, taken together, offer a highly sophisticated discussion about the proper meaning of the concept of liberty, and chiefly center on the coherence of Pettit's first, and Skinner's main, claim: that there can be unfreedom without interference. While it is no surprise that the most vigorous challenge to republican freedom should have come from advocates of the negative view of liberty as non-interference, it is perhaps more unexpected that the challenge has taken the form of calls for a *rapprochement*. In their chapters, Matthew Kramer and Ian Carter both argue that the pure negative theory of freedom is more capacious than republicans recognize, and is thus able to accommodate domination and dependence, as well as interference, as reductive of liberty. This is because their revised theory of negative liberty diverges from the traditional Hobbesian paradigm in two important ways. First, freedom is reduced by potential as well as by actual interference, as exemplified by cases of subtle coercion, threats, arrogant displays of superiority and so forth. Second, freedom is reduced not only by the removal of single options, but also by the foreclosing of sets of options. Thus, when faced with the highwayman's threat ("your money or your life"), I am, on the Hobbesian view, free to keep my money and free to keep my life (I am not physically prevented from doing either) but, on the "new" negative theory, what I am not free to do is to keep both my money and my life: I am not free, that is, to exercise both options conjunctively. By analogy, if I am dominated, I may be able to exercise most of my liberties, but my overall liberty is reduced by the fact that I cannot exercise them in conjunction with (for example) non-deferential behavior toward my dominator.

Thus negative liberty theorists contend that readiness to interfere – which is what republican domination amounts to – reduces freedom, because of the need for the dominated to engage in patterns of behavior intended to ward off the threat of interference. As a result, in Kramer's words, "there is no need whatsoever to go beyond a theory of negative liberty for this important insight into the working of despotism." Carter, likewise, suggests that it is possible to derive "equivalent judgments" about degrees of freedom and unfreedom arrived at by the republican and the pure negative conception of freedom. However, an important difference between advocates of pure negative liberty and republicans has emerged from their engagement with Pettit and Skinner's writings on liberty. While Carter and Kramer concede to republicans that mere exposure to the power of another (as opposed to the actual experience of that power) can be an instance of unfreedom, they insist that freedom is negatively and proportionally affected only in relation to the probability of the power being actually exercised. Thus, if we live under the power of a benign master – or a Gentle Giant, in Kramer's example – whose actual willingness ever to interfere with our lives is negligible, we (*contra* republicans) cannot be said to be unfree. This is the core of the pure negative challenge to republican freedom. In their wide-ranging chapters, both Carter and Kramer develop a number of other thought-provoking objections to the republican theory of freedom. Yet their main claim is that the theory of negative liberty is compatible with the thought that we can be unfree when, *but only to the extent that*, we are subjected to a *plausible* threat of interference.

It is naturally on this claim that Skinner and Pettit, in wholly original chapters written specifically in response to Carter's and Kramer's, focus their attention. In the process, they considerably refine the conceptual apparatus of republican liberty, and clarify some of its central tenets. Their central move is to deny that slaves, even if they have a benign master, can ever be considered free. For republicans, it is not the probability, but the mere possibility, of the exercise of power that matters to liberty. Skinner goes even further, and argues that the originality of the republican view is entirely to disconnect the presence of unfreedom from the likelihood of interference. We are unfree just by being dependent on the will of others, because everything we do, we do *cum permisso*, by their leave and under their control. We are unfree when our fate depends on the dispositions – however benign or gentle – of our princes. Unless they are strictly unable, rather than merely disinclined, to exercise arbitrary power over us, Skinner advises us not to "put . . . thy trust in princes." Skinner also corrects what he takes to be the unduly psychological interpretation of freedom that may have been detected in his previous writings. There, he extensively chronicled the republican concern for the way in which servitude breeds servility, indolence, and self-censorship, thus reducing agents' freedom of action without overt interference. Skinner is now keen to reiterate that such foreclosing of options usually accompanies, but does not itself define, the basic "existential condition" of slavery. In his sharp formulation, mere subjection to arbitrary power is what makes us unfree.

In his chapter, Pettit clarifies the central concept of arbitrary power and its connection with freedom as non-interference by introducing the notion of *alien control*. Republican freedom, on his new formalization, can be defined as the absence of alien or alienating control on the part of other persons – the absence, that is, of control which negatively affects the agent's freedom of choice. Importantly, both alien and non-alien control can materialize with or without interference. Alien control without interference – the classic case of republican unfreedom – obtains even when the agent is not aware of living under such control, and independently acts as his controller wishes, because all his choices are invigilated, however implicitly, by his controller. Such control is "alien" if it removes options, replaces options, or otherwise undermines what Pettit calls the "deliberative assumptions of personal choice." Like Skinner, Pettit asserts that when such situations of alien control obtain, a low probability of actual interference is only small consolation to the controlled agent. As he puts it, "alien control will remain in place so long as the agent can interfere or not interfere, whatever the reduced probabilities of interference that are dictated by the agent's nature."

The alternative scenario – that of non-alien control with interference – allows Pettit to expand on and formalize the second postulate of his theory of republican freedom, namely, that interference *per se* need not reduce freedom – only alien interference does. This possibility is evidently discarded by negative liberty theorists, and Carter specifically excludes from his discussion what he calls Pettit's "moralized" conception of freedom. By this he means that, by making reference to interference that tracks an agent's avowed interests, or is adequately checked or countered by the agent, as not limiting but enhancing freedom, Pettit smuggles in normative judgments about the legitimacy of certain kinds of interference (cf. also McMahon 2005). Pettit has retorted that his definition of arbitrary power is factual not evaluative (Pettit 2006). Yet it remains the case that if, as they do, republicans value liberty, and believe that certain forms of interference do not limit but enhance liberty, they will look favorably upon them. Thus republicans have long insisted, *contra* Hobbesians and utilitarians, that non-arbitrary laws do not limit freedom but enhance it. A law penalizing physical assault promotes my freedom by protecting me against potential assault, and securing me with a kind of shielded standing against the alien (and in this case violent) interference of others. A standard critique of this view, paradigmatically articulated by William Paley, Jeremy Bentham, and Henry Sidgwick (Kelly 2001), is that republicans simply confuse liberty with the security of liberty. The law may make my freedom (as non-interference) more resilient over time, but it does not constitute it. Republicans, it is further suggested, are vulnerable to Rousseau's notorious paradox, that we can be "forced to be free" by the law. If I myself commit assault and go to prison, should I still be called free? While the standard liberal solution to this problem is to say that liberties can be reduced only for the sake of other liberties (Rawls 1971: 204), so that lesser liberties (that of being uninterfered with if I commit assault) are "traded" against more important ones (that of being free of assault from others), Pettit's republican reply is to draw a qualitative distinction between the greater evil of domination (which leaves us "unfree") and the lesser evil of interference (which leaves us "non-free"). Generally, interference by a non-arbitrary state, one suitably invigilated and checked by the constitutional people, does not compromise republican freedom.

Leaving aside the claim that non-arbitrary interference enhances *freedom*, the idea that interference by the state in the lives of its citizens should be responsive to the latter's interests and convictions is a fairly uncontroversial tenet of most schools of democratic liberalism. As both Charles Larmore (2001) and Henry Richardson (2002) have pointed out, Pettit's concept of non-arbitrariness is perfectly compatible with liberal understandings of the common good, founded on basic ideals of equality and respect for individuals. Wherein, then, lies the distinctiveness of the republican approach? Two points, a conceptual and a normative point, can be made at this stage (others will emerge later in our discussion). Conceptually, Pettit's concept of non-domination is more comprehensive and thus more "parsimonious" (List 2006) than any liberal ideal. This is because non-domination makes definitional connections between the ideals of liberty, the rule of law, popular contestation and the common good. Thus, on the republican reading, I am free only if I am recognized by others as enjoying a status that resiliently protects me against alien interference and guarantees my equal status as a citizen living in community with others. In a word, I am free as a citizen of a particular state, a state that promotes the common good of non-domination. Non-domination thus supports the Rousseauian connection between *liberté* on the one hand, and *égalité* and *fraternité* on the other (Spitz 1995; Pettit 1997a: ch. 4). For most liberals, by contrast, the ideals appealed to by republicans have at best independent value and are contingently, not necessarily, related. (Of course, whether republican parsimony is a virtue or a vice is a highly disputed matter, and even writers sympathetic to republicanism have pointed out that the ideal of non-domination may not be robust enough by itself to support the range of republican normative ideals (Richardson 2002; Dagger 2006).) However, secondly, the tight conceptual fit between freedom and forms of political rule has strengthened the republican normative commitment to the political institutionalization of non-domination. Republicanism, after all, was historically a theory of popular self-rule and democracy. But how, and how much, should the people participate in politics to be free of domination? To this second, crucial theme we now turn.

2. Institutionalizing Self-Rule

In his chapter, David Miller sharply lays out the daunting challenges facing republicans in their attempt to adapt republican political forms to contemporary conditions. A long-standing republican concern was with the appropriate *size* of the republic. While classical city-states could be ruled by the popular will because they were small and relatively homogeneous, they were also prone to majority tyranny and foreign domination. To these republican maladies, large-sized republics could, under certain conditions, provide republican remedies. Thus representation, federalism and constitutional checks and balances were conceived of by later republicans, notably Madison, as institutional devices intended to preserve the liberty and public spirit cherished by republicans. Miller is doubtful that the conditions under which such remedies can truly protect republican values easily obtain today. Specifically, he takes aim at those who wish to see republican values realized within the transnational European Union. He develops two chief objections to what he calls "Euro-republicanism." The first is that, as national identity historically provided the foundation for the civic trust underpinning republican citizenship in large societies, nations-states today behave like "factions" at the European level by promoting their own national interests above that of a EU-wide common good. Moreover, they remain the primary repository of citizens' allegiance and sense of belonging, and the distinctiveness of their heritage and culture makes it very unlikely that a genuinely European "constitutional patriotic" sentiment will emerge. Thus the "motivational" preconditions for European citizenship are not present. The second objection to Euro-republicanism is that it "makes virtue out of complexity" by describing existing power arrangements in the EU as a republican "mixed constitution" which preserve citizens' liberty as non-domination while offering multiple avenues for democratic participation. Miller, for his part, is skeptical about the democratic, and therefore republican, credentials of the European Union. Complexity makes for opacity, he says: the EU is more of an oligarchic than a democratic regime, and the constitutional protection of rights furthers liberal ideals rather than republican ideals of civic engagement. Thus the "institutional" preconditions for European citizenship are not present either. In this way, Miller can be said to illuminate the two challenges that contemporary republican democracy has to confront. The first, the "motivational" challenge, looks for suitable modern substitutes for civic virtue capable of generating trust and solidarity between citizens. The second, the "institutional" challenge, asks how popular self-rule can be operationalized in large and complex polities. In what follows, we investigate how republicans have sought to address both challenges, starting with the latter.

There are two distinct questions underlying the institutional challenge for republicans. The first concerns the *form* that self-rule should take, and the second its *scope*. As regards *form*, republicans agree that, for the state not to dominate them, the people must in some way be involved in its government, but they disagree as to how. Advocates of contestatory democracy, of which Pettit is the most prominent, endorse a fairly minimalist version of popular involvement, seeing majority tyranny and "populism" as one of the chief forms of domination. In the old republican adage, the people want not to be a master, but to have no master. Thus power should be dispersed, not concentrated at any point, and there should be constitutional constraints on its exercise – notably a bill of rights (Pettit 1997a: 181). Pettit's republic is designed to ensure that the government can reliably track the common interests of its citizens, who can then contest and review decisions through judicial, tribunal, ombudsman-like, multi-cameral, and localized institutions. In Pettit's recent words, the people should be able to act as "editors" of policy in addition to the more traditional authorial role they play through their elected representatives (Pettit 2001a: 162–3). Advocates of participatory democracy, for their part, doubt that contestatory democracy is sufficient to guarantee the non-dominated status of all citizens, and have argued for more robust forms of self-government. More avenues for the political involvement of citizens – proposals include referendums, internet democracy, workplace democracy, town meetings, citizens' juries, compulsory voting – are necessary for the voice of disadvantaged groups to be heard (Southwood 2002; Dryseck 2000; Barber 1984). Advocates of deliberative democracy share Pettit's concerns about the dangers of untamed majoritarianism, but believe that democracy, conceived as rational deliberation about ends and values or "public autonomy" (Richardson 2002), has internal self-correcting tendencies. In a democracy organized deliberatively, all have an equal chance to speak, decisions are publicly made on the basis of the best argument presented, and citizens' initial preferences and values are transformed in the process of interacting with others, generating virtuous circles of trust and participation (Sunstein 1988; Cohen 1989; Habermas 1994, 1996; Miller 2000). Thus deliberative democracy is an important corrective to the kind of unprincipled interest-group politics that has long been the chief target of republicans.

In his chapter, Richard Bellamy both surveys the variety of republican proposals for reform of existing liberal democracy and defends his own version, which might be called realist democracy. It is realist in two ways. First, drawing on a more radical reading of Machiavelli than the one espoused by Pettit (cf. also McCormick 2001; Maddox 2002; Maynor 2003: ch. 5), Bellamy argues that conflicts of values and interests are an ineliminable part of politics, which republican political arrangements are designed to tame and control, but cannot eliminate. Second, Bellamy suggests that existing, ordinary politics – the rough-and-tumble of adversarial party politics – exhibit more republican features than republican philosophers have cared to notice. Only the procedural fairness inherent in "one person one vote" politics guarantees the non-domination of citizens. Thus Bellamy distances himself from those republicans who seek to rationalize or purify democratic outcomes, either by giving a semi-objective, consensual content to the public interest (contestatory republicans) or by rationalizing the democratic process so that it produces consensual outcomes (deliberative republicans). He specifically targets the republican conversion to legal constitutionalism, according to which non-arbitrary power and the rule of law are best guaranteed if certain matters are de-politicized and entrusted to judicial vigilance (Sunstein 1988; Michelman 1988; Richardson 2002; Pettit 1997a). Bellamy argues instead in favor of a "political constitutionalism," where the constitution is identified with the body politic itself, and where the rule of law ultimately depends on the rule of men – on the actual ability of citizens to have a say in the way their collective life is to be organized. Thus, in Bellamy's realist republicanism, it is through ordinary politics (such as voting in open elections) that common liberty as non-domination is best preserved. While Bellamy would agree with Miller that supranational political institutions should not seek to reproduce the motivational conditions which historically made the nation-state the natural site for active republican citizenship, he has also been one of the chief advocates of the view that existing EU politics – shorn of a formal constitution and bill of rights – have built-in republican qualities, notably that of offering multi-level checks and balances, as well as the potential for the development of transnational, *ad hoc* forms of participatory citizenship.

This question of the *scope* (or boundaries) of republican citizenship is further taken up by James Bohman in his chapter on transnational democracy and cosmopolitan republicanism. Noting that Pettit himself is agnostic as to the size and scope of the republic, Bohman argues that Pettit's ideal of non-domination as contestation is particularly well-suited to transnational politics. Bohman sees globalization as having generated new "circumstances of politics," where unchecked arbitrary power is exercised across national borders with far-reaching but highly differentiated impact on groups and individuals worldwide; and where no supranational cooperative scheme or "basic structure" through which citizens could collectively self-govern can (or should) exist. Thus Bohman agrees with Miller and Bellamy that there can be no self-government where there is no constituted *demos*, but suggests a thinner form of democracy, rooted in the accountability of transnational economic and political organizations to ordinary citizens (Bohman 2004). In his contribution to this volume, Bohman draws on republican anti-colonial and anti-imperial literature to suggest, *contra* Miller, that membership in a single political community is insufficient for robust non-domination. As nineteenth-century republicans were well aware, there was a link between the oppression of foreign people and the corruption of democracy at home; and the only way to check the tendencies of "bounded" democracies to become corrupt was to create federations of republics. The EU can be seen as an approximation of this cosmopolitan republicanism, as it offers multiple avenues for citizens to contest the arbitrary exercise of power. The EU is also beginning to give effect to what Bohman calls the "democratic minimum" – the basic "right to have rights" (to use Hannah Arendt's phrase) which can be universally claimed, notably by stateless persons and other "denizens." In this way, the most basic right that human beings have *qua* human is, properly speaking, a *political* right, the right to belong politically, the right to have a voice, the right not to be dominated. Thus Bohman's republican cosmopolitanism substantially differs from the dominant liberal cosmopolitanism – which detaches human rights from political membership – while considerably expanding the cosmopolitan scope of republican ideals.

3. Motivating Self-Rule

One question raised by Bohman's contribution is that of the motivational basis of cosmopolitan republican citizenship. What exactly will motivate individuals to engage in transnational practices of democratic engagement, and how can they meaningfully see themselves as "citizens of the world?" This takes us back to Miller's second challenge to contemporary republicans, which is rooted in the thought that, for people to discharge their duties as citizens, they must identify with one another and share strong bonds of fellowship – which for Miller must be those of national identity (Miller 2000). Most republicans would agree with Miller that republican citizenship is underpinned, not only by good laws and institutions, but also by supporting norms of civic virtue or civility (Pettit 1997a; Dagger 1997). This is because republican citizenship is (reasonably) demanding: it requires that people willingly share in practices of social cooperation (such as wealth distribution), be able to make compromises for the sake of the common good, and also that they be ready to defend the institutions of their common liberty. Cosmopolitan republicans, however, have denied that such virtues can only manifest themselves as expressions of national fellow-feeling. Republicans should champion the universal promotion of democracy and liberty as non-domination, and as they care about their common liberty, so they will care about the common liberty of others (Viroli 1995; Nabulsi 1999; White 2003a). They will also be particularly concerned about the ways in which both are negatively affected by global interdependency and by the dominating power of powerful countries and corporations (Bohman, this volume). Common concerns and special obligations, therefore, arise beyond the nation-state. One could even say that *only* a republican conception of citizenship can do justice to the new global "circumstances of politics" where, in the absence of institutionalized spheres of rights and obligations, the political will to counter arbitrary power and structures of domination must partly rely on the civic virtue of ordinary people organized in transnational social movements (Chung 2003).

More generally, many have challenged Miller's idea that republican civility must be rooted in cultural affinity, even within established states. If "democracy needs patriotism," as Charles Taylor memorably put it (Taylor 1996), it need not be a patriotism based on thick cultural or historical bonds. Thus Jürgen Habermas has argued that the connection between republicanism and nationalism was a contingent, not a necessary, one; today, republican values of trust and solidarity can be underpinned by a "constitutional patriotism" (*Verfassungspatriotismus*), an inclusive political identity which can motivate citizens to feel "politically responsible for each other" (Habermas 1996: 286) without having to share a thickly constituted collective identity. On this view, love of country and love of liberty are mutually supportive: republicans do not support the thoughtless nationalism of "my country for good or ill," but rather endorse the critical patriotism of "my country for the values it realizes (or should realize)." In Maurizio Viroli's more "rooted" version of republican patriotism, "democratic politics do not need ethno-cultural unity; they need citizens committed to the way of life of the republic" (Viroli 1995: 176). Thus, on the new republican account of patriotic virtue, it is sufficient that citizens identify with the shared institutions and practices that have arisen out of social and political inter-dependency and underpin the feeling they have of sharing a common fate (Mason 2000). These sentiments appear to tie into a kind of Tocquevillian patriotism where democratic citizens view their contri-bution to the maintenance of the political community as being part of a common endeavor that they share with others and one in which they have part ownership. Seen in this manner, contributing to the main-tenance of the republic helps citizens have a proprietary orientation to the state and its laws and institutions that helps to bind the citizenry together in a common enterprise. In Iseult Honohan's illuminating ana-logy, citizens relate to one another, neither as strangers nor as family, but rather as *colleagues*: people with different memberships and values, connected through involuntary institutional membership, whom we treat as relative equals, owe special obligations to, and with whom we share common concerns (Honohan 2001). Such a political and institutional account of the motivational foundations of civic virtue allows republicans to expand the scope of citizenship beyond national bound-aries, as we have seen. It also allows them to reflect on the forms of social and political solidarity compatible with the religious and cultural diversity of contemporary states – a theme which has recently come back to the fore, and has long been central to non-Anglophone tradi-tions, such as French republicanism (Schnapper 1988; Laborde 2008). Yet questions remain about whether republican civic virtue really is compatible with modern values of individualism, universalism, and inclusion, as our next sections will show.

4. Taking Rights Seriously?

A common complaint against republican political theory is that it does not take individual rights seriously enough. Classical republican soci-eties were pre-modern, pre-individualistic societies where citizens had limited moral life independently of the community to which they belonged. Modern individualism, by contrast, is based on the intuition that individuals, as "self-originating sources of claims" (Rawls 1971), are entitled to live their own life in their own way. It is true that some republicans have joined in with communitarian critiques of liberalism to denounce the social disintegration and moral anomie to which the right-based liberal society is prone, and have expressed nostalgia for a more morally and socially homogeneous society organized around a unitary common good (Oldfield 1990; Sandel 1996; Pangle 1988). However, the dominant interpretation of republicanism – the one which is broadly reflected in this volume – fully endorses the moral individualism and ethical pluralism of modern society, and does not deny the existence and importance of individual rights. None the less, republicans are skeptical of accounts of rights that totally abstract from the political conditions of their formulation, realization, and protection. Take, as a fairly representative sample, the views of five of the authors represented in this volume. In the 1980s, Skinner interpreted the Machiavellian tradition of thinking about liberty as asserting that individual liberties and rights are not safe unless citizens are prepared to participate in politics in order to secure them (Skinner 1983, 1984) – an account believed to be compatible with Rawls' defense of republican participation as instrumental to the defense of liberties (Rawls 1993; Patten 1996). Bellamy and Miller have argued that the content of rights should be deliberated upon politically, rather than derived *a priori* and handed over to an undemocratic judiciary. Bohman has suggested that the most basic right we have as human beings is the right of membership, the right to belong to a non-dominating political community. And along with liberal republicans, such as Cass Sunstein, for whom a number of basic rights – rights of conscience, speech, association – are indispensable pre-requisites for republican deliberation (Sunstein 1988), Pettit has conceded that certain legal or constitutional rights may be essential to achieve freedom as non-domination (Pettit 1997a: 101, 181). Yet generally, the vocabulary of rights is better suited to sanction *acts* of interference than to address *relationships* of domination and, as Pettit noted, the freedom of slaves, workers, and women has historically been more effectively furthered by their gaining more power (or "anti-power") than by their being granted formal rights (Pettit 1999: 304).

There is a related sense in which the ideal of non-domination can be seen to be adverse to the notion of individual rights. Non-domination, as conceived by Pettit, is a *consequentialist* ideal. This means that it refers to a goal – the overall reduction of arbitrary power in society – to be promoted by social institutions, rather than a constraint on the latter's actions (the protection of "natural" rights would be such a constraint). In his chapter in this volume, Richard Dagger critically examines the implication of republican consequentialism for Pettit's (and John Braithwaite's) theory of punishment (Braithwaite & Pettit: 1990). The aim of the criminal justice system, for Pettit and Braithwaite, is to promote overall non-domination (or *dominion*) in society. Consequentialist approaches to punishment are often criticized for failing adequately to explain why punishing an innocent person could never be justified (if, for example, it was effective in calming a nearly hysterical public in the midst of a series of horrible crimes). Pettit and Braithwaite retort that dominion is a special kind of good, one that can be promoted or maximized without threat to individual rights or to considerations of justice, because people would in fact be dominated if they suspected that the state would be unscrupulous in respecting their rights. Dagger is sympathetic to Pettit's approach but takes seriously the retributivist objection that only backward-looking considerations, such as consideration of guilt and innocence, can ensure that the rights of the innocent will be protected. He shows that, in recent works, Pettit has developed such a backward-looking theory of punishment as rectification, which turns out, on closer inspection, to be compatible with Antony Duff's influential communicative retributivism. Dagger concludes that republicans can and should be retributivists, without losing sight of their central intuitions – that the chief point of punishment is the restoration of citizenship in the community, and that citizenship is not only a legal status but also an intersubjective standing. But how inclusive can republican citizenship be? This is the subject of our next section.

5. Status, Inclusion, Emancipation

Traditionally, republican citizens were arms-bearing, property-owning men – a small minority enjoying a privileged status based on the honored virtue of (material, moral, and political) independence. Citizenship, then, was a positional good, whose value depended on others not having it (Honohan 2002: 258). The modern republic, influenced by the democratic, universalist revolutions of the late eighteenth century, is, by contrast, a single-status society, one where the equal status of citizen-ship is (asymptotically at least) extended to all persons. Even one of the last "frontiers" of modern citizenship – the frontier of the nation-state – is being lifted by those republicans who argue that "denizenship," the lack of a right to have any right at all, is the worst form of domination. Non-citizens, then, are dominated, and immunity from domination is construed as a kind of universal primary good (Bohman, this volume). Thus, while in classical republics the status of citizenship recognized and rewarded existing social standing, in modern republics it is citizenship that grants and protects social standing. All the same, republican citizen-ship remains a particular kind of intersubjectively validated social status, not merely a legal entitlement. It is more demanding and hence, in light of contemporary universalist egalitarianism, more radically inclusive than standard interpretations of citizenship. This (perhaps unexpected) claim can be vindicated in two ways. First, republicans will seek ways to give political voice to excluded groups in society, typically through repre-sentation in deliberative settings. Because (deliberative) republicans do not set limits as to who can enter public deliberation, and on which terms, they are better able actively to respond to cultural diversity than other traditions (Miller 2000: chs. 3 and 9). Further, because to be a citizen is intimately tied up with enjoying a certain status in com-munion with others, and having your voice authorized by others – what Pettit calls discursive control (Pettit 2001a: 140) – republicanism is sen-sitive to the subtle ways in which groups marked out as "different" are being dominated. Thus, they can be dominated if they are not allowed to speak for themselves, are subjected to demeaning images of their iden-tity, and are made to feel vulnerable to the decisions and opinions of others. Even in the absence of interference, discrimination or other-wise unjust treatment, they are not secure in their status as citizens: the price of liberty, for them, is eternal discretion. This is not to say that republican theorists should therefore espouse the "politics of recogni-tion," if we mean by this that for people to be secure in the enjoyment of a non-dominated status, their particular identities must be given spe-cial protection and public recognition. Instead of the fixed representa-tion of differences, republicans tend to favor inclusive participation in deliberation with others.

The second way in which republican citizenship has more radically inclusive implications than standard interpretations of citizenship is that it is concerned with protecting individuals, not only from the *imperium* of the state, but also from the private *dominium* of other citizens and groups in society (Pettit 1997a: ch. 5). While the republican school of thought has thus far concerned itself more with political than with social domination, there is no doubt that the demand to be freed from domination was historically a profoundly radical call, as it targeted the structural and institutional contexts that produced inequalities in power relations in society. Pettit even suggests that the republican ideal of non-domination was abandoned in the late eighteenth century because it was seen to have too radical implications in a democratic age: it would have required the overturning of deeply inegalitarian social relations, such as those between men and women or between masters and servants, and therefore was discarded in favor of the less demanding ideal of non-interference (Pettit 1997a: 47–9, 77–8). Yet Karl Marx's discussion of wage slavery and alienation was permeated by a critique of the evils of dependency. Likewise, Mary Wollstonecraft's and J. S. Mill's writings on the subjection of women drew on the ideal of independence to stress that "no slave is a slave to the same lengths, and in so full a sense of the word, as a wife is" (Mill 1970, in Pettit 1997a: 139; cf. also James 1992). Now, it is true that republicanism and feminism do not form a *prima facie* "plausible alliance" (Phillips 2000): republicanism was his-torically a masculinist, militaristic ideology whose vision was rooted in a highly gendered separation between the public world of rational deliberation, politics, and war on the one hand, and the private world of domesticity, emotionality, and the body on the other. However, the republican ideal of freedom from domination is potentially attractive to feminists for four main reasons. First, on a republican view, there is more to the ideal of liberty than merely to be "left alone," as in the crudest versions of negative liberty. Second, interference itself may not be the chief obstacle to liberty, as some forms of caring and benevolent ("non-alien" in Pettit's words) interference actually increase a person's freedom. Third, domination, contrary to interference, is a structural, institutional, and collective social fact, which applies to systems, not only to individual actions, and can thus best capture the functioning of what feminists call "patriarchy" or "male domination." Fourth, the structural nature of domination can explain phenomena such as those of the "con-tented slave" or the "tamed housewife" – cases in which individuals are not aware they are being dominated.

In her contribution to this volume, Marilyn Friedman endorses the first two lines of argument. She begins by praising Pettit for denying that "the best thing that people can do for each other is to get out of each other's way," although she argues that his ideal of independence is still vulnerable to the feminist objection that it underestimates the value of relationships of interdependence and dependency. Caretakers – say, parents – have capacities for arbitrary power as well as for benevolent, non-arbitrary caring, and men–women relationships are likewise too complex to be reduced to simple patterns of domination. Friedman suggests that we should distinguish between *acts* of domination and *relationships* of domination. More broadly, she is skeptical about the third and fourth lines of argument referred to above. The potentially collectivist and objectivist features of non-domination conflict with her liberal, individualistic feminism. Friedman is not convinced that the elimination of domination, understood as the mere capacity for the exercise of power, is a realistic or attractive ideal; and she argues that domination is best conceived of as actual or attempted arbitrary interference. She also worries about the paternalistic implication of liberating people from forms of domination that they are not aware of, and argues that non-arbitrary interference should track people's ideas about their interests, not their (externally defined) interests. Finally, Friedman points out that the fact that women are dominated as a group does not mean that all women are dominated, and she offers a more individualistic interpretation of domination. Her chapter is therefore a good place to identify the lines of debate between liberal and radical interpretations of social domination.

6. Social and Economic Republicanism

A common critique of republicanism is that, because it is primarily a theory of political citizenship, it is relatively indifferent to questions of socio-economic justice and equality (Goodin 2003: 62). Yet there is little evidence for this: traditional republicanism was deeply concerned about the effects of the emergence of the "commercial society" on civic virtue, and recent republican contributions to the "political economy of citizenship" have been substantial and, if anything, have grown in size and scope over recent years (Sandel 1996; Sunstein 1997; Allen & Regan 1998; White 2003b; Pettit 2006; Dagger 2006). In Gerald Gaus's perceptive albeit critical assessment, contemporary republicanism can be seen as a post-socialist critique of market society (Gaus 2003).

Republicans value the *market economy* for instrumental reasons, and because private property, as Rousseau insisted, guarantees citizens' self-sufficiency and independence (Pettit 2006). But they argue that the market by itself cannot secure equal non-domination, and they object to the *market society*, where market relations spill into, and corrupt, parts of life where they should not reign supreme (Dagger 2006).

More specifically, republicans have made four contributions to current debates about economic and social issues. First, non-intervention by the state in the economy should not be seen as a natural state of affairs from which deviations are *prima facie* illegitimate. Markets are not "natural" but political and institutional artifacts, and the distribution of existing entitlements may reflect unjust background conditions; thus democracies can legitimately override markets if this is necessary to promote non-domination (Sunstein 1997). Second, citizens should receive a basic income, not as an unconditional right, but as a "civic minimum" tied to their status as citizen and guaranteeing their independence (White 2003b). Third, republicans are as concerned about the relative as about the absolute position of the worst-off; they are as concerned, that is, with reducing gaps in living standards and lifestyles between the rich and the poor. This is because, as Michael Sandel puts it, "inequality undermines freedom by corrupting the character of both rich and poor and destroying the commonality necessary to self-government" (Sandel 1996: 330). Republican civic virtue is underpinned by an egalitarian ethos, a spirit of "social equality": if inequalities become too large, citizens will no longer see themselves as sharing the same fate and might default on their obligations of justice and solidarity. Inequality further undermines self-government by increasing disparities of political influence and thus corroding the value of equal citizenship. Thus republicans have been keen severely to limit the effects of wealth in the political process, notably through profound reforms of campaign financing (Sunstein 1988: 1552). Fourth and last, republicans, like socialists, have been concerned not only with issues of distribution but also with issues related to production and working conditions. The "political economy of citizenship" is designed to control the effects of economic arrangements on the independence and civic virtue of the citizenry (Sandel 1996). Much work remains to be done on republican political economy, and although the topic is not directly addressed in our volume, we expect it to be one of growing importance and relevance in years to come.

Conclusion

We hope we have said enough to convince skeptics that the republican contribution to contemporary political theory should not be summarily dismissed. Republicans have been articulating a political theory of citizenship which is conceptually parsimonious – organized as it is around the concept of freedom as non-domination – and normatively attractive – concerned as it is with the struggle against contemporary forms of arbitrary power. The contributions assembled in this volume further demonstrate the richness, originality, and diversity of contemporary republican thought. They also illustrate the vitality of current debates about and within republicanism. Thus in the first section, Skinner and Pettit respond to the searching criticisms of Kramer and Carter; in the second section, the exchanges between Miller, Bellamy, and Bohman testify to the strength of inter-republican debates about the nature of republican democracy; and in the third section, Dagger and Friedman critically apply the concept of non-domination to the areas of punishment and gender. Overall, this volume aims to provide the basis for a new (and overdue) assessment of republican political theory. A year before the publication of Pettit's *Republicanism*, Alan Patten had advanced the proposition that "either there is no interesting disagreement between liberals and republicans, or there is, but not one which should concern liberals" (Patten 1996: 27). The contributions assembled in the current volume show that the republican theory of citizenship as non-domination should be at the very least "interesting" to liberals – and others. Whether, and where, there is a "disagreement" between them is a question that can only be settled through further careful investigation.

ACKNOWLEDGMENTS

Thanks to Richard Bellamy, Meghan Benton, Philip Pettit, and Quentin Skinner for their comments on an earlier draft of this introduction.

Republicanism and Contemporary Political Theory: Key Texts

Please note that this bibliography is thematic and not simply alphabetical. Different texts by the same author may appear in different sections.

1. GENERAL

Brennan, G. and Lomasky, L. (2006). "Against Reviving Republicanism." *Politics, Philosophy, and Economics*, 5(2), 221–52.

Dagger, R. (1997). *Civic Virtues: Rights, Citizenship and Republican Liberalism*. Oxford: Oxford University Press.

Dagger, R. (2004). "Communitarianism and Republicanism." In G. Gaus and C. Kukathas (eds.), *Handbook of Political Theory*. London: Sage.

Goodin, R. (2003). "Folie Républicaine." *Annual Review of Political Science*.

Jennings, J. and Honohan, I. (eds.) (2005). *Republicanism in Theory and Practice*. London: Routledge.

Hakonseen, K. (1993). "Republicanism." In P. Pettit and R. Goodin (eds.), *Handbook of Contemporary Political Philosophy*. Oxford: Blackwell.

Honohan, I. (2002). *Civic Republicanism*. London: Routledge.

Maynor, J. (2003). *Republicanism in the Modern World*. Cambridge: Polity.

Oldfield, A. (1990). *Citizenship and Community: Civic Republicanism and the Modern World*. London: Routledge.

Pettit, P. (1997). *Republicanism: A Theory of Freedom and Government*. Oxford: Oxford University Press.

Pettit, P. (1999). "Republicanism: Once More with Hindsight." postface to paperback edition of *Republicanism*. Oxford: Oxford University Press.

Skinner, Q. (1997). *Liberty before Liberalism*. Cambridge: Cambridge University Press.

Spitz, J.-F. (1995). *La Liberté Politique*. Paris: Presses Universitaires de France.

Spragens, T., Jr. (1999). *Civic Liberalism: Reflections on our Democratic Ideals*. Lanham, MD: Rowman and Littlefield.

Terchek, R. (1996). *Republican Paradoxes and Liberal Anxieties: Retrieving Neglected Fragments of Political Theory*. Lanham, MD: Rowman and Littlefield.

Viroli, M. (2001). *Republicanism*. New York: Hill and Wang.

Weinstock, D. and Nadeau, C. (eds.) (2004). *Republicanism: History, Theory and Practice*. London: Frank Cass.

2. HISTORY

Bailyn, B. (1967). *The Ideological Origins of the American Revolution*. Cambridge, MA: Harvard University Press.

Baron, H. (1955). *The Crisis of the Early Italian Renaissance: Civic Humanism and Republican Liberty in an Age of Classicism and Tyranny*. Princeton, NJ: Princeton University Press.

Bock, G., Skinner, Q., and Viroli, M. (eds.) (1990). *Machiavelli and Republicanism*. Cambridge: Cambridge University Press.

Fink, Z. S. (1962). *The Classical Republicans: An Essay in the Recovery of a Pattern of Thought in 17th Century England*. Evanston, IL: Northwestern University Press.

McCormick, J. (2001). "Machiavellian Democracy: Controlling Elites with Ferocious Populism." *American Political Science Review*, 95(2), 297–313.

McCormick, J. (2003). "Machiavelli against Republicanism: On the Cambridge School's 'Guicciardinian Moments.'" *Political Theory*, 31(5), 615–43.

Nelson, E. (2004). *The Greek Tradition in Republican Thought*. Cambridge: Cambridge University Press.

Pangle, T. (1988). *The Spirit of Modern Republicanism: The Moral Vision of the American Founders and the Philosophy of Locke*. Chicago: University of Chicago Press.

Pocock, J. G. A. (1975). *The Machiavellian Moment: Florentine Political Thought and the Atlantic Republican Tradition*. Princeton, NJ: Princeton University Press.

Skinner, Q. (1978). *The Foundations of Modern Political Though*, 2 vols. Cambridge: Cambridge University Press.

Skinner, Q. (1997). *Liberty before Liberalism*. Cambridge: Cambridge University Press.

Skinner, Q. (2002b). *Visions of Politics, Vol. II: Renaissance Virtues*. Cambridge: Cambridge University Press.

Skinner, Q. and van Gelderen, M. (eds.) (2005). *Republicanism, A Shared European Heritage*. Cambridge: Cambridge University Press.

Spitz, J.-F. (1995). *La Liberté Politique*. Paris: Presses Universitaires de France.

Tuck, R. (1990). "Humanism and Political Thought." In A. Goodman and A. MacKay (eds.), *The Impact of Humanism on Western Europe*. London: Longman.

Wood, G. (1969). *The Creation of the American Republic, 1776–1787*. Chapel Hill, NC: University of North Carolina Press.

Wootton, D. (1994). *Republicanism, Liberty and Commercial Society, 1649–1776*. Stanford, CA: Stanford University Press.

3. FREEDOM AND NON-DOMINATION

Brennan, G. and Hamlin, A. (2001). "Republican Liberty and Resilience." *The Monist*, 84(1), 45–59.

Carter, I. (2000). "A Critique of Freedom as Non-domination." *The Good Society*, 9(3), 43–6.

Goldsmith, M. M. (2000). "Republican Liberty Considered." *History of Political Thought*, 21(3), 543–59.

James, S. (1992). "The Good-enough Citizen: Citizenship and Independence." In S. Bock and S. James, *Beyond Equality and Difference: Citizenship, Feminist Politics and Female Subjectivity*. London: Routledge.

Kelly, P. (2001). "Classical Utilitarianism and the Concept of Freedom: A Response to the Republican Critique." *Journal of Political Ideologies*, 6(1), 13–31.

Kramer, Matthew H. (2003). *The Quality of Freedom*. Oxford: Oxford University Press.

Laborde, C. (2006). "Female Autonomy, Education, and the *Hijab*." *Critical Review of International Social and Political Philosophy*, 9(3), 351–77.

Larmore, C. (2001). "A Critique of Philip Pettit's Republicanism." *Philosophical Issues*, 11, 229–43.

Maynor, J. (2003). *Republicanism in the Modern World*. Cambridge: Polity Press.

Patten, A. (1996). "The Republican Critique of Liberalism." *British Journal of Political Science*, 26(1), 25–44.

Pettit, P. (1993). "Negative Liberty, Liberal and Republican." *European Journal of Philosophy*, 1(1), 15–38.

Pettit, P. (1996). "Freedom as Antipower." *Ethics*, 106(3), 576–604.

Pettit, P. (1997a). *Republicanism: A Theory of Freedom and Government*. Oxford: Oxford University Press.

Pettit, P. (1997b). "Republican Political Theory." In A. Vincent (ed.), *Political Theory: Tradition, Diversity and Ideology*. Cambridge: Cambridge University Press.

Pettit, P. (1999). "Republican Freedom and Contestatory Democratization." In I. Shapiro and C. Hacker-Cordon (eds.), *Democracy's Value*. Cambridge: Cambridge University Press.

Pettit, P. (2000). "On Republicanism: Reply to Carter, Christman, and Dagger." *The Good Society*, 9(3), 54–7.

Pettit, P. (2001a). *A Theory of Freedom: From the Psychology to the Politics of Agency*. Cambridge: Polity Press.

Pettit, P. (2001b). "Capability and Freedom: A Defense of Sen." *Economics and Philosophy*, 17, 1–20.

Pettit, P. (2002). "Keeping Republican Freedom Simple: On a Difference with Quentin Skinner." *Political Theory*, 30(3), 229–356.

Pettit, P. (2003). "Agency-Freedom and Option-Freedom." *Journal of Theoretical Politics*, 15(4), 387–403.

Phillips, A. (2000). "Feminism and Republicanism: Is this a Plausible Alliance?" *Journal of Political Philosophy*, 8(2), 279–93.

Skinner, Q. (1978). *Foundations of Modern Political Thought*, 2 vols. Cambridge: Cambridge University Press.

Skinner, Q. (1981). *Machiavelli*. Oxford: Oxford University Press.

Skinner, Q. (1983). "Machiavelli on the Maintenance of Liberty." *Politics*, 18(2), 3–15.

Skinner, Q. (1984). "The Idea of Negative Liberty: Philosophical and Historical Perspectives." In R. Rorty, J. Schneewind and Q. Skinner (eds.), *Philosophy in History*. Cambridge: Cambridge University Press.

Skinner, Q. (1990a). "Machiavelli's *Discorsi* and the Pre-humanist Origins of Republican Ideas." In G. Bock, Q. Skinner and M. Viroli (eds.), *Machiavelli and Republicanism*. Cambridge: Cambridge University Press.

Skinner, Q. (1990b). "The Republican Ideal of Political Liberty." In G. Bock, Q. Skinner and M. Viroli (eds.), *Machiavelli and Republicanism*. Cambridge: Cambridge University Press.

Skinner, Q. (1991). "The Paradoxes of Political Liberty." In D. Miller (ed.), *Liberty*. Oxford: Oxford University Press.

Skinner, Q. (1992). "On Justice, the Common Good and the Priority of Liberty." In C. Mouffe (ed.), *Dimensions of Radical Democracy*. London: Verso Press.

Skinner, Q. (1996). *Reason and Rhetoric in the Philosophy of Hobbes*. Cambridge: Cambridge University Press.

Skinner, Q. (1997). *Liberty Before Liberalism*. Cambridge: Cambridge University.

Skinner, Q. (2002a). "A Third Concept of Liberty." *Proceedings of the British Academy*, 117, 237–68.

Spitz, J.-F. (1994). "The Concept of Liberty in a Theory of Justice and its Republican Version." *Ratio Juris*, 7(3), 331–47.

Rawls, J. (1971). *A Theory of Justice*. Cambridge, MA: Harvard University Press.

Rawls, J. (1993). *Political Liberalism*. New York: Columbia University Press.

Wall, S. (2001). "Freedom, Interference and Domination." *Political Studies*, 49(2), 216–30.

4. LAW, DELIBERATION AND DEMOCRACY

Barber, B. (1984). *Strong Democracy: Participatory Politics for a New Age*. Berkeley, CA: University of California Press.

Bellamy, R. (1999). *Liberalism and Pluralism: Towards a Politics of Compromise*. London: Routledge.

Braithwaite, J. and Pettit, P. (1990). *Not Just Deserts: A Republican Theory of Criminal Justice*. Oxford: Oxford University Press.

Cohen, J. (1989). "Deliberation and Democratic Legitimacy." In A. Hamlin and P. Pettit (eds.), *The Good Polity*. Oxford: Oxford University Press.

Drysek, J. (2000). *Deliberative Democracy and Beyond*. Oxford: Oxford University Press.

Ferry, L. and Renaut, A. (1992). *From the Rights of Man to the Republican Idea*. Chicago: University of Chicago Press.

Habermas, J. (1994). "Three Normative Models of Democracy." *Constellations*, 1(1), 1–10.

Habermas, J. (1996). *Between Facts and Norms: Contributions to a Discourse Theory of Law and Democracy*. Cambridge: Polity Press.

List, C. (2006). "Republican Freedom and the Rule of Law." *Philosophy, Politics, and Economics*, 5(2), 201–20.

Maddox, G. (2002). "The Limits of Neo-Roman Liberty." *History of Political Thought*, 23(3), 418–31.

McMahon, C. (2005). "The Indeterminacy of Republican Policy." *Philosophy and Public Affairs*, 33(1), 67–93.

Michelman, F. (1988). "Law's Republic." *Yale Law Journal*, 97(8), 1493–1537.

Miller, D. (1995). "Citizenship and Pluralism." *Political Studies*, 43, 432–50.

Miller, D. (2000). "Is Deliberative Democracy Unfair to Disadvantaged Minorities?" In D. Miller, *Citizenship and National Identity*. Cambridge: Polity Press.

Pettit, P. (2000). "Democracy, Electoral and Contestatory." *Nomos*, 42. New York: New York University Press.

Richardson, H. (2002). *Democratic Autonomy: Public Reasoning about the Ends of Policy*. Oxford: Oxford University Press.

Sandel, M. (1996). *Democracy's Discontent: America in Search of a Public Philosophy*. Cambridge, MA: Harvard University Press.

Southwood, N. (2002). "Beyond Pettit's Neo-roman Republicanism: The Deliberative Republic." *Critical Review of International Social and Political Philosophy*, 5(1), 16–42.

Sunstein, C. (1988). "Beyond the Republican Revival." *Yale Law Journal*, 97(8), 1539–90.

5. PATRIOTISM, MULTICULTURALISM AND COSMOPOLITANISM

Bohman, J. (2004). "Republican Cosmopolitanism." *Journal of Political Philosophy*, 12(3), 336–52.

Chung, R. (2003). "The Cosmopolitan Scope of Republican Citizenship." *Critical Review of International Social and Political Philosophy*, 6(1), 135–54.

Dagger, R. (1985). "Rights, Boundaries and the Bond of Community: A Qualified Defense of Moral Parochialism." *American Political Science Review*, 79, 436–47.

Dagger, R. (2001). "Republicanism and the Politics of Place." *Philosophical Explorations* 4(3), 157–73.

Favell, A. (2001). *Philosophies of Integration*. London: Routledge.

Habermas, J. (1994). "Struggles for Recognition in the Democratic Constitutional State." In C. Taylor and A. Gutmann (eds.) *Multiculturalism*. Princeton, NJ: Princeton University Press.

Habermas, J. (1996). "The European Nation-State: Its Achievements and its Limits." In G. Balakrishnan (ed.), *Mapping the Nation*. London: Verso.

Habermas, J. (1999). *The Inclusion of the Other: Studies in Political Theory*, eds. C. Cronin and P. De Greiff. Cambridge: Polity Press.

Honohan, I. (2001). "Friends, Strangers or Countrymen? Citizens as Colleagues." *Political Studies*, 49(1), 51–69.

Laborde, C. (2002). "From Constitutional to Civic Patriotism." *British Journal of Political Science*, 32, 591–612.

Laborde, C. (2008). *Critical Republicanism*. Oxford: Oxford University Press.

Mason, A. (2000). *Community, Solidarity and Belonging*. Cambridge: Cambridge University Press.

Miller, D. (1995). *On Nationality*. Oxford: Oxford University Press.

Miller, D. (2000). *Citizenship and National Identity*. Cambridge: Polity Press.

Miller, D. (2000). "Bounded Citizenship." In Miller, *Citizenship and National Identity*. Cambridge: Polity Press.

Nabulsi, K. (1999). *Traditions of War: Occupation, Resistance and the Law*. Oxford: Oxford University Press.

Schnapper, D. (1988). *Community of Citizens*. Piscataway, NJ: Transaction.

Taylor, C. (1995). "Cross Purposes: The Liberal–Communitarian Debate." In Taylor, *Philosophical Arguments*. Cambridge, MA: Harvard University Press.

Taylor, C. (1996). "Why Democracy Needs Patriotism." In J. Cohen (ed.), *For Love of Country: Debating the Limits of Patriotism*. Boston: Beacon Press.

Viroli, M. (1995). *For Love of Country: An Essay on Nationalism and Patriotism*. Oxford: Oxford University Press.

White, S. (2003a). "Republican Cosmopolitanism." In D. A. Bell and A. De-Shalit, *Forms of Justice: Critical Perspectives on David Miller's Political Philosophy*. Lanham, MD: Rowman and Littlefield.

6. SOCIAL EQUALITY AND CIVIC VIRTUE

Allen, A. and Regan, M. (1998). *Debating Democracy's Discontent: Essays on American Politics, Law and Public Philosophy*. Oxford: Oxford University Press.

Burtt, S. "The Politics of Virtue Today: A Critique and a Proposal." *American Political Science Review*, 87, 360–8.

Callan, E. (1997). *Creating Citizens: Political Education and Liberal Democracy*. Oxford: Oxford University Press.

Dagger, R. (1997). *Civic Virtues: Rights, Citizenship and Republican Liberalism*. Oxford: Oxford University Press.

Dagger, D. (2006). "Neo-Republicanism and the Civic Economy." *Philosophy, Politics, and Economics*, 5(2), 151–73.

Fallon, R. (1989). "What is Republicanism, and What is Worth Retrieving?" *Harvard Law Review*, 102(7), 1695–1735.

Gaus, G. (2003). "Backwards into the Future: Neo-Republicanism as a Post-socialist Critique of Market Society." *Social Philosophy and Politics*, 20, 59–91.

Herzog, D. (1989). "Some Questions for Republicans." *Political Theory*, 14, 473–93.

Mouritsen, P. (2003). "What's the Civil in Civil Society? Robert Putnam, Italy and the Republican Tradition." *Political Studies*, 51(4), 650–69.

Patten, A. (1996). "The Republican Critique of Liberalism." *British Journal of Political Science*, 26, 25–44.

Pettit, P. (2006). "Freedom in the Market." *Philosophy, Politics, and Economics*, 5(2), 131–49.

Putnam, R. (1994). *Making Democracy Work*. Cambridge, MA: Harvard University Press.

Putnam, R. (2000). *Bowling Alone*. New York: Simon and Schuster.

Sandel, M. (1996). *Democracy's Discontent: America in Search of a Public Philosophy*. Cambridge, MA: Harvard University Press.

Sunstein, C. (1997). *Free Markets and Social Justice*. New York: Oxford University Press.

White, S. (2003b). *The Civic Minimum: On the Rights and Obligations of Economic Citizenship*. Oxford: Oxford University Press.

Part I

Republican Freedom and its Critics

Chapter 2
Liberty and Domination

Matthew H. Kramer

In an array of influential writings stretching over a quarter of a century, Quentin Skinner has repeatedly challenged the modern conception of negative liberty developed by Isaiah Berlin and many other theorists.[1] He has sought to draw attention to some once vibrant but now largely peripheral traditions of thought – especially the civic-republican or neo-Roman tradition – in order to highlight what he sees as the limitedness and inadequacies of the currently dominant ways of thinking about freedom. His complaint for many years was that modern liberals are blind to the instrumental freedom-preserving role of civic virtue.[2] More recently, Skinner has joined Philip Pettit in maintaining that the liberal conception of freedom is itself inadequate. Whereas previously he had presumed that civic republicans were at one with present-day liberals in taking freedom to be a negative condition of unconstraint, he now differentiates between them with reference to the breadth of the category of "constraints." According to him, the civic republicans were more perspicacious than the twentieth-century thinkers in recognizing the freedom-impairing effects produced by conditions of domination and dependence. This new claim by Skinner about domination, along with similar claims by Pettit, will undergo scrutiny in this essay. Although Skinner and Pettit disparage the liberal conception of unfreedom as unduly narrow, it will prove to be more capacious than the republican approach which they eloquently champion. It fully encompasses their approach, while also extending further.

Matthew H. Kramer

The Republican Understanding of Freedom

Until publishing *Liberty Before Liberalism* in 1998, Skinner always contended that the civic-republican conception of freedom was the same as the conception espoused by modern negative-liberty theorists. He criticized those present-day theorists for their supposed inattentiveness to the connections between the good of the public and the preservation of individual liberty, but he sided with them in their "negative" understanding of freedom. What he endeavored to show, in other words, was that the doctrine of negative liberty is perfectly compatible with a political credo that adjures people to devote themselves to the common weal. Until 1998, he never assailed the negative-liberty stance itself; he frowned only upon the ostensibly inadequate way in which that stance has been developed by its modern votaries.

Skinner has recently altered his position and has now submitted that the fundamental conception of freedom upheld by the civic-republican writers was more subtle and expansive than that championed by the negative-liberty theorists. On the one hand, he continues to maintain that the civic-republican writers adhered to a negative rather than positive account of freedom. That is, he still affirms that liberty does not amount to the performance of certain actions or the exercise of certain faculties or the following of certain procedures or the attainment of certain goals. On the other hand, he declares that the republicans were more perceptive in apprehending the sources of unfreedom than are the modern exponents of the idea of negative liberty. According to Skinner, unfreedom arises not merely when somebody is prevented from ϕ-ing by someone else,[3] but also when somebody is dominated by someone else. Domination consists in a state of subordination or subjugation, whereby somebody's latitude-to-ϕ is dependent on the tolerance or leniency of someone else. When a person P is in such a state of dependence with regard to ϕ-ing, his ability to ϕ is not sufficient to render him free-to-ϕ. In other words, if his being unprevented from ϕ-ing is at the whim of someone else who enjoys a position of dominance over him, we cannot correctly attribute to P the freedom-to-ϕ. Or so we are now told, in *Liberty before Liberalism*.

Skinner believes that the civic republicans' conception of freedom, as he newly recounts it, was significantly different from the negative-liberty theorists' conception. My terse rehearsal of his new position has so far accentuated the apparent divergence between the republican conception and the modern negative conception, by focusing on particular freedoms (that is, by focusing on each freedom-to-ϕ). Such a focus does create the appearance that "free" and "freedom" as used by civic republicans were quite different in meaning from those terms as used by negative-liberty theorists. However, as will be seen shortly, Skinner himself does not elaborate his new stance with reference to particular liberties; he concentrates instead on the overall dependence and overall liberty of each person. In light of that orientation, his attempt to distinguish his republican understanding of freedom from the negative-liberty theorists' understanding is more vulnerable than it otherwise would be. At any rate, even if Skinner were to develop his position in the direction sketched by my last paragraph, it would prove unsustainable as a conception of freedom that is distinct from the negative-liberty theorists' conception.

Central to Skinner's discussion in *Liberty before Liberalism* is a distinction between two ways in which a person can be made unfree: force or the coercive threat of force, and domination. When a person is prevented by someone else from engaging in certain activities or combinations of activities, she has obviously been made unfree *pro tanto*. Like the negative-liberty theorists, Skinner accepts as much and indeed insists as much. However, he also insists that dependence is a separate mode or source of unfreedom, and he maintains that it is overlooked by the aforementioned theorists. Dependence, the product of domination, gives rise to a situation of unfreedom because it renders a person's latitude precariously contingent on the forbearance of a dominant person. Somebody in a position of dependence cannot afford to ignore or flout the wishes of the person to whom she is subordinate. Hence, even if the dominant party is uninclined to interfere much at all with the leeway of the dependent person, the relationship between them is not unconstrained. So long as the situation of domination persists, that relationship is marked overtly or implicitly by the dependent person's need to seek or retain the good grace of the other party.

Skinner contends that the negative-liberty theorists and their intellectual precursors (such as Thomas Hobbes and William Paley) have declined to acknowledge the character of dependence as a state or source of unfreedom. He suggests that they distinguish between freedom and the security of freedom, and that they do not classify encroachments on the latter as restrictions on the former (Skinner 1998: 80). Thus, because a posture of dependence impairs only the security of one's freedom without necessarily reducing the extent of that freedom in any way, it should not be viewed as a species of unfreedom at all. Such is the claim which Skinner ascribes to the modern negative-liberty theorists and their philosophical forebears.

As will be seen, people on both sides of the debate charted by Skinner are confused. Civic republicans and some negative-liberty theorists alike have erred in overstating the difference between the dependence of a dominated person and the confinedness of a person who is thwarted from ϕ-ing. What the civic republicans have regarded as two varieties of unfreedom will turn out to be two aspects of a single type of unfreedom. Likewise, what some negative-liberty theorists have perceived as a dichotomy between unfreedom and insecurity will turn out to dissolve into a single complicated condition of unfreedom.

To arrive at these conclusions, we shall have to be attentive to three main considerations: (1) the division between the particular liberties and the overall liberty of each person; (2) the role of probabilities in ascriptions of freedom and unfreedom; and (3) the twofold temporal indexes of each particular freedom (namely, the time at which a particular freedom exists and the time of the action or process or condition to which the particular freedom pertains). Once we have taken those factors duly into account, we shall find that Skinner's new approach – however powerful it may be – is no more successful than his erstwhile approach in showing that modern theories of negative liberty do not compare well with civic-republican theories.

The Restrictive Effects of Domination

As I have argued at length elsewhere, the overall freedom of each person P is largely determined by the range of the combinations of conjunctively exercisable opportunities that are available to him.[4] If P is free to ϕ, but if his ϕ-ing will sharply reduce his future opportunities, then his freedom-to-ϕ does not add much to his overall liberty (since only a small number of the combinations of conjunctively exercisable freedoms that make up his overall liberty will each include his freedom-to-ϕ as an item). If most of the opportunities available to P at any given time are similarly hemmed in – perhaps because most activities are forbidden by severe and well-enforced laws – then his overall liberty is highly straitened, notwithstanding that his particular liberties at the time might be numerous. Thus, if a situation of domination eliminates some of *P*'s combinations of conjunctively exercisable freedoms, it curtails his overall liberty. If the eliminated range is substantial, then so too is the curtailment. Consequently, insofar as we have good grounds for thinking that a relationship of domination will indeed produce an effect of that sort, we ipso facto have good grounds for deeming such a relationship to be inimical to *P*'s freedom. That verdict follows straightforwardly from the doctrine of negative liberty; there is no need to augment or modify that doctrine in order to reach such a verdict.

On the basis of Skinner's illuminating expositions of civic-republican worries about domination, we have ample reasons indeed for believing that the dependence of a dominated person will impair her freedom in the way just described. Though her state of dependence might eliminate very few of her particular freedoms, it will eliminate the conjunctive exercisability of many such freedoms and will thereby significantly reduce her overall liberty. Specifically, the combinations of conjunctively exercisable liberties that will typically be removed are those which include freedoms to engage in patterns of behavior that are not deferential toward the dominant party. Because somebody who makes use of such freedoms will arouse the ire of the dominant party and will thereby trigger harsh penalties, those freedoms are not exercisable conjunctively with any freedoms that would be scotched by the penalties. Myriad combinations-of-liberties, every one of which would be a conjunctively exercisable set in the absence of domination, will each contain liberties that are not conjunctively exercisable in the presence of domination. As a consequence, the dependent person's overall liberty is seriously constricted. We can discern as much on the basis of a negative theory of liberty alone, without any need for the putatively supplementary theses of civic republicanism.

Skinner repeatedly makes clear that a relationship of dominance and dependence does indeed cabin freedom in the manner outlined by my last paragraph. As he writes, for example, when summarizing James Harrington's remarks on the autocratic regime in Constantinople:

> If you are a subject of the sultan, . . . your freedom in Constantinople, however great in extent, will remain wholly dependent on the sultan's goodwill. . . . You will find yourself constrained in what you can say and do by the reflection that, as Harrington brutally puts it, even the greatest bashaw in Constantinople is merely a tenant of his head, liable to

lose it as soon as he speaks or acts in such a way as to cause the sultan offence. (Skinner 1998: 86)

Skinner quotes and paraphrases many similar statements propounded by other civic-republican writers. We shall look here at only a couple of the germane passages. When synopsizing the views of Algernon Sidney concerning despotic regimes (such as that of Charles II), Skinner declares that "Sidney . . . emphasises the life of extreme precariousness that everyone is made to suffer under such forms of government. . . . The outcome of living under such a regime . . . is that everyone lives in continual fear and danger of incurring the tyrant's displeasure. It becomes everyone's chief preoccupation 'to avoid the effects of his rage'" (Skinner 1998: 91–2). Skinner offers a cognate observation when recounting the attitude of civic republicans toward the untrammeled discretion of tyrants: "[I]f you live under any form of government that allows for the exercise of prerogative or discretionary powers outside the law, you will already be living as a slave. . . . The very fact . . . that your rulers possess such arbitrary powers means that the continued enjoyment of your civil liberty remains at all times dependent on their good-will. But this is to say that you remain subject or liable to having your rights of action curtailed or withdrawn at any time" (Skinner 1998: 70).

As has been indicated, the freedom-corroding effects of domination are readily explicable within my theory of negative liberty. When the civic-republican writers attacked despotic and autocratic regimes, they vividly captured the ways in which those regimes cut off the conjunctive exercisability of various liberties. When a ruler wields tyrannical power, many of the freedoms of citizens to engage in non-obsequious patterns of behavior will no longer be exercisable conjunctively with their freedoms to engage in any modes of conduct that would be prevented by the tyrant's penalties for insufficient deference. There is no need whatsoever to go beyond a theory of negative liberty for this important insight into the workings of despotism. Nonetheless, Skinner resolutely endeavors to put some distance between the civic-republican approach and that of the negative-liberty theorists. He contends that the republican campaign against tyranny was informed by a more expansive sense of the nature of unfreedom.

Skinner sounds this theme at a number of junctures, such as the following: "The thesis on which the [civic-republican] writers chiefly insist, however, is that it is never necessary to suffer . . . overt coercion in order to forfeit your civil liberty. You will also be rendered unfree if you merely fall into a condition of political subjection or dependence, thereby leaving yourself open to the danger of being forcibly or coercively deprived by your government of your life, liberty or estates" (Skinner 1998: 69–70). A similar message emerges in the course of Skinner's discussion of Sidney: "As Sidney makes clear, it is the mere possibility of your being subjected with impunity to arbitrary coercion, not the fact of your being coerced, that takes away your liberty and reduces you to the condition of a slave" (Skinner 1998: 72). A host of other statements along the same lines bestrew Skinner's piquant and informative account of seventeenth-century republicanism. His reason for insisting on the point is most directly expressed in the following passage:

> What the [civic-republican] writers repudiate *avant la lettre* is the key assumption of classical liberalism to the effect that force or the coercive threat of it constitute the only forms of constraint that interfere with individual liberty. The [civic-republican] writers insist, by contrast, that to live in a condition of dependence is in itself a source and a form of constraint. As soon as you recognise that you are living in such a condition, this will serve in itself to constrain you from exercising a number of your civil rights. This is why they insist . . . that to live in such a condition is to suffer a diminution not merely of security for your liberty but of liberty itself. (Skinner 1998: 84, footnotes deleted.]

Skinner's attempt to stake out the distinctiveness of the civic-republican understanding of freedom and unfreedom is unsuccessful. His expositions make clear that the republican analyses do not advance at all beyond a theory of negative liberty that properly distinguishes between particular freedoms and overall freedom. Indeed, in two important respects (which will be specified shortly), the civic-republican conception of liberty and unfreedom – at least as described by Skinner – is unduly narrow rather than commendably wide-ranging.

According to the conception of unfreedom that I have espoused elsewhere,[5] the preventative factors that give rise to unfreedoms are other people's actions and dispositions. There is no suggestion whatsoever that the unfreedom-engendering conduct must occur by certain routes, such as the actual application or coercive threat of force. The freedom-reducing effects of domination occur so long as some people are at the mercy of others and are therefore obliged to propitiate those others in order to escape their wrath. If the dependent people give offense to the dominant parties, they will suffer fierce retaliation. In those circumstances, freedoms to engage in nondeferential patterns of behavior are no longer exercisable conjunctively with freedoms to engage in any patterns of behavior that would be precluded by the retaliatory measures which the insufficient deference will trigger. In this manner, the situation of domination impairs the overall liberty of each dependent person. In connection with this point, the exact nature of the techniques by which the dominant parties exert their ascendance is almost wholly immaterial. Whether those parties impose their sway through the frequent application of violence and the issuance of overt threats, or whether they impose it instead more subtly by constantly displaying their superiority in ways that render largely superfluous the use of outright threats and force, their dominance means that many freedoms that would otherwise be conjunctively exercisable are not so. When a negative-liberty theorist recognizes that the conjunctive exercisability of those freedoms has been removed, he is not automatically presuming that the removal must have been due to the actual wielding of violence or explicit threats. After all, a reduction in the freedom of some person P occurs whenever P would be prevented from ϕ-ing if he were to endeavor to ϕ, and whenever he would be prevented from performing certain actions together if he were to endeavor to perform them together. In other words, the occurrence of the reduction does not necessarily involve any actual endeavor and thus does not necessarily involve any actual obstruction; the endeavor and the obstruction can remain hypothetical. If the only door to a room would be immediately locked in the event that a man inside were to attempt to leave, then he is unfree-to-leave regardless of whether the attempt and the locking ever actually take place. Given that a reduction in freedom does not perforce presuppose the actual occurrence of preventative steps, it obviously does not perforce presuppose the actual occurrence of preventative steps of certain specified types. Hence, Skinner goes astray when he repeatedly declares that negative-liberty theorists acknowledge only force and patent coercion as sources of unfreedom.

In two respects, as has been stated, Skinner's civic-republican account of freedom and unfreedom is narrower – not broader – than the negative-liberty account. First, in the final passage quoted above, Skinner suggests that unfreedom arises only "[a]s soon as you recognize that you are living in such a condition." By contrast, a sound theory of negative liberty does not set any such limitation on the emergence of unfreedom. If a man is in a room where the only door has been firmly locked by someone else, then he is unfree-to-depart irrespective of whether he knows that the door cannot be opened. Of course, he will not *feel* unfree unless he does apprehend that he is confined to the room; but he will *be* unfree even if he remains ignorant of his plight. Much the same can be said with reference to a relationship of domination. A dependent person might never become aware of her position as such. That is, she might fail to grasp that her combinations of conjunctively exercisable opportunities are diminished by the dominance of someone else, who will punish her severely if she engages in behavior that displeases him. If she fortuitously avoids such behavior, and if she does not otherwise become aware of her subordination, then she will not *feel* unfree in her position of dependence. As a result, she will probably not adopt the sycophantic mien of a knowingly subjugated person. Nonetheless, she will *be* unfree in many respects so long as the dominant person's ascendance decreases the range of her combinations of conjunctively exercisable liberties. Her unfreedom is independent of her knowledge of her unfreedom. (Of course, nothing said here has been meant to suggest that a dependent person is very likely to remain ignorant of the lowliness and precariousness of her condition. As Pettit has argued, a situation of dominance and subjection will typically impress itself upon the consciousness of each party involved, who will also grasp that the other party harbors a corresponding awareness of their relationship [Pettit 1997: 58–61]. Nevertheless, even in the unusual circumstances where this typical situation of common knowledge does not obtain, the structure of mastery and subordination restricts the overall liberty of the person who occupies the inferior position in the structure.)

A second inadvisably cramping feature of civic republicanism is its apparent assumption that unfreedom comes about only by way of conduct that is *intended* to cause such an effect. Although the civic republicans correctly perceived that deliberate violence and coercion are not the only sources of unfreedom, they unwisely adduced only one further source: domination. Like the wielding of force and coercion, the exercise or sustainment of domination is intentional rather than inadvertent. It is thus the sort of activity which the civic republicans would recognize as generative of unfreedom. The importance of intentionality or deliberateness in the conduct that produces unfreedom is manifest within the work of the present-day republican writer Pettit, who explicitly excludes "non-intentional obstruction" from the set of factors that give rise to unfreedom (Pettit 1997: 26). Pettit explains his position on this matter as follows: "Were non-intentional forms of obstruction also to count as interference, that would be to lose the distinction between securing people against the natural effects of chance and incapacity and scarcity and securing them against the things that they may try to do to one another. This distinction is of the first importance in political philosophy, and almost all traditions have marked it by associating a person's freedom with constraints only on more or less intentional interventions by others" (Pettit 1997: 52–3). Pettit's explanation does not support our limiting of the sources of unfreedom to intentional obstructions or interventions. Instead, it supports our limiting of those sources to any obstructions or restraints that have been imposed on some person(s) by the actions or dispositions-to-perform-actions of some other person(s), whether the effects of the actions/dispositions are intentional or unwitting. Causal attributability along those lines is precisely what my own theory of negative liberty specifies as the key requirement that must be satisfied if a constraint on freedom is to count as an instance of unfreedom.

To be sure, Pettit's category of "intentional interventions" is more expansive than would normally be true of a category so labeled. It apparently includes "the sort of action in the doing of which we can sensibly allege negligence" (Pettit 1997: 52). Exactly why Pettit designates negligently produced results as "intentional" is unclear; in any case, his somewhat idiosyncratic classification renders less objectionable his insistence that unfreedom must be due to intentional obstructions. Still, even though negligent actions are comprehended within his array of unfreedom-engendering factors, his account remains too narrow. It should encompass all types of human actions rather than only some types. Among the potential sources of unfreedom, the sundry unintentional effects of other people's actions and dispositions-to-perform-actions should be included – even if the occurrence of those inadvertent effects is not due to negligence at all. Given Pettit's desire to distinguish between the results of sheer chance or incapacity or scarcity and the results of other people's endeavors, we should mark the divide between "not free" and "unfree" by differentiating between any states of preventedness that are not causally ascribable to other people's actions and any states of preventedness that are so ascribable. Such a differentiation will have placed the unintentional effects of non-negligent actions among the possible sources of unfreedom.

Before we move on, we should glance at an example that helps to underscore the drawbacks of distinguishing between the intentional effects and the unintentional effects of human actions, for the purpose of ascertaining whether someone has been made unfree.[6] Suppose that Mark and Molly are both in a room, and that they are endowed with roughly equal strength. Simon shuts and locks the only means of exit from the room. Knowing that Molly is inside, Simon has locked the door because he wants to confine her there. Simon knows nothing of Mark's presence in the room – either because Simon has been negligent or because there were no reasonable grounds for him to be aware of Mark's location. (Mark may have been hidden from view, such that even a careful and attentive person would not have been able to espy him.) If we correlate the "intentional"/"unintentional" dichotomy with the distinction between "unfree" and "not free," we shall have to conclude that Simon's act of locking the door has made Molly unfree-to-leave but has made Mark merely not-free-to-leave. In other words, we arrive at the verdict that a single human act which imposes exactly the same physical constraints on two people of similar capacities has affected their unfreedom in markedly different ways. Such a verdict is unacceptable for any nonmoralized account of freedom and unfreedom. We can and should acknowledge that Molly has been wronged to a greater degree than Mark, but we should not accept that the severity of the wrong bears even tenuously on the question whether Mark has been rendered unfree-to-leave-the-room by Simon. That question is a factual inquiry about one of Mark's inabilities and about the causes thereof, rather than an inquiry about the morality of Simon's action or about anyone's intentions. Certainly if we aim to give due heed to the distinction which Pettit highlights – the distinction between the results of natural incapacity or chance or scarcity and the results of human activity – we should conclude that both Molly and Mark have become unfree-to-leave as a consequence of Simon's locking of the door.

The Gentle Giant

Skinner and especially Pettit broach the possibility of a relationship of dominance and dependence that eliminates very few of the dependent person's combinations of conjunctively exercisable freedoms. If the ascendant party in the relationship is sufficiently tolerant and undemanding, then his tendency to retaliate in the event of contumacious behavior by the subordinate party might be extremely slight – so slight as to constitute virtually no impingement on the subordinate party's overall freedom. Insofar as we assess this situation by reference to the doctrine of negative liberty, then, we shall have to conclude that the indulgent dominator's sway has no significant impact on the freedom of the dominated person. Indeed, the dominator might not reduce the inferior person's overall freedom to any greater extent than would the presence of someone else who lacks a position of dominance altogether. In the eyes of the negative-liberty theorists, accordingly, the soft-hearted dominator's superiority is not in itself a source of unfreedom; everything hinges on what the dominator does with his superiority. Such, at any rate, is the view ascribed to the negative-liberty theorists by Skinner and Pettit. For the proponents of the civic-republican conception of freedom, by contrast, the superiority of the dominator is in itself a source of unfreedom. Though the ascendant person might not interfere with any of the subordinate person's projects and activities, the very structure of their relationship – a relationship of outright superiority and inferiority, in which the former party is sufficiently powerful to impose his will on the latter party if he chooses – is a situation of dependence and thus of unfreedom. Whenever the sustainment of someone's overall liberty hinges on the good will of other people (who might be impeccably benevolent indeed), his liberty has thereby been curtailed.

Skinner suggests this line of thought at several junctures, most directly in the following passage (part of which was quoted earlier):

> [I]f you live under any form of government that allows for the exercise of prerogative or discretionary powers outside the law, you will already be living as a slave. Your rulers may choose not to exercise these powers, or may exercise them only with the tenderest regard for your individual liberties. So you may in practice continue to enjoy the full range of your civil rights. The very fact, however, that your rulers possess such arbitrary powers means that the continued enjoyment of your civil liberty remains at all times dependent on their goodwill. (Skinner 1998: 70)

Pettit has more insistently sounded this theme, as he seeks to accentuate the ostensible divergences between his own conception of freedom and the conception put forward by the negative-liberty theorists. He repeatedly adverts to the possibility of dominators whose benignly uninterfering obligingness ensures that their power does not cause any significant loss of day-to-day latitude for the people under their sway. For example, near the outset of his discussion of the contrasts between the republican account and the negative account of freedom, he submits that "I may be dominated by another – for example, to go to the extreme case, I may be the slave of another – without actually being interfered with in any of my choices. It may just happen that my master is of a kindly and non-interfering disposition" (Pettit 1997: 22). Pettit persistently harks back to this example of the indulgent master, in order to emphasize that a structure of domination does not necessarily remove particular freedoms or impair overall freedom as defined by the negative-liberty theorists. The example illustrates his general thesis that the unfreedom of domination exists whenever powerful people *can* inflict oppression, rather than only when they *do* inflict oppression. "Domination can occur without interference, because it requires only that someone have the capacity to interfere arbitrarily in your affairs; no one need actually interfere" (Pettit 1997: 23). Accordingly, an absence of domination consists in the absence of anyone's ability to exploit others for his or her own gain.

Pettit recurrently maintains that the negative conception of liberty contrasts sharply with his own conception. We are told again and again that negative-liberty theorists believe that no unfreedom is engendered when "some people hav[e] dominating power over others, provided they do not exercise that power and are not likely to exercise it" (Pettit 1997: 9). Now, before we continue to explore the possibility of an indulgently uninterfering dominator, we should note that Pettit frequently has some quite different possibilities in mind when he writes about the unlikelihood of a dominator's interference. Often, what he means when he talks about the improbability of interference is that the subordinate person in a hierarchical relationship can behave with enough sycophancy or cunning to forestall any angry exertions of force by the ascendant person. Through sufficient groveling or sufficient furtiveness and shrewdness, a subjugated person can guard against triggering the wrath of her master and can thereby save herself from being physically battered or trammeled. On the many occasions when Pettit refers to toadying and stealthiness as patterns of conduct that can make the interference of a dominator unlikely, he is committing an error which I have already criticized.[7] He is failing to recognize that the overall freedom of each person is largely determined by the range of the combinations-of-conjunctively-exercisable-liberties available to her. Inasmuch as' we do take due account of that point, we can see that the overall freedom of a subordinate person *P* is significantly impaired when she has to resort to obsequiousness or unobtrusiveness in order to stave off a dominant person's punitive measures. Far from being a situation wherein interference is unlikely, *P*'s plight is a situation wherein interference is occurring extensively. That interference does not come about through the actual application of violence (*ex hypothesi*), but it consists in the undoing of the conjunctive exercisability of many opportunities – opportunities that could have been exercised conjunctively in the absence of the dominant party's sway. In the presence of that sway, if *P* acts in any manner that is insufficiently humble or furtive, she will not also be able to act in any manner precluded by the retaliation that will be undertaken against her as a response to her perceived audacity. Her freedom to act in the former manner is not exercisable conjunctively with her freedom to act in the latter manner, because of the dominant party's preparedness to remove the latter freedom if the former freedom is acted upon. Hence, under any tenable account of negative liberty, we must conclude that *P*'s overall freedom is substantially reduced by her subjection to the dominant party. Contrary to what Pettit contends, the dominance of that party is indeed being exerted – not through the actual infliction of violence (which is unnecessary in the circumstances), but through the party's readiness to inflict violence. That very readiness eliminates many combinations of conjunctively exercisable freedoms for *P*.

In short, if Pettit's remarks about the unlikelihood of a dominator's interference are to stand any chance of going beyond arguments that have already been countered in this essay, they will have to be construed as pertaining only to contexts in which the ascendant parties are too obliging or uninterested to obstruct the activities of the inferior parties. To drive home his point with reference to such contexts, Pettit distinguishes between the mere *improbability* of domination and the *infeasibility* thereof. Whereas the uninterfering disposition of a master can render highly unlikely the application of physical force, the only veritable guarantee against the wielding of such force is the dismantling of the whole structure of mastery and subjugation. As Pettit writes:

Seeing an option as an improbable choice for an agent, even as a van-
ishingly improbable choice, is different from seeing it as a choice that is
not accessible to the agent: seeing it as a choice that is not within the
agent's power. Thus the fact that another person is unlikely to interfere
with me, just because they happen to have no interest in interfering, is
consistent with their retaining access to the option of interfering with
me. . . . And so it is quite possible for me to be forced to think of myself
as subordinate to someone who is no more likely to interfere with me
than I am to interfere with them. (Pettit 1997: 88)

This distinction between the mere unlikelihood and the impossibility
of oppression is crucial for Pettit's republican position. We should
therefore note an array of objections to his use of that distinction –
objections that are cumulatively fatal to his insistence on the distinctiveness of the republican conception of freedom and unfreedom.

First, when Pettit repeatedly relies on a dichotomy between not being
endowed with sufficient strength for the exploitation of others and not
being inclined to avail oneself of that strength, he is doing so in order
to differentiate between a situation where dominating interference is
impossible and a situation where such interference is merely improbable.
"The point is not just to make arbitrary interference improbable; the
point is to make it inaccessible" (Pettit 1997: 74). This impossibility/
improbability distinction is deeply problematic, since the availability
or unavailability of resources essential for domination is always itself
a matter of greater or lesser probability. Only in a utopian fantasy can
the emergence of domination and its effects be strictly ruled out. In
any possible world outside such a fantasy, the most that can be done is
to render domination highly unlikely.

To be sure, the focus of the probabilistic calculations will not always
be the same for Pettit as for his opponents. Someone adopting Pettit's
position has to inquire about the likelihood that any person or group
of people will be able to gain access to means of oppressive power.
Pettit's opponents, by contrast, have to inquire about the likelihood that
any person or group capable of wielding oppressive power will choose
to make use of that capability. Now, Pettit's republican institutional
proposals will aim to minimize the first of these probabilities – the
probability that people will become capable of acting as dominators –
but will never reduce it to zero. Were anyone to think that that risk
can indeed be altogether removed, he or she would be indulging in

irresponsibly wishful dreaming; such dreaming may be suitable for the conclusion of a fairy tale, but it should not enter into political philosophy. Within the domain of political philosophy, both the inquiry associated with Pettit's stance and the inquiry associated with his opponents' stance are about contingencies that can never be ruled out categorically for the future. Instead of a sharp division between a quest for the infeasibility of oppression and a quest for the mere unlikelihood thereof, the split between Pettit and his opponents is nothing more than a matter of alternative foci concerning the ineliminable risk of the onset of domination. Pettit concentrates on minimizing the chance that anyone will come to occupy a position of ascendance, while his opponents concentrate on minimizing the chance that the powers of any such position will be exerted. In each case, the goal pursued is improbability rather than strict impossibility.

A second objection to Pettit's argument goes together well with the first. Not only are both sides of the debate between Pettit and his opponents focused on probabilities, but furthermore they will very often be focused on the same set of probabilities. For anyone who desires to minimize the likelihood of the exercise of oppressive powers, the best route will typically be to minimize the accumulation of such powers in the first place. Once those powers have been amassed by some person or group of people, the chance of their being exerted is typically extremely high; almost always, then, the freedom-constricting consequences of relationships of domination can most effectively be averted if the relationships themselves are nipped in the bud. A reliance on the sheer benevolence or indifference of people in positions of dominance is a far, far less effective tack. Skinner and Pettit quote a myriad of thunderous declamations by republicans who warned of the corruptions and temptations to which the holders of autocratic power are prone. We have no reason whatsoever to doubt the pertinence of those warnings. Indeed, Pettit's acute awareness of the tendency of powerful people to make use of their dominance is precisely what lies behind his assumption that subordinate people must normally resort to flattery or diffidence in order to stave off harsh penalties. Tyrants and masters and other power-holders usually take advantage of their superiority in any number of ways that impair the overall liberty of their underlings to varying extents. Thus, if one's aim is to lower the probability of impairments of each person's liberty as much as possible, one should generally resist the establishment of positions of dominance – even if one believes that some specific occupants of those positions will be scrupulously unassertive in the exercise of their powers. Such forbearance (whether due to benignity or to indifference) is very seldom to be found among power-holders, as the civic republicans themselves would heartily agree. It should hardly ever be counted on.

A third objection pertains to the rare circumstances in which people capable of systematically exploiting and mistreating others are wholly uninclined to do so. In any such set of circumstances, where the probability of serious encroachments by a dominant person on the overall liberty of his or her contemporaries is practically nil, we should acknowledge as much in our measurements of freedom. That is, we should acknowledge that the redoubtable might of the person does not lessen anyone else's overall liberty significantly. A rather far-fetched example should illustrate this point. Suppose that, in a community not far from some hills, a gigantic person G is born. From adolescence onward, G is far larger and stronger and swifter and more intelligent than any of his compatriots. If he wished, he could arrogate to himself an autocratic sway over his community by threatening to engage in rampages and by coercing some of the residents into serving as his henchmen. Were G so inclined, no one would dare to resist his bidding. He is well aware of this state of affairs. Ergo, as a matter of sheer capability – which, as has already been mentioned, is the determinative factor for someone's status as a dominator (Pettit 1997: 23, 52, 54–5) – G clearly occupies a position of dominating ascendance. In fact, however, he loathes the idea of becoming a tyrant; his principal desire is to seclude himself altogether from his community. He does indeed depart therefrom, in order to reside in a cave among the nearby hills where he contentedly feeds off natural fruits and wildlife and where he spends his time in solitary reflection and reading and exercise. In these circumstances G is a dominator (according to Pettit's criteria for that status), but he is not significantly reducing the overall liberty of anyone else. Given his formidable strength and size, he could impose his will on others if he so chose. However, given his inclinations and self-sufficiency, there is no prospect of his doing so. Because of his reclusive disposition, the likelihood of his expunging many liberties of his contemporaries – or many of their combinations of conjunctively exercisable liberties – is effectively zero. His abstention from exerting his formidable powers against his fellows is a product of inveterate traits of his personality, and is thus not something that is liable to change. Those ingrained features of his character are as much facts of his existence as are his size and physical strength. If we described him as rendering his contemporaries unfree in many respects simply by dint of his dominating capacity, we would be misrepresenting his situation rather than illuminating it.[8] His withdrawal from his community to the cave reveals the potential gap between dominance and the engendering of unfreedom. Though that gap is prodigiously uncommon, it is certainly possible.

This point becomes even more palpable when we consider an example of a dominator who is subordinated by someone whom he himself could oppress. Let us ponder a scenario involving Lennie and George (who bear a considerable resemblance, though not a perfect resemblance, to their namesakes in John Steinbeck's *Of Mice and Men*). Lennie is nearly as strong and large and swift-footed as G in my previous example, but he is less intelligent and free-spirited. George is much smaller and weaker than Lennie, but his domineering tough-mindedness offsets his physical deficiencies. Although Lennie is physically much more powerful than George, and although the intellectual disparity between the two men is not vast, the differences between their temperaments eventuate in the wholesale domination of the more brawny man by the more diminutive. George continually browbeats Lennie into performing countless menial tasks that serve George's needs and comfort, and he insists on getting his way whenever Lennie forms intentions that are at odds with his own. He terrorizes Lennie with his fits of temper and his piercing insults; Lennie, thoroughly overmastered and intimidated by George, is his dutiful servant. Now, even if this scenario were to be moderated by the addition of some ties of friendship and protection between the two men, the basic point highlighted by it would remain prominent. Somebody fully capable of dominating another person – somebody whom Pettit's analysis will therefore classify as a dominator – can turn out to be exploited and bullied by that other person. If we were to describe George as having been made unfree by Lennie's dominating strength, we would be distorting his situation even more markedly than a cognate description of G's compatriots in my previous example would distort *their* situation.

Admittedly, it might be that George's irascible and imperious behavior is itself necessary to ward off domination by Lennie. If George's aggressively tyrannical conduct is indeed a means of defending his own overall liberty, then that liberty has been diminished by Lennie's daunting presence. After all, were George to abstain from his domineering surliness under such circumstances, he would very quickly render himself unfree to undertake any projects or activities that would be precluded by Lennie's assumption of the ascendant posture in their relationship. Under such circumstances, that is, Lennie's latent disposition to exert his might has extinguished the conjunctive exercisability of many of George's liberties. Nonetheless, this feature of the situation is purely contingent. We can just as easily imagine that a softening of George's demeanor would produce less dramatic effects. Perhaps it would not induce any substantial changes at all in the subordinate posture of Lennie, who might be unshakably habituated to George's dominance. Or, what is slightly more plausible, the growing emollience of George might simply induce Lennie to become less dutiful and subservient without actually prompting him to act despotically toward George. Instead of inverting the previous relationship of mastery and submission, Lennie might simply opt to live alongside George as an equal. Or perhaps he would separate from George and go his own way. Whatever might be the precise outcome of a marked alteration in George's authoritarian mien, it would not necessarily involve any significant loss of liberty for George himself (especially if the baseline for measuring the loss is a situation in which neither of the two men dominates the other). In that case, his currently overbearing behavior is not a means of safeguarding his own freedom against the potential dominance of Lennie, but is straightforwardly a means of coercing and manipulating the bulkier man. Such a state of affairs can obtain even though Pettit's analysis of domination clearly generates the conclusion that Lennie is a dominator. Someone can qualify as a possessor of that status – as defined by Pettit – without significantly impairing the overall freedom of anyone else.

In short, in the very rare circumstances where relationships of domination genuinely involve extremely low probabilities of nontrivial encroachments on the freedom of subordinate people, we should not characterize the state of subordination as a state of unfreedom. When we examine the posture of the gigantic recluse G as a dominator *vis-à-vis* the other members of his community, and when we examine the posture of Lennie as a dominator *vis-à-vis* George, we shall be misunderstanding those situations if we maintain that G and Lennie have significantly abridged the overall freedom of the people to whom they are hugely superior physically. Pettit's republican inclination to equate domination and unfreedom does not illuminate such situations.

Before we move on from this discussion of probability, we should very briefly note that most of the principal contentions herein about the curtailment or noncurtailment of overall freedom are applicable *mutatis mutandis* to the inexistence or existence of particular freedoms. If it is virtually certain that somebody in a dominant position will use his ascendance to prevent a subordinate person S from ϕ-ing in the event that S endeavors to ϕ, then we are warranted in saying that S is unfree to ϕ. We can for most purposes leave implicit any probabilistic qualifications. By contrast, if the likelihood of the powerful person's prevention of S from ϕ-ing (in the event of S's endeavoring to ϕ) is lower but still nontrivial, then our statements about S's unfreedom-to-ϕ should be overtly probabilistic. Finally, if the likelihood of the powerful person's prevention of S from ϕ-ing in the event of S's endeavoring to ϕ is exceedingly small – as it clearly is in the case of G or Lennie above, for most specifications of the "ϕ" variable – we shall be amply warranted in affirming that S is free to ϕ (*vis-à-vis* the powerful person). Once again, any probabilistic qualifications can for most purposes be left implicit. In other words, with regard to the reduction or non-reduction of a person's overall freedom, and with regard to the inexistence or existence of any of a person's particular freedoms, our basic focus in a context of domination should be the same. The crucial consideration in such a context is not the sheer fact of the domination, but the probability that that fact will result in the prevention of certain actions or combinations of actions.

Time for a Change

The last paragraph's terse remarks on particular freedoms can serve well as a transition to the topic of this closing discussion, where we look at the impact of domination on a subordinate person's ability to perform particular actions at specified times. As has been observed, Skinner and Pettit and other republicans have generally expounded their doctrine with reference to overall freedom and unfreedom rather than with reference to particular liberties. However, a shift of orientation from the former to the latter will enable us to detect some further complexities in republican ascriptions of freedom and unfreedom. Specifically, we shall explore here some difficulties relating to the flow of time.[9]

Let us concentrate on a scenario involving a huge bully Barry and a much smaller lad Ernest. Ernest keenly desires to eat a russet apple that is on a table very close to the spot where Barry is now standing. Barry indicates loudly and unmistakably that he will prevent Ernest from eating or even touching the apple if the smaller boy attempts to gain possession of it. He positions himself squarely between Ernest and the apple, and thereby blocks off the only route of access to the piece of fruit. A relationship of domination clearly obtains between the two boys. Feeling famished, and avidly enthusiastic about russet apples in any event, Ernest becomes despondent and desperate. He pleads with Barry to step aside, but the bully is unyielding. Ernest falls to his knees and grovels, and he even kisses Barry's feet while exhorting the brawny boy to desist from preventing his consumption of the apple. Barry, delighted by this confirmation of his extravagant sense of his own worth, eventually relents and moves away in order to give Ernest access to the table. While Barry watches from a short distance, Ernest joyously grabs the apple and consumes it with gusto.

Let us designate as "$t6$" the time at which Ernest takes hold of the russet apple. Manifestly he is free at $t6$ to clutch the apple at $t6$, since necessarily he is able to perform an action which he in fact does perform. Somewhat less obviously, he has also been free at each earlier juncture to grab the apple at $t6$. Let us designate the earliest relevant juncture – say, the point at which Barry initially decides to prevent Ernest from getting hold of the apple – as "$t1$." We may designate some of the intervening moments as "$t2$," "$t3$," "$t4$," and "$t5$." Ernest at $t1$ (and at every subsequent stage) is free to gain possession of the apple at $t6$, for there is at least one course of conduct open to him at $t1$ that will enable him to acquire the apple at $t6$. Retrodictively we can easily know as much, because Ernest in fact does acquire the apple at $t6$. Quite a different matter is our knowing at $t1$ whether Ernest is free at that very moment to clutch the apple at $t6$. At any rate, either retrospectively or prospectively, we can correctly ascribe to Ernest just such a freedom.

Now, this analysis of the situation may seem insensitive to the harsh and dispiriting constraints imposed by domination. After all, my account maintains that Ernest is free at every stage ($t1, t2, \ldots t6$) to grab the apple at $t6$. Yet, as we have been told, he manages to get the apple at that time only by having resorted to a series of self-abasing maneuvers of the most humiliating sort. Operating within the severe confines established by Barry's powerful presence, Ernest has had to undergo considerable anguish and ignominy in the struggle to achieve his objective. Yet my ascription to him of freedom at every stage might appear to suggest that his plight has not been significantly different from a situation in which his access to the apple is never obstructed at all. If the need for arduous efforts of cajolery by him is deemed to be fully consistent with his constant possession of the freedom-to-clutch-the-apple-at-$t6$, then my exposition might seem to be portraying those efforts as largely indistinguishable from his simply walking up and snatching the apple without any opposition. Given that the particular freedom (Ernest's freedom-to-clutch-the-apple-at-$t6$) is said to exist at every juncture in the face of Barry's pugnacity, the contrast between a stifling ordeal of domination and a refreshing lack of domination may appear to be disregarded by my analysis. Were that contrast indeed slighted by a negative-liberty approach, the republican criticisms of such an approach could have a new lease on life.

In fact, however, the gap between the presence and the absence of domination can be charted precisely and illuminatingly within a negative-liberty account. Three chief points should be emphasized. First, as has already been intimated, any prospective attribution to Ernest of the freedom-at-$t1$-to-hold-the-apple-at-$t6$ will be fiendishly problematic indeed. Because of Barry's bulk and temperament, the chances of Ernest's becoming able to gain access to the russet apple at $t6$ are shuddersomely slim at $t1$ (and at $t2$ and $t3$). In light of the meagerness of those chances, any apposite prospective attribution of unfreedom – any apposite claim at $t1$ that Ernest at $t1$ is unfree to acquire the apple at $t6$ – will be subject to only a light probabilistic qualification. When somebody propounds such an attribution, she submits that Ernest despite his best efforts will be unfree at $t6$ to hold the russet apple at that time, but she adds that at $t1$ there is a small chance that her prediction of unfreedom-at-$t6$ will turn out to be false. Conversely, any apposite prospective attribution to Ernest of the freedom-at-$t1$-to-grab-the-apple-at-$t6$ will be subject to a stringent probabilistic qualification. If the probability is specified accurately, then a claim of this type will exactly correspond (in content) to an accurate retrospective account of Ernest's situation at $t1$. In any accurate predictive statement at $t1$ about the possible success of Ernest's persistent endeavors to become free at $t6$ to clutch the apple at $t6$, and in any accurate retrodictive statement made later, an ascription of freedom will be accompanied by an acknowledgment of the unlikelihood of his success. Both the heavily qualified prospective ascription of freedom and the heavily qualified retrospective ascription will have drawn due attention to the repressiveness of domination. In each case, the emphasis lies on the preventative force of Barry's minatory presence and on the consequent cabinedness of Ernest's ability at $t1$ to grab the apple at $t6$. Stringent probabilistic qualifications underline the narrowness of Ernest's room for maneuver. (Those qualifications from a retrodictive vantage point do not, of course, pertain to the likelihood after $t6$ that Ernest was free at $t1$ to grip the apple at $t6$. From such a vantage point, we can know with certainty that he was so free. Instead, the probabilistic qualifications pertain to the likelihood at $t1$ of Ernest's being free at that time to grab the apple at $t6$.)

In short, any accurate ascription to Ernest of the freedom-at-$t1$-to-get-the-apple-at-$t6$ will be no more neglectful of his dominated abjection than will an accurate ascription to him of the unfreedom-at-$t1$-to-get-the-apple-at-$t6$. A severe probabilistic qualification attached to the former ascription or a light probabilistic qualification attached to the latter ascription will equally well indicate the likelihood at $t1$ of Ernest's being unfree to clutch the apple at $t6$. Here the effect of the probabilistic caveats, in other words, is to highlight the misery of his plight. They enable us to be aware of the grim efforts by Ernest that were essential for the realization of his liberty-at-$t6$-to-grip-the-apple-at-$t6$. Qualified by such caveats, prospective or retrospective claims about Ernest's freedom at $t1$ can fully take into account the oppressiveness of Barry's dominance at that time.

As we gauge the pertinence of the doctrine of negative liberty in coming to grips with domination, then, one key point to be noted is the probabilistic character of nearly all retrospective and prospective attributions of freedom. When the probabilistic aspect of any such attribution is expressed overtly – as it very frequently should be – the limitedness of the freedom enjoyed under conditions of oppressive power is readily apparent. A second principal point deserving attention here is the revealingness of any accurate accounts of Ernest's situation at $t1$ (or at $t2$ or at $t3$) that are neither predictive nor retrodictive. When the topic under consideration is Ernest's freedom-at-$t1$-to-grab-the-apple-at-$t1$, a negative reply is clearly in order. At $t1$, Ernest is unfree to clutch the apple at $t1$. Hence, whatever freedom he may have at that moment in connection with clutching the apple at $t6$ is not paralleled by any comparable freedom in connection with clutching the apple at $t1$ itself. Much the same can be said about his posture at $t2$ and $t3$. He at $t2$ is unfree to hold the apple at $t2$, and he at $t3$ is unfree to hold the apple at $t3$. When the two temporal indexes in each attribution of freedom or unfreedom are simultaneous, what becomes plain is that Ernest's freedom at $t1$ (or $t2$ or $t3$) concerning the grabbing of the apple in the future is conjoined with his *un*freedom at $t1$ (or $t2$ or $t3$) concerning the grabbing of the apple in the present. In other words, although the apple might become available to Ernest hereafter – as it in fact does, through his genuflections – it is currently unavailable to him because of Barry's obstruction. Thus, when we ascribe to Ernest the freedom-at-$t1$-to-seize-the-apple-at-$t6$, we do not have to rely solely on probabilistic qualifications in order to capture the bleakness of his plight. We can and should also stress that his freedom pertaining to a future act of seizure is combined with his unfreedom pertaining to a current act of seizure. That unfreedom does not negate that instance of freedom, of course, but it does hem in that instance of freedom quite severely. By highlighting what Ernest cannot now do, we place in context the fact that he might be able to perform a certain action subsequently. Even if the likelihood of his future ability were greater than it is, it would be tempered by his present inability.

To perceive a third way in which a negative-liberty analysis can pinpoint the divergences between the presence and the absence of domination, we should suppose that $t4$ is the moment at which Barry relents and decides to let Ernest have the apple. We should furthermore suppose that $t5$ is the moment at which Barry becomes unable to prevent Ernest from clutching the apple. (At that moment – presumably, only a split-second before $t6$ – Barry is no longer able to reach Ernest in time to avert the clutching.) At $t4$, the probability of Ernest's being free at $t6$ to grab the apple at $t6$ will have increased dramatically, and that probability at $t5$ will have become 100 percent or virtually 100 percent. Even more important for our present focus is the change in Barry's position. At $t1$, $t2$, and $t3$, Barry is able and therefore free to obstruct Ernest from getting hold of the apple. At $t5$ he is no longer able, as has been stipulated. At $t4$, and at each moment between $t4$ and $t5$, the situation is somewhat more complicated. On the one hand, as has been stated, the probability of Barry's continuation of his obstruction diminishes greatly at $t4$. On the other hand, his ability to preclude Ernest from snatching the apple will continue until $t5$. That is, the state of affairs in the interval between $t4$ and $t5$ is plainly a situation that would be characterized by Skinner and Pettit as domination without interference. An analysis of the sort carried out here can illuminate the precise structure of non-interfering dominance in the interaction between Barry and Ernest.

Of course, a full examination of this matter requires us to look beyond Barry's particular freedom-to-stop-Ernest-from-grabbing-the-apple-between-*t4*-and-*t5*. We have to inquire whether Barry's exercise of that freedom would detrimentally affect his subsequent freedoms. In other words, we have to investigate the combinations-of-conjunctively-exercisable-liberties that constitute his overall freedom. If Barry can thwart Ernest's efforts with impunity – as my scenario has implicitly assumed – then his exercise of his freedom to block those efforts would not occasion the elimination of any of his own subsequent liberties. In such circumstances, we should designate Barry as a dominator even if he is not disposed to interfere with Ernest (as is true after *t4*). That same designation will be pertinent if Barry's exercise of his freedom would have only a small negative effect on his other liberties. By contrast, if a lot of his subsequent freedoms would be negated by dint of his exercising his liberty to thwart Ernest's striving, Barry is not appropriately characterized as a dominator; or, at any rate, he is not appropriately characterized as a dominator simply because he can prevent Ernest from getting the apple. Suppose, for example, that his prevention of Ernest from clutching the apple would lead to the levying of serious penalties on himself. In that event, at least with regard to the modes of behavior under consideration here, Barry is not a dominator *vis-à-vis* Ernest. His ability to interfere is not a product of a clear ascendance.

In any case, whether or not a full exploration of Barry's position would yield the conclusion that his ability to obstruct Ernest is indicative of domination, an analysis in line with the doctrine of negative liberty enables us to specify quite exactly the nature of noninterfering dominance. If the following four conditions obtain, then the relationship between any two people X and Y in connection with any type of activity A is pro tanto a relationship of domination without interference: (1) X will not seek to prevent Y's performance of A and will not in fact prevent it; (2) X is able to prevent Y from performing A; (3) X would not suffer any significant adverse consequences if he availed himself of his ability to prevent Y from performing A; (4) Y is not able to prevent X from performing A, or would suffer significant adverse consequences if he did prevent X from performing A. These four conditions can of course obtain when Y is free at some time t to do A at some time later than t. We have seen as much in the scenario of Barry and Ernest. Hence, an ascription to Ernest of the freedom-at-*t4*-to-gain-hold-of-the-apple-at-*t6* is entirely consistent with the proposition that Ernest at *t4* is still under the dominance of Barry. Furthermore, an ascription to Ernest of the freedom-at-*t1*-to-grab-the-apple-at-*t6* is fully consistent with the proposition that until *t4* the domination of him at the hands of Barry (in respect of the apple) is marked by interference rather than by non-interference. Though Ernest cannot be endowed with the freedom-at-*t1*-to-gain-hold-of-the-apple-at-*t1* unless Barry's domination at that time (in respect of the apple) is marked by non-interference, he can perfectly well be free-at-*t1*-to-gain-hold-of-the-apple-at-*t6* even if Barry's domination at *t1* is actively obstructive.

A Pithy Conclusion

As this essay has sought to show, the powerful efforts by Skinner and Pettit to drive a wedge between their republican conception of freedom and the negative-liberty conception have come to nought. Quite inadequate as a basis for a *distinctively* republican understanding of freedom and unfreedom is a focus on domination; conclusions arising from that focus can be elaborated rigorously with the categories and techniques of a modern negative-liberty theory. Although civic republicanism as a general political doctrine can perhaps lay claim to distinctiveness, it does not provide an analysis of the concept of freedom that goes beyond the negative-liberty approach in any significant way. When fine distinctions are duly taken into account, the modern exponents of negative liberty can fare well in a confrontation – and a reconciliation – with their civic-republican counterparts.

NOTES

1   For a book-length critique of Skinner and Philip Pettit, see the second chapter of Kramer 2003. The present essay draws heavily on section 2.3 of that chapter, albeit with many modifications. Throughout this essay, I use "freedom" and "liberty" interchangeably.

2   For citations to the principal writings by Skinner in which he voices this complaint, see Kramer 2003: 14 n. 1. For a powerful riposte to this strand of Skinner's work, see Patten 1996: 28–36. For my own rejoinders to this strand of Skinner's work, see Kramer 2003: 105–24.

3   I use the "ϕ" variable to denote a person's performance of some action or existence in some state or undergoing of some process.

4   I argue for this point throughout *The Quality of Freedom* – especially in that book's fifth chapter. For an excellent critique of Pettit that bears several resemblances to my critique of Skinner in this section, see Carter 1999: 237–45. A combination of conjunctively exercisable opportunities is a set of opportunities that can all be exercised together simultaneously and/or sequentially.

5   That conception is encapsulated in a U Postulate: "A person is unfree to φ if and only if both of the following conditions obtain: (1) he would be able to φ in the absence of the second of these conditions; and (2) irrespective of whether he actually endeavors to φ, he is directly or indirectly prevented from φ-ing by some action(s) or some disposition(s)-to-perform-some-action(s) on the part of some other person(s)" (Kramer 2003: 3).

6   My example builds on a laconic remark in Parent 1974: 159.

7   Pettit resorts to the same general line of argument in his more recent reflections on the topic; see Pettit 2001: 136–8.

8   Pettit himself occasionally offers analyses that are roughly in accordance with what I am claiming here. See especially Pettit 1997: 64, 262, 266–7.

9   For a general discussion of the bearing of time on freedom, see Kramer 2003: 76–91.

REFERENCES

Carter, Ian (1999). *A Measure of Freedom*. Oxford: Oxford University Press.

Kramer, Matthew (2003). *The Quality of Freedom*. Oxford: Oxford University Press.

Parent, William (1974). "Some Recent Work on the Concept of Liberty." *American Philosophical Quarterly*, 11, 149–67.

Patten, Alan (1996). "The Republican Critique of Liberalism." *British Journal of Political Science*, 26, 25–44.

Pettit, Philip (1997). *Republicanism: A Theory of Freedom and Government*. Oxford: Oxford University Press.

Pettit, Philip (2001). *A Theory of Freedom*. Cambridge: Polity Press.

Skinner, Quentin (1998). *Liberty before Liberalism*. Cambridge: Cambridge University Press.

Chapter 3
How are Power and Unfreedom Related?

Ian Carter

Matthew Kramer's contribution to this volume is concerned not with the acceptability or otherwise of republican political prescriptions, but with the meaning of freedom. The thrust of his argument, or at least of a part of it, is that republicans fail to provide an adequate justification for their rejection of the negative definition of freedom assumed by contemporary liberals, given that the liberal definition can be shown to imply exactly those judgments about unfreedom that the republicans use to motivate the rejection. Even if republicans are right in accusing certain liberals of a blindness to the freedom-restricting nature of domination, they are wrong to lay the blame on the negative conception of freedom, and should instead accuse those liberals of failing fully to comprehend certain characteristics and implications of their own conception of freedom. Rather than doing this, they err with those liberals in embracing the same inadequate understanding of negative freedom and in seeing the liberal conception of freedom as therefore hostile to republican political prescriptions. I am in agreement with Kramer on this issue, and have presented an argument along similar lines in previous work (Carter 1999: chs. 7 & 8, in particular pp. 237–45; Carter 2000).

In what follows, I shall first attempt to clarify and reinforce this line of reasoning by presenting it as an argument about the way in which freedom is related to certain forms of social power. These considerations support the claim, already advanced by Kramer and myself, that the negative view of freedom (or rather, a particular negative definition to be clarified below) implies comparative judgments about people's freedom that are, to all intents and purposes, equivalent to those comparative judgments implied by the republican view of freedom (or rather,

58

one influential republican definition of freedom to be clarified below). I shall call this thesis the "equivalent-judgments thesis." According to the equivalent-judgments thesis, while two people are in disagreement about how freedom is to be defined, they can nevertheless be shown to give very similar answers to questions like "Who is freer than whom?," "Has this person's freedom been reduced?," and "How is freedom distributed in society?"

Now the equivalent-judgments thesis constitutes an answer to the republican critique of negative freedom, but it does not amount to the claim that the two rival definitions of freedom are themselves equivalent, nor does it entail that one definition should be preferred to the other. Equivalent judgments about freedom might be reached because the phenomena respectively identified by the two definitions are ultimately the same (one being reducible to the other), but they might also be reached because the two phenomena are distinct but empirically correlated. This is a point that my previously published critique of the republican conception failed to clarify. In the present contribution, I shall therefore go on to ask whether and how far the phenomena identified by republican and liberal conceptions of freedom can indeed be thought of as distinct.

My critique of the republican conception of freedom will concentrate on the work of Philip Pettit, but I shall also refer to the equally influential writings of Quentin Skinner, in particular where he clearly agrees or disagrees with Pettit. Skinner himself prefers the term "neo-Roman" to "republican," but to simplify I shall use the latter term in a generic sense when discussing the two authors together.

Social Power

Since the relation between power and freedom is central to the difference between republicans and liberals, it is important for us to have in mind a clear and plausible account of power (which I am here assuming to be short for "social power," or power as an interpersonal relation). Let us say that A exercises power over B when A's behavior induces B to modify her course of action in accordance with A's interests (Stoppino 2007; Carter 2007). This is a broad definition, allowing us to classify as exercises of power all situations in which B's actions track the interests of A in a way that they would not have done in the absence of the relevant behavior on the part of *A*. The most obvious cases of power are those of coercion (the threat of violent, economic or symbolic sanctions). But an offer will also count as an exercise of power, on this broad definition, if *A*'s offer to reward *B* is sufficiently attractive to induce *B* to perform some action (in *A*'s interests) that *B* would not otherwise have performed. And power is also exercised by *A* when *B*'s conformity to *A*'s interests is an "anticipated reaction" (Friedrich 1963: ch. 11): *A* may not make a threat or an offer, but *B* may rightly anticipate that, were her own behavior not to conform to *A*'s will, *A* would nevertheless impose a sanction or withhold a benefit. Republicans do not themselves speak of "anticipated reactions," but the concept seems to me to cover the many cases they cite of *B* living "under the thumb" of *A*, feeling forced to "curry favor" with *A*, having to remain "continually on guard" against provoking *A*, and so on.

Rather than *exercising* power over *B*, *A* may simply *have* power over *B*, which is to say that *A* has the *possibility of exercising* power over *B*. The concept of exercising power can be called an "exercise concept," and the concept of having power an "opportunity concept" (cf. Taylor 1979; Carter 2004). *A* can have power over *B* without exercising it, which is to say that *A* does not actually behave so as to modify *B*'s behavior in accordance with *A*'s interests even though *A* has the opportunity to do so.

It is important to emphasize that cases of anticipated reaction are themselves cases in which power is *exercised* by *A*, for in such cases *B* actually modifies her behavior in accordance with *A*'s interests. Even though *A* does not issue a threat or an offer, *A*'s past behavior or *A*'s occupying a certain role is sufficient to induce in *B* the belief that, were *B* not to do *x*, *A* would impose a sanction or withhold a benefit, and is thus sufficient to bring about *B*'s doing *x* (in *A*'s interests). Cases of anticipated reaction may *look like* cases of *A* merely "having" power over *B* without exercising it, but this is only because in such cases *A does* have (but does not exercise) *another* kind of power over *B*, namely coercive or remunerative power. Another feature of anticipated reactions worth noting is that, whereas in the case of an explicit (and successful) threat or offer *A* necessarily exercises power intentionally over *B*, in the case of an anticipated reaction *A*'s exercise of power may or may not be intentional. Where *A*'s power (exercised through anticipated reaction) is non-intentional, *A* exercises something like what Pettit calls "virtual control," only becoming fully conscious of *B*'s conformity to her will where that conformity ceases (Pettit 2001: 38–9).

Coercion, remuneration, and anticipated reactions do not themselves exhaust the concept of social power, either as an exercise concept or as an opportunity concept. *A* may modify *B*'s behavior without *B*'s knowledge, through various forms of manipulation: for example, by influencing the kind or amount of information available to *B*, or by influencing the behavior of third parties in such a way as to modify *B*'s behavior indirectly. And *A* may also modify *B*'s behavior non-manipulatively (that is, with *B*'s knowledge of the fact) but by means other than prospective sanctions or rewards: for example, by arguing with *B* and rationally persuading her to modify her behavior in *A*'s interests, or simply by setting an example (Stoppino 2007). These changes in behavior might be in *B*'s interests too, but they will still be the product of a power relation on the definition I am assuming.

Having distinguished between these various forms of power, we need to ask which of them constitute limitations of *B*'s freedom, and why. Very few political philosophers would see *all* kinds of power (on this broad definition) as limiting the freedom of those subject to them. Even republicans do not generally see offers or rational persuasion as freedom-limiting. For Pettit, freedom is the absence of domination, and domination is constituted only by a subset of the set of forms of power just mentioned. However, the contention of both Pettit and Skinner is that liberals adopt an overly narrow account of what constitutes a constraint on freedom, so that they nevertheless exclude too many forms of power from the relevant set – most importantly, cases of anticipated reaction, and the fact of a person having power without exercising it.

Negative Freedom

The liberal conception of freedom that I shall assume here is sometimes referred to as "pure negative freedom." On this conception, a person is unfree to perform some action if and only if some other person renders that action physically impossible (Taylor 1982; Gorr 1989; Steiner 1994; Carter 1999; Kramer 2003). I shall call defenders of this conception of freedom "pure negative theorists."

In the present context, pure negative freedom should be thought of as a relation between persons, for it limits the class of freedom-restricting obstacles to those created by other persons. In the present context, then, both power and pure negative freedom are social relations. Pettit (2003: 387–8) attributes to pure negative theorists the view that all cases of physical impossibility count as instances of unfreedom – not only those whose source lies in the actions of other human agents, but also those that are self-inflicted or have natural causes. However, this is not a correct representation of most contemporary pure negative theorists. Neither do I share Pettit's view (2000) that pure negative theorists *cannot justify* limiting their attention to humanly caused obstacles. They limit their attention in this way because they see their conception of freedom as a *political* conception. In this, pure negative freedom is surely no different from freedom as non-domination or as the absence of dependence (the conceptions favored by republicans). For it is no less plausible to talk, in a non-political context, of our being dominated by, or dependent on, the weather, gravity, bodily needs, and so on, than it is to point out that these natural phenomena physically prevent us from performing certain actions.

On the pure negative view, freedom is an "opportunity concept" rather than an "exercise concept." Freedom is about the doors that are open rather than about which doors one goes through or how one goes through them. It is about possible actions rather than actions that are actually performed. An important example of an exercise concept of freedom, for our purposes, is the concept of "acting freely." One might say that I act freely in doing x if I do x voluntarily, where to do x voluntarily is to do it for certain reasons rather than others. Serena Olsaretti suggests, for example, that I do x unfreely (or involuntarily) if the reason I do x is that I have no acceptable alternative (Olsaretti 2004: ch. 6).

The most famous defender of the pure negative conception of freedom is Thomas Hobbes. Hobbes believed, as do contemporary pure negative theorists, that when a highwayman confronts you with the alternatives "Your money or your life," you are free to refuse to hand over the money, as it is not physically impossible, but only very costly, for you to do so. Hobbes, however, failed to distinguish adequately between the concept of freedom to act and that of acting freely, and therefore also held, less plausibly, that when you in fact hand over your money, you do so freely. Contemporary pure negative theorists, on the other hand, are generally sensitive to this distinction, and deny that in handing over the money you are acting freely (or else abstain from pronouncing on the issue). It is therefore a misrepresentation of their overall view of such cases to call it "the Hobbesian view" (Pettit 2001: 46). The pure negative conception is not a conception of free action, and pure negative theorists are not therefore committed to the view that an agent's having a minimum of rational control over her actions is sufficient for her to be described as acting freely. The pure negative view says that where A makes B do x by threatening severe sanctions, A leaves B free to do not-x, but it does not say that when B actually does x she does so freely or voluntarily. A's power can be coherently said to reduce the freedom or voluntariness with which B acts while nevertheless not removing any particular freedoms-to-act on the part of B.

One reason why Pettit lumps the contemporary negative theorists in with Hobbes may be that he has unconsciously projected onto the former his own belief – which is shared by Hobbes and which provides the organizing principle of his book *A Theory of Freedom* – that a political conception of freedom should be continuous with, and built on, a theory of freedom of the will. Contemporary theorists of negative freedom tend, however, not to share that belief. On the contrary, they see it as essential to a political conception of freedom that the validity of such a conception should prescind from psychological or metaphysical questions about freedom of the will. (Whether or not they are right about this is another matter.)

If, however, coercive power and the phenomenon of anticipated reactions represent curtailments of the "freedom with which people act" rather than of their "freedom to act," it might then be asked why freedom-to-act (rather than acting freely) should be seen as the politically salient concept of freedom. If it is admitted that the pure negative conception of freedom does not construe such forms of power as inimical to freedom, and one of the reasons we are interested in a political conception of freedom is to justify limiting or controlling such forms of power, should we not reject the pure negative conception of freedom? This is the conclusion that Kramer and I have sought to counter by means of what I have called the "equivalent-judgments thesis." In our view, the pure negative conception of freedom implies, contrary to first appearances, that when A exercises coercive power over B, or when B's behavior is motivated by the anticipation of a sanction, or indeed when A merely *has* these forms of power without exercising them, A *is* generally limiting B's freedom-to-act, and to an extent that more or less mirrors that to which republicans normally see A as limiting B's freedom. Being subjected to these forms of power generally implies strong limits not just on the freedom with which one acts, but also on one's freedom-to-act.

Two Features of Non-domination

Before turning to the equivalent-judgments thesis, I need to qualify that thesis by pointing out that it applies only to a particular republican conception of freedom. More precisely, it applies to a conception of freedom that only partly coincides with Pettit's notion of freedom as non-domination.

As Pettit defines it, non-domination contrasts with non-interference (the absence of obstacles imposed by other agents) in two ways. First, a person can be dominated without suffering any actual interference. This is said to occur in the case of successful threats (where the sanction is never applied), in the case of anticipated sanctions (where a threat is not even issued), and in the case of power that is possessed without being exercised. But Pettit also claims, secondly, that a person can suffer interference without being dominated. This is said to occur when the interference is in the interests of the person interfered with, and is thus "non-arbitrary" interference. Interference without domination is, for Pettit, interference without unfreedom.

Now the republican conception of freedom that forms the main object of my critique – the conception to which the equivalent-judgments thesis applies – is a conception that contrasts with freedom as non-interference in only the first of the above ways. What is the justification for this restriction of the object of my critique?

I think that there are important independent reasons for rejecting the second feature of freedom as non-domination. A first reason is that it conflicts with a basic intuition about unfreedom that is shared not only by liberals but also by a number of republicans. According to that intuition, being prevented physically by someone else from doing something is a sufficient condition for being unfree to do that thing. If one denies this, and says instead that interference with B in the interests of B is not a restriction of B's freedom, then one runs counter to the common understanding of paternalist intervention as intervention that can reduce a person's freedom in her own interests.

A second, more fundamental objection to Pettit's notion of "interference without unfreedom" is that it appears to *moralize* the concept of freedom. A moralized definition of freedom states that obstacles do not restrict one's freedom as long as they are morally legitimate obstacles. For example, libertarians often assume a rights-based moralized definition of freedom when they claim that a minimal state leaves everyone's freedom perfectly intact. The assumption, here, is that obstacles are sources of unfreedom only if they violate property rights. Critics have rightly pointed out that this definition fails to treat freedom as an independent ideal. By defining freedom in terms of the political ideals to be defended (in this case, private property and the minimal state), it prevents us from defending those ideals as good on the grounds that they promote freedom (Cohen 2006).

On Pettit's definition of freedom, obstacles are restrictions of your freedom only if they do not track your avowed interests. This he sees as implying that "neither a tax levy, nor even a term of imprisonment, need take away someone's freedom" (Pettit 1997: 56 n. 3). For there is such a thing as "friendly coercion" which does not restrict the freedom of the coerced, given that it tracks their avowed interests. Thus, Ulysses is not unfree when, sailing past the sirens, his sailors refuse to unbind him from the mast of his ship, given that they are following his orders in refusing to do so. Now it might be suggested that, because Pettit is referring to *avowed* interests, no independent moral considerations come into play here. It is not obvious, however, why an individual who is coerced in the collective interest is to be seen as analogous to Ulysses in this respect. For it is difficult to imagine a justly convicted thief affirming an interest in being imprisoned (analogous to that of Ulysses in being bound to the mast) either before or during the term of imprisonment, although this may happen in rare cases of extreme penitence. Such cases aside, while even larcenous people may avow a common interest in the institutions of private property and progressive taxation, they almost certainly also consider it to be in their personal interest to be treated as an exception.

Unless the common interest is defined very narrowly, in terms of Pareto-superiority, there will be conflicts between one's personal interest and the common interest. Where such conflicts occur, I can see no reason for privileging the common interest over the agent's personal interest in deciding which obstacles count as instances of unfreedom, unless this reason consists in a moral point of view – a point of view having to do with the proper role of the state and the proper procedures determining public policy. To be sure, this may be the moral point of view of many of the citizens themselves, but it is no less a moral point of view for that. It will still be true that what constitutes a constraint on one's freedom depends on which obstacles one considers to be morally right, not just on which obstacles one considers to be in one's interests. Thus, while Pettit maintains that "there is no reference to any independent value, only to the expectations that people hold in regard to the state" (2000: 55), it nevertheless seems to me that such "expectations" can be interpreted as resting either on personal interests or on moral values, and that Pettit privileges the interpretation in terms of moral values.

Skinner clearly rejects this moralized element of Pettit's conception of freedom: for those neo-Roman writers whose conception of freedom he is particularly interested in rehabilitating, "the exercise of force or the coercive threat of it" is a sufficient condition for the existence of unfreedom.

> Pettit imputes to the defenders of "republican" freedom the view that, since it is only arbitrary domination that limits individual liberty, the act of obeying a law to which you have given your consent is "entirely consistent with freedom." The writers I am discussing never deal in such paradoxes. For them the difference between the rule of law and government by personal prerogative is not that the former leaves you in full possession of your liberty while the latter does not; it is rather that the former only coerces you while the latter additionally leaves you in a state of dependence. (Skinner 1997: 83 n. 54)

More recently, Skinner has suggested that Pettit's notion of freedom as non-domination is "more or less equivalent" to the neo-Roman conception of freedom as "absence of dependence" (Skinner 2002: 255 n. 99). Nevertheless, not only the above quote but also the general thrust of his argument in *Liberty before Liberalism* suggest that we should understand the relevant equivalence to be between freedom as the absence of dependence and the first (but not the second) aspect of freedom as non-domination. On this view, the second aspect of non-domination is presumably what is covered by the "less" in "more or less equivalent."

The Equivalent-judgments Thesis

Let us proceed, then, on the assumption that we are dealing with a republican conception of freedom that affirms only the first of the two features of Pettit's definition of freedom. On this conception, while we should reject the view that there can be interference without unfreedom, we should nevertheless affirm that there can be unfreedom without interference. The equivalent-judgments thesis answers the accusation that liberal theorists of negative freedom are necessarily blind to cases of unfreedom without interference.

Since the argument in support of the equivalent-judgments thesis has already been rehearsed elsewhere, including in this volume, I shall limit myself here to summarizing its main points and then addressing some objections.

On the pure negative conception, freedom consists in the absence of prevention. As Hillel Steiner points out, this prevention can be either *actual* or *subjunctive*: one is negatively unfree to do x not only if someone has *already* foreclosed the option of doing x, but also if, *were* one to attempt to do x, someone *would* act so as to foreclose one's doing x (Steiner 1994: 33–41). If one applies this point to sets of actions rather than only to single actions, one can see that situations of coercion will generally register as situations in which freedom is restricted even where no sanction is carried out. For, when A coerces B into doing x, B is, typically, subjunctively prevented by A from performing various sets of actions – that is, all sets of actions containing both not-x and one or more of the actions that would be foreclosed by the threatened sanction. Were B to attempt to perform one of these sets of actions, A would physically prevent it. B is therefore unfree to perform that set. Moreover, in line with our intuitions about degrees of freedom, the severer the sanction threatened, the greater the reduction in B's freedom is likely to be, given the likely effect on B's set of sets of available actions.

This point applies as much to anticipated reactions as to coercion. The reason for this is that what is essential to unfreedom, on the pure negative conception, is not the fact of issuing threats, but the foreclosing of options or sets of options. What makes coercion a limitation of freedom is not, then, the fact of coercion as such, but a deeper underlying phenomenon that is present both in cases of coercion and in cases where B anticipates a sanction. In both cases, A exercises power over B because B fears some sanction, and in both cases A is generally rendering B unfree to perform various sets of actions, despite not making B unfree to perform any single action considered in isolation. So while the republican theorist points out that in the case of anticipated reactions as well as in that of coercion, B is "dependent on A's will" –

that is, B must seek A's approval for the realization of her projects, must conform her behavior to A's interests, curry favor with A, and so on – the pure negative theorist points out that B's degree of non-prevention is correspondingly reduced because B's available options (or sets of options) are restricted by A. And the pure negative theorist notes, in addition, that the degree of limitation of B's options (or sets of options) is roughly isomorphic with the degree to which we tend to see B as dependent on A for the realization of her projects. That prevention of options (or sets of options) should be seen as the fundamental freedom-limiting factor, because the same factor is present in all instances of unfreedom, including those of sheer brute force (where A does not exercise power over B's will). It is indeed an interesting feature of the pure negative conception that, despite involving a particularly narrow construal of constraints, it actually accommodates a much wider range of situations of unfreedom than does the rival conception of negative freedom frequently cited by Skinner and Pettit: freedom as the absence of direct force or coercion.

It should be emphasized that the relation between the unfreedom of B and certain forms of power of A is, on the above account, an empirical generalization. And, like any empirical generalization, it is therefore subject to exceptions. A first exception is where A either does not intend to carry out the threatened sanction (A is in fact bluffing) or is unable to do so, yet, since B is unaware of this, A's threat or B's anticipation of A's reaction still represents a successful exercise of power by A (i.e. B's choice still conforms to A's will in a way that it would not have done had B been fully informed). A second possibility is that the threatened or anticipated sanction would consist in inflicting harm on some third party, C, whom B cares about (hence the success of the threat), rather than on B herself.

Pettit and I disagree over the importance to be attributed to these counterexamples (Carter 1999: 229–31; Pettit 2000; Pettit 2001: 46–7). One reason why they are insufficient to move me to abandon the pure negative conception is that I see a liberal, negative conception of freedom as ultimately motivated by the need to provide an account of one of the underlying values motivating liberal political prescriptions. The negative account of freedom is therefore essentially a *political* conception of freedom. And in the power relations with which political theory is concerned, exceptions of the kind just mentioned do not seem to play a significant role. Consider first the case of bluffing. It is simply unrealistic to think that bluffing can play a significant role in those *stabilized relations of power* that are at work in political life – that is, relations of power that are generalized over a large number of actors and over long stretches of time. The statistical probability of any law failing to give rise to at least one offence is trivially low, and once offenders are seen to go unpunished the bluff is revealed. Rulers who fail, whether out of reluctance or out of incapacity, to carry out the relevant sanctions, fail to exercise stabilized power of the sort associated with deterrents (anticipated or threatened costs).

The second kind of exception constitutes a stronger counterexample than the first. For while it is true that legal systems generally *do not* provide for sanctions inflicting harm on innocent third parties, so that the exceptions will affect very few actual freedom judgments, this is not something that can or should be ruled out. The force of the counterexample has been somewhat dampened by an argument of Kramer to the effect that, even where the threatened sanctions harm *C* rather than *B*, *B*'s freedom is reduced by *A* in as much as the sanctions would affect *B*'s ability to perform actions or undergo processes that depend on *C*'s presence or cooperation (Kramer 2003: 156–69, 195–204). However, this argument admittedly fails to show that *B*'s freedom is reduced *as much as* where the same sanction is directed at *B*.

But there is also a more fundamental difference between Pettit and myself that needs to be taken into account in assessing the force of these counterexamples. Pettit sees the relation between *A*'s domination and *B*'s unfreedom as a necessary one, and for this reason cannot tolerate exceptions to the rule that when *A* dominates *B*, *B* is unfree. I, on the other hand, see the relation as a contingent one. I see the liberal's opposition to certain forms of power as an opposition that is based on a strong empirical correlation between these two phenomena. The validity of my argument therefore depends not so much on its ability to accommodate all the counterexamples as on the overall strength of the empirical correlation it posits.

Let us now turn to situations where *A* merely *has* power over *B* but does not *exercise* it. Republicans claim that here, too, *B* is rendered unfree, and that negative conceptions are unable to capture this unfreedom. Both Skinner and Pettit have repeatedly pointed to the mere exposure to the power of another (as opposed to the actual experience of that power) as a clear case of unfreedom (Skinner 1997: ch. 2; Pettit 1997: chs. 1 & 2; Pettit: 2001: ch. 6).

Kramer and I have tried to answer this point by appeal to the probabilistic assessments inevitably involved in all judgments about the presence of particular freedoms and about degrees of overall freedom. Judgments about freedom concern actions that take place at a time subsequent to the freedom being predicated of the agent (regardless or whether that time is in the past, present or future) and involve counterfactual claims about hypothetical preventions. They are therefore necessarily characterized by a degree of uncertainty. It is virtually impossible for me to be certainly free at time t to perform some action that occurs later than t. And since we should not like to describe as equally free at time t a person who is (at time t) 95 per cent likely to be prevented from doing x (at $t+1$) should she try, and a person who is (at time t) only 5 per cent likely to be so prevented, our judgments about the presence of freedoms, or about varying degrees of overall freedom, must take account of such varying degrees of probability as can be reasonably judged at time t (Carter 1999: 189–91, 233–4; Kramer 2003: 76–91, 174–8). While Pettit and Skinner insist that unfreedom is created by the mere possession of power (even in the absence of its exercise), then, the pure negative theorist points out that, where A's mere opportunity to exercise power has some degree of *probability* of being exercised, then B's unfreedom is to that same degree limited. And it would again be a very unrealistic theory of politics that conceived of opportunities for the exercise of power as being accompanied, except in rare cases, by a trivially low probability of that exercise taking place. Where A's capacity and opportunity to make threats is superior to B's, but A does not exercise this superior coercive power, A usually exercises power over B thanks to the law of anticipated reactions. And in those cases in which A does not exercise power even in this way, the probability of those exposed to coercive power nevertheless coming to experience it is generally kept above a certain minimum by two factors: first, A's own behavior might change at any moment, for whatever reason; secondly (and perhaps more importantly), since power (as well as health and life itself) is never fully guaranteed, A might at any moment be replaced as the holder of the relevant institutional position of power by some as yet unknown person. Thus, even if the power is not exercised by A, the same power may still be exercised by A' (or A'', or A''', . . .).

It is this uncertainty about a possible exercise of power that *explains why* we feel unfree even when merely "exposed" to it, and *why* we so often conform our behavior to the will of those who "merely" possess it. For suppose that there really were a case of a trivially low probability of some opportunity-to-exercise-power being converted into exercised power. This would have to be true, presumably, on the basis of some iron law of human nature internally constraining A's behavior, as well as that of any successors of A subsequent to A's hypothetical replacement as the holder of the relevant position of power. In such a case, to the extent that our political prescriptions are based on the value of B's freedom, we ought not to be particularly worried by such a "possibility" of power being exercised. After all, *ex hypothesi*, the law of human nature just referred to is an extremely reliable one, in which case it protects B from arbitrary interference no less efficiently than do the institutional safeguards commonly prescribed by republicans. (Needless to say, neither liberals nor republicans are naïve enough to believe in such an iron law.)

So runs the argument that Kramer and I have sought to present in favor of the equivalence of the judgments about degrees of freedom and unfreedom arrived at on a republican conception of freedom and on the pure negative conception. The argument is not, in my view, either "dismissive" or "dogmatic" (Skinner 2002: 262, 265, respectively). It is not dismissive, as it takes seriously the republican concern with certain forms of power, but tries to show, through detailed analytical argumentation, that the negative conception of freedom is in fact compatible with the view that those forms of power are inimical to freedom. Neither does the argument proceed on the dogmatic assumption that the negative conception is the correct or "true" conception. Rather, it aims to show that republicans have failed in their attempt to identify significant shortcomings in a conception of freedom that liberals have striven to explicate and to refine in such a way as to capture one of their fundamental political ideals.

Resilient Non-interference and Absence of Dependence

In my previously published presentation of the argument from equivalent judgments, I assumed that for the republicans against whom that argument was directed, freedom is to be understood as "resilient non-interference" – a term I took from one of Pettit's early articles on freedom (Pettit 1993; but see also Pettit 1997: 24). I considered this to be the appropriate way of characterizing a republican conception of freedom that affirms the first but not the second aspect of Pettit's notion of non-domination – that is, Pettit's currently affirmed conception of freedom shorn of its moralized element. Resilient non-interference, as Pettit conceives it, implies something more than the absence of actual interference. One can enjoy the absence of actual interference while still depending on the will of another, because that other is still in a position to interfere, as a result of which one is never completely protected against ill will on his or her part, and must continually take measures to avoid incurring it. Pursuing resilient non-interference at a political level implies that power in society be structured in such a way as to guarantee the absence of interference, and in this sense one's independence of others' wills.

Skinner has objected to my characterization of the republican conception in terms of resilient non-interference, pointing out that on the neo-Roman conception, unfreedom should be characterized not in terms of "interference . . . of any kind," but in terms of subjection to the will of another, and that "this is unquestionably to speak of an alternative theory of liberty, since it is to claim that freedom can be restricted and constrained in the absence of any element of interference or even any threat of it" (Skinner 2002: 262–3). The restriction of freedom "in the absence of any element of interference or even any threat of it," however, is exactly the scenario that the notion of resilient non-interference was brought in to cover: the notion arises exactly out of the idea that one is less free by virtue of the mere possibility of interference, regardless of whether one is actually interfered with or is even subject to the threat of it. Thus, on both characterizations of republican freedom – freedom as resilient non-interference and freedom as subjection to the will of another (or absence of dependence) – restrictions on freedom can occur "in the absence of any element of interference or even any threat of it," as indeed they can on the pure negative conception of freedom. One may describe the situation enjoyed as one of absence of dependence or as one of resilient non-interference, but the degrees of the phenomenon one has identified will still vary in ways that are more or less isomorphic with variations in overall extents of pure negative unfreedom. So, at any rate, runs the argument from equivalent judgments. It was for this reason that I saw this argument as applying not only to Pettit's conception of freedom (shorn of its moralized element), but also to that of Skinner.

As well as reiterating the republican belief in the *non*-equivalence of liberal and republican freedom judgments, Skinner affirms that the two conceptions of freedom are ultimately distinct because their proponents "hold rival views about the underlying concept of autonomy": proponents of the view of freedom as non-interference "are committed to the view that the will is autonomous so long as it is neither threatened nor coerced," whereas on the neo-Roman argument the will cannot be autonomous "unless it is also free from dependence on the will of anyone else" (Skinner 2002: 263).

Three points need to be made in answer to this claim. First, theorists of negative freedom are not, as such, committed to any particular view about the conditions under which the will is autonomous (even though, as we saw in discussing the distinction between "freedom to act" and "acting freely," Hobbes happens to have been so committed). Such theorists generally claim that the negative definition prescinds from questions about the nature of the will and the conditions for its autonomy or freedom. A classic statement of this view is to be found in the work of J. P. Day (1987: 16), according to whom "there is no connexion between Freedom and the Will." Secondly, it follows from the point just made that the negative conception of freedom (to act) is compatible with the view that the will cannot be autonomous unless it is free from dependence on the will of anyone else. Thirdly, assuming the truth of the equivalent-judgments thesis, and regardless of their views on autonomy, pure negative theorists can agree that those whose will is dependent (in the republican sense) are generally lacking in freedom (to act).

There is nevertheless an important point in Skinner's response that needs further attention. For even if the freedom-judgments arrived at on the basis of the liberal and republican definitions of freedom are indeed equivalent, it may still be true that the two *definienda* are distinct phenomena. This distinctness might be thought to be an important fact in its own right. And there is no doubt that the possibility of this distinctness is obscured by an exclusive concentration on the interpretation of republican freedom as resilient non-interference. Resilient non-interference is a more likely candidate for reducibility to non-prevention than is the absence of dependence, for the latter can more plausibly be interpreted as *consisting*, at least in part, in the fact of the will being autonomous (in the sense of not depending on other wills).

In order to address this issue we need to be clearer about what it is that might *explain* the truth of the equivalent-judgments thesis. A first possible explanation is that the distinctness of the phenomena identified by the liberal and republican definitions of freedom is only apparent, and that one of the phenomena is in fact reducible to the other. If the two phenomena are ultimately one and the same, it should not surprise us that they imply equivalent freedom judgments. A second possible explanation is that, while the two phenomena are indeed distinct, there is nevertheless such a strong empirical correlation between them that variations in one (greater or lesser increases or decreases) are mirrored by variations in the other. The first kind of explanation seems to be the appropriate one where the two phenomena in question are non-prevention and resilient non-interference. In this case, the equivalent-judgments thesis can be explained by saying that degrees of resilient non-interference are ultimately reducible to degrees of non-prevention (once the latter are properly understood as taking into account sets of actions and degrees of probability of prevention). In the case of absence of dependence, on the other hand, it is not so obvious which of the two explanations is the appropriate one. On the one hand, absence of dependence might simply be explicated in terms of the resilience of non-interference, in which case the first kind of explanation will apply. Here, one's "subjection to the will of another" is to be interpreted as *an interpersonal relation between actions* – i.e. as being present or absent to the extent that the realization of one's projects does not depend on certain actions (or omissions) of others, where those others are in a position to abstain at will from performing those actions (or omissions). (The reference to others abstaining "at will" explains why we nevertheless speak in this case of subjection *to the will* of another.) On the other hand, absence of dependence might be explicated in terms of the autonomy of the agent's will, in which case the second kind of explanation will apply. Here, one's "subjection to the will of another" is to be interpreted more directly as *an interpersonal relation between wills* (be these actual wills or hypothetical wills) – i.e. as being present or absent to the extent that the decisions one makes, or the decisions available to one, are not determined (in certain specified ways) by the decisions of others. In my view, there is evidence for both of these interpretations in the writings of Pettit and Skinner. The second interpretation is pointed to most clearly in Pettit's recent book *A Theory of Freedom*.

Is Dependence a Relation Between Wills?

The challenge for those who see dependence as (partly or wholly) a relation between wills is to show that *only certain* forms of power imply dependence. For if such a view includes too many forms of power as sufficient conditions for dependence, then that conception will fail to reflect republican intuitions about freedom. The equivalent-judgments thesis will have been contradicted, but in a way that will leave most republicans siding with the idea of dependence as a relation between actions.

With this challenge in mind, let us consider the possibility of accommodating the view, commonly held by both liberals and republicans, that coercive threats generally limit freedom whereas conditional offers generally do not. When *A* offers *B* some commodity or service that *B* needs or desires, *B*'s decision to accept the offer and to make use of the commodity or service would seem to depend on *A*'s will. Can those who see dependence as a relation between wills consistently deny that this relation between *A* and *B* is a case of dependence?

Pettit attempts to deny it in the following way. Having freedom, he says, is a matter of enjoying a certain discursive status, where to enjoy such a status is to be recognized as capable of providing reasons and to be treated by others as a co-reasoner. It is to "have the ratiocinative capacity for discourse and the relational capacity that goes with enjoying discourse-friendly linkages with others" (Pettit 2001: 72–3). When a person is subject to brute force or to coercive threats she does not enjoy this status, for she is not being respected as a co-reasoner and is instead being subjected to the will of another irrespective of her capacity to provide reasons. If I coerce you I will no longer be "discoursing with you from the base-line of all the considerations that were relevant prior to the threat." I am "not content just to discourse with you about what the pre-existing considerations require," and have as a result "deprived you of the capacity to be moved as . . . [those] pre-existing reasons require" (2001: 74–5). Offers, on the other hand, are "discourse friendly." Offers respect the pre-existing considerations of their recipients, and do not remove those recipients' capacity to be moved by such considerations.

From the point of view of the theorist concerned with dependence, this seems rather a rosy picture of offers. The image conjured up is one in which *A*, with *B*'s interests at heart (and perhaps even without regard for her own interests), simply gives *B* an additional option that is preferable (in terms of *B*'s pre-existing reasons for action) to the options previously available. An example might be where *B* has a pre-existing reason for getting home in a hurry, and *A* therefore offers *B* a lift in her car.

This, however, is an example of an altruistic unconditional offer, not of a conditional offer. The case we need to consider is one where *A* makes *B* an offer in *A*'s own interests and hopes to gain from *B*'s acceptance. This is what happens in most voluntary contractual agreements. It happens, for example, where *A* offers *B* a lift in return for a fee. The challenge, for those who see freedom as (partly or wholly) a relation between wills, is to accommodate the common view that such conditional offers do not *worsen* *B*'s situation in terms of freedom – i.e. that they do not make *B* *less* free than she would otherwise have been.

Conditional offers are clearly exercises of power, in as much as they involve an exercise of *A*'s capacity to modify *B*'s will with respect to the various courses of action available. This is a feature that conditional offers share with threats. Whereas before *A*'s successful intervention *B* preferred doing *x* to doing not-*x*, after the intervention *B* prefers not-*x*. In both cases of successful intervention, *B*'s non-compliance would leave *B* worse off than her compliance, and this depends, *inter alia*, on *A*'s probable responses to *B*'s non-compliance (*A*'s carrying out the sanction or not giving the offered reward).

The difference between a threat and an offer is that relative to the course of events that would have occurred in the absence of *A*'s intervention, *B*'s compliance with an offer leaves her better off (and her non-compliance leaves her situation unchanged) whereas her compliance with a threat leaves her worse off (and her non-compliance leaves her worse off still) (Steiner 1994: 24–5). But does this mean that the threat, and not the offer, lessens *B*'s *discursive status*? This will depend on the effects of these interventions on *B*'s "capacity to be moved as the pre-existing reasons require." There are two ways in which *A* can limit this capacity of *B*: on the one hand, *A* may intervene so as to *outweigh* *B*'s pre-existing reasons by creating new, weightier reasons for *B*; on the other hand, *A* may make it more *psychologically difficult* for *B* to be moved by those pre-existing reasons. Since either of these views might provide the best interpretation of Pettit's basis for distinguishing between threats and offers in terms of discursive status, let us consider them in turn.

Suppose we say that threats are discourse-unfriendly because they introduce new reasons that outweigh *B*'s pre-existing reasons. Consider the following example. I have information about a gang of criminals that I could pass on to the police, but which I do not pass on for fear of violent sanctions on the part of those criminals. The police, knowing I have this information, threaten to torture me if I do not provide it.

Thus, my pre-existing reason for not passing on the information (minimizing the probability of being subjected to criminal violence) is now outweighed by my new reason for passing on the information (avoiding imminent torture by the police). Notice, however, that this outweighing of pre-existing reasons is also a feature of conditional offers. Suppose that the police do not threaten me with torture but nevertheless successfully induce me to provide the same information in exchange for $100,000. In this case, I have a new reason for providing the information (the receipt of $100,000), which outweighs the pre-existing reason for not doing so (minimizing the probability of the criminal aggression). The offer, no less than the threat, outweighs my pre-existing reasons for action.

In answer to this last point it might be suggested that we should distinguish between fundamental and non-fundamental reasons, and that offers respect pre-existing *fundamental* reasons whereas threats do not. Thus, in making the offer, the police respect, and indeed reinforce, the fundamental pre-existing reason consisting in the desirability of accumulating wealth (and all the other fundamental reasons that typically accompany this). An *immediate*, non-fundamental pre-existing reason (that of minimizing the probability of the criminal aggression) is outweighed, but my *fundamental* pre-existing reasons are not outweighed. Again, however, the same can be said of the threat in the above example, and with equal plausibility. For it is equally plausible to say that I have a fundamental pre-existing reason consisting in the maintenance of my bodily integrity, and that the threat of torture outweighs not this fundamental reason but only the more immediate reason of minimizing the probability of being subjected to criminal aggression. The fundamental reason of bodily integrity is left in place, and is indeed acted on in avoiding the greater evil of police torture. In each of the two cases, then, *A*'s intervention is such that *B*'s compliance will allow *B* to satisfy a relevant pre-existing *fundamental* reason (a concern with wealth or a concern with bodily integrity). And in each of the two cases *A*'s intervention is such that it becomes irrational for *B* to act on the basis of a certain pre-existing *immediate* reason (minimizing the probability of the criminal aggression).

It is true, as Pettit implies, that the offer does not rule out *A* and *B* continuing to discourse on the merits of *B*'s remaining silent in order to avoid the possible criminal aggression. But then, neither does the threat rule out such continued discourse on the merits of *B*'s remaining silent for that same reason. And if one denies this, and claims instead, with Pettit, that the threat has "pre-empted such unfettered discussion" (Pettit 2001: 74), it is unclear why one should not say the same of the offer.

Suppose it is suggested that we interpret the "pre-emption of unfettered discussion" as involving the outweighing of *fundamental* reasons. A threat, after all, *can* outweigh a fundamental pre-existing reason, even if the above example of a threat does not do so. Imagine, for example, that I am myself a member of the criminal gang mentioned earlier, and am strongly committed to showing loyalty to my partners in crime. In this case, the threat of torture outweighs my fundamental reason of loyalty. Once again, however, the same is true of offers: these, too, can outweigh fundamental reasons even though the offer in the example discussed above did not do so. For we can similarly imagine my being a member of the criminal gang and the police making me the offer of $100,000. In this case the issuing of the successful offer, no less than that of the successful threat, shows utter contempt for my pre-existing fundamental reason for remaining silent. To be sure, an offer has to be fairly strong (i.e. generous) in order to outweigh a fundamental reason, but then a threat also has to be fairly strong (i.e. severe) in order to do so.

Suppose, then, that we instead say that what distinguishes threats and offers in terms of their effect on discursive status is *B*'s *internal capacity* to be moved by pre-existing reasons. Perhaps it is in *this* sense that in the example where *B* is a member of the criminal gang, the offer respects *B*'s pre-existing attachment to loyalty whereas the threat does not. Thus, it might be said that in the case of torture it is very difficult, psychologically, for *B* to act from loyalty to her fellow criminals, whereas in the case of the offer of $100,000 it is much easier for her not to comply with *A*'s will. But this, again, is not a sound basis for distinguishing between threats and offers. The degree of power of an intervention, and the corresponding degree of ease with which *B* *could* refuse compliance with *A*'s will, does not depend on whether the intervention is a threat or an offer, but on how far apart on *B*'s scale of value are the consequences of compliance with *A*'s will and the consequences of non-compliance. Compare *A*'s offer to pay *B* $10,000 if *B* runs an errand, with *A*'s threat that if *B* does not run the errand she will pull *B*'s hair. Although the offer of $10,000 is probably one we feel capable of refusing, most of us would find it more difficult to refuse this offer than to ignore the threat of having our hair pulled. (The evaluative distance for

B between complying and not complying may of course be strongly influenced by her absolute level of well-being prior to *A*'s intervention.)

Pettit also suggests that "non-discursive" forms of power are freedom-limiting because they "diminish in some measure the agent's fitness to be held responsible" (Pettit 2001: 79). This, indeed, is what Pettit sees as the ultimate test for deciding whether or how far a person is free in given situations (and he applies the test explicitly to threats and offers, at p. 23). Thus, when *A* induces *B* to do *x* by means of a threat, *B*'s fitness to be held responsible for doing *x* is generally diminished, whereas the same is not true where *A* induces *B* to do *x* by means of an offer. Pettit's claim that threats and offers have different effects on discursive status can be interpreted as merely illustrative of this ultimate reason for saying that threats are freedom-limiting and offers are not. And it may still be possible that while the illustration fails, this ultimate reason still stands, and in some sense serves to explain why we think of *B* as lacking in independence of the will in the case of threats but not of offers. (Let us leave aside here the question of how attributions of responsibility could ever *explain* independence of the will in spite of the fact that we normally think of the former as consequent upon the latter.)

I would suggest, however, that there are many cases of threats that we intuitively see as freedom-limiting but which do not diminish *B*'s fitness to be held responsible upon choosing to comply. It is important here to distinguish between diminished responsibility and diminished praise or blame: *B*'s fitness to be held responsible is only one of the factors affecting the degree of praise or blame attributable to *B*, and a threat or offer might affect the latter without diminishing *B*'s fitness to be held responsible. Consider the case of a threat where the act of compliance is morally despicable and the threatened sanction is bearable, if severe. Imagine, for example, that *B* is threatened with the sack if she does not execute a number of innocent people. We might just consider *B* less *blameworthy* for having carried out the executions than someone who would have carried them out for fun rather than to save their job, but we do not tend to consider *B* less fit to be held responsible for having done so. The same point applies, conversely, to offers. Suppose that *B* saves a drowning child only because she stands to gain a reward of $1,000. While we do not tend to consider her any less fit to be held responsible for having saved the child, we might well consider her less *praiseworthy* than someone who does so purely out of a sense of duty.

Again, the two kinds of intervention would appear to be symmetrical in their effects.

There remains of course the fact that conditional offers are generally welcomed by their recipients whereas coercive threats (at least, those that Pettit calls "hostile" coercive threats) are generally unwelcome. This, however, is simply the distinction I made at the outset between offers and threats, and does not itself imply that the two kinds of intervention differ in terms of their impact on their recipients' degrees of dependence of the will. All it implies is that some kinds of dependence are preferred to others.

In the light of the above arguments, I conclude that republicans who define dependence as a relation between wills (and freedom as the absence of dependence) continue to owe us an explanation of why, if one's freedom is restricted by the receipt of threats (or indeed by mere exposure to their possibility), one's freedom is not similarly restricted by the receipt of attractive offers (or indeed by others merely being in a position to make them).

There *is* an intuitively appealing way of interpreting dependence that allows us to distinguish between threats and offers, and that is by conceiving of dependence as a relation between *actions*, in the way outlined earlier. On this view, threats generally increase our dependence because, as an empirical rule, they decrease our probable scope for action by making more of our courses of action dependent on the actions of others. In this sense of dependence, offers generally make us *less* dependent. But if dependence is interpreted in this way, then we are back to explaining the equivalent-judgments thesis in the first of the two ways outlined at the end of the last section. In this case, "freedom as absence of dependence" and "freedom as absence of prevention" produce equivalent judgments about freedom because the two terms ultimately denote the same phenomenon.

Power and Unfreedom as Contingently Related

To the extent that one accepts the notion of freedom as a relation between actions, one has to admit that the relation between the power of *A* and the unfreedom of *B* is, as I suggested earlier, a contingent one. After all, power is, at least in part, a relation between wills. Only if dependence is defined as a relation between wills can we say that when *A* exercises or possesses power over *B*, *A* limits *B*'s freedom *by definition* rather than as a matter of empirical generalization.

We have seen that the idea of dependence as a relation between wills (coupled with the idea of freedom as the absence of dependence) lets in too many forms of power as freedom-limiting. Even leaving aside this criticism, however, there is a reason for preferring the view of power and unfreedom as distinct but empirically correlated phenomena. This reason has to do with the kind of normative work we expect the concept of freedom to be doing in the construction of a political theory.

The contingent link between power and pure negative unfreedom might be thought to be a weaker one than the definitional link between power and unfreedom as a relation between wills. It true that it is a weaker link in the sense that it admits the possibility of exceptions to the rule that when *A* exercises certain forms of power, *B*'s freedom is limited. But there is another sense in which the contingent link is a stronger link: it provides a stronger *justificatory tool*. The discovery (or the stipulation) of a logical link between two terms does no more than clarify the meaning of those two terms. The discovery of an empirical correlation, on the other hand, tells us something about the world. As a result, it allows us to establish normative relations of justification between the two phenomena. The fact that freedom logically entails the absence of certain forms of power implies only that freedom is appropriately defined as the absence of those forms of power. The fact that freedom is empirically correlated to the absence of those forms of power, on the other hand, implies that it is possible to justify, in the name of freedom, certain normative attitudes toward those forms of power. This point is similar to the one made earlier against moralized conceptions of freedom. It is not helpful to praise property rights as good for freedom if one then goes on to define freedom in terms of respect for property rights. Similarly, it is not helpful to condemn certain forms of power as producing unfreedom if one then goes on to define unfreedom in terms of those forms of power. In both cases, freedom falls out of the picture as an independent ideal, since the justificatory work is done not by freedom or unfreedom but by the concept in terms of which freedom or unfreedom is defined.

One can only usefully condemn certain forms of power as bad for freedom if one sees one's subjection to those forms of power and one's suffering of the corresponding unfreedom as distinct but empirically related phenomena. Recognizing the contingency of the relation between unfreedom and certain forms of power would provide republican political theory with a justificatory tool which, by defining one phenomenon in terms of the other, it has hitherto tended to deny itself.

ACKNOWLEDGMENTS

I am grateful to Matthew Kramer, Valeria Ottonelli, and Hillel Steiner for their helpful comments on an earlier draft of this essay.

REFERENCES

Carter, I. (1999). *A Measure of Freedom*. Oxford: Oxford University Press.

Carter, I. (2000). "A Critique of Freedom as Non-domination." *The Good Society*, 9(3), 43–6.

Carter, I. (2004). "Choice, Freedom and Freedom of Choice." *Social Choice and Welfare*, 22, 61–81.

Carter, I. (2007). "Social Power and Negative Freedom." *Homo Oeconomicus*, 24.

Cohen, G. A. (2006). "Capitalism, Freedom and the Proletariat." In D. Miller (ed.), *The Liberty Reader*. Boulder, CO: Paradigm Publishers.

Day, J. P. (1987). *Liberty and Justice*. London: Croom Helm.

Friedrich, C. J. (1963). *Man and his Government*. New York: McGraw-Hill.

Gorr, M. J. (1989). *Coercion, Freedom and Exploitation*. New York: Peter Lang.

Kramer, M. H. (2003). *The Quality of Freedom*. Oxford: Oxford University Press.

Olsaretti, S. (2004). *Liberty, Desert and the Market*. Cambridge: Cambridge University Press.

Pettit, P. (1993). "Negative Liberty, Liberal and Republican." *European Journal of Philosophy*, 1, 15–38.

Pettit, P. (1997). *Republicanism: A Theory of Freedom and Government*. Oxford: Oxford University Press.

Pettit, P. (2000). "Reply to Carter, Christman and Dagger." *The Good Society*, 9(3), 54–7.

Pettit, P. (2001). *A Theory of Freedom*. Cambridge: Polity.

Pettit, P. (2003). "Agency-freedom and Option-freedom." *Journal of Theoretical Politics*, 15, 387–403.

Skinner, Q. (1997). *Liberty before Liberalism*. Cambridge: Cambridge University Press.

Skinner, Q. (2002). "A Third Concept of Liberty." *Proceedings of the British Academy*, 117, 237–68.

Steiner, H. (1994). *An Essay on Rights*. Oxford: Blackwell

Stoppino, M. (2007). "A Formal Classification of Power." *Homo Oeconomicus*, 24.

Taylor, C. (1979). "What's Wrong with Negative Liberty." In A. Ryan (ed.), *The Idea of Freedom*. London: Oxford University Press.

Taylor, M. (1982). *Community, Anarchy and Liberty*. London: Cambridge University Press.

Chapter 4
Freedom as the Absence of Arbitrary Power

Quentin Skinner

I

I have two principal aims in this chapter,[1] the first of which is to furnish an historical sketch of what has come to be known as the "republican" theory of freedom. This terminology is owed to Philip Pettit, who has done more than anyone to make republicanism a living force in contemporary political philosophy (Pettit 1997, 2001, 2002). Like Pettit, to whom I owe an obvious debt, I was originally motivated to reconsider the republican theory in part because it seemed to me to offer a corrective to the blinkered assumptions underlying current discussions of negative liberty (Skinner 1998 and 2002a). This suggestion has since been further explored in a number of valuable works, but the view that republicanism has anything distinctive to contribute to the analysis of freedom has at the same time been sharply criticized. The attack has come from several different quarters, but perhaps the most challenging questions have been raised by Ian Carter and Matthew Kramer. Both have aired their doubts in major books on the theory of freedom, and both have restated and extended their critiques in their contributions to the present volume. My second aim in what follows will accordingly be to try to assess how far they have succeeded in establishing that, as they maintain, the features taken by Pettit and myself to be distinctive of the republican understanding of freedom can all be accommodated within the framework of their own rival theory of negative liberty (Carter 1999: 237–45; Kramer 2003: 91–149).

II

Before embarking on my historical sketch, I need to stress that I speak of the "republican" theory solely in order to remain in line with the other contributors to this volume. My own preference would be to avoid the label, which seems to me misleading as a way of describing the theory I want to discuss. It is true that, in the early-modern heyday of the theory, no one who claimed to be a republican (in the strict sense of being an opponent of monarchy) failed to espouse the so-called republican theory of liberty. But the same theory was also espoused by a number of writers – for example, John Locke – who would have been horrified to be described as republicans. I should prefer to speak of the theory as neo-Roman, in acknowledgment of its inspiration and provenance, but I seem to have lost this part of the argument.

Within Anglophone political discourse, the republican theory first rose to prominence in the course of the disputes between crown and parliament preceding the outbreak of the English civil wars in 1642. The protagonists of parliament chiefly complained that a number of specific rights and liberties were being undermined by the crown's legal and fiscal policies. But they argued at the same time that these infringements amounted to mere surface manifestations of a deeper affront to liberty. What basically troubled them was that, by emphasizing its prerogative rights, the crown was laying claim to a form of discretionary and hence arbitrary power that gave it the means to undermine specific rights and liberties with impunity.

Before going further, I need to acknowledge that in the above summary I have reformulated my original account of the views put forward by the crown's adversaries. Initially I took them to be saying that civic liberty can equally well be subverted either by acts of arbitrary interference or else by background conditions of domination and dependence (Skinner 1998: 82–3). But Pettit rightly questioned this formulation, observing that the capacity to engage in acts of arbitrary interference depends upon the prior possession of arbitrary power, and thus that the underlying presence of such power must constitute the fundamental affront to liberty (Pettit 2002). I am happy to accept this correction, for it now seems to me that this is certainly the sense of priorities we encounter among the early critics of the Stuart monarchy.

The claim that liberty is subverted by arbitrary power soon began to be widely taken up. A full history of this republican commitment would need to encompass at least four later phases of English public debate. First of all, it was partly in the light of this argument that parliament sought to legitimize the abolition of the monarchy and the establishment of the "free state" in 1649. We accordingly find the republican theory vehemently reaffirmed in the course of the 1650s by such leading apologists for the English commonwealth as Marchamont Nedham, John Milton, William Sprigg, and above all James Harrington in his *Oceana* of 1656. Next, the theory was further developed in the closing decades of the seventeenth century as part of the reaction against the renewed defense of monarchical absolutism, especially as mounted by Sir Robert Filmer in his posthumously published *Patriarcha*. William Petyt, Algernon Sidney, James Tyrrell, and most notably John Locke in his *Two Treatises of Government* all invoke a republican understanding of liberty in responding to Filmer's arguments. Within a generation, the same understanding was widely deployed as a means of denouncing the arbitrary powers allegedly wielded by the executive under the long ascendancy of Sir Robert Walpole. To this end the republican theory was reshaped by such radical whigs as John Trenchard and Thomas Gordon in the 1720s, and later by numerous propagandists associated with Bolingbroke and his circle in the following decade. Finally, the same theory was pressed into a different kind of ideological service when it was used by Joseph Priestley, Richard Price, and other supporters of the American colonists against the British crown in the 1770s. It was only with the rise of classical utilitarianism in the same period that the republican theory finally began to be widely challenged and repudiated.

As I began by noting, the distinctive contention uniting these various strands of thought is that the mere presence of arbitrary power has the effect of undermining political liberty. We next need to note that this commitment was in turn expressed in the form of a more specific claim about freedom and servitude. The basic argument on which the republican theorists take their stand is that the presence of arbitrary power within a civil association has the effect, as they like to phrase it, of converting its members from the status of free-men into that of slaves.

The classic account of this contrast between *servi* and *liberi homines* can be found in the *Digest* of Roman Law, but the same distinction was taken up into English law at a very early date. We find it further explored in the opening chapters of Bracton's thirteenth-century treatise on the laws of England, and Bracton's analysis subsequently exercised an overwhelming influence. Within this legal tradition, a slave is always defined as someone who is subject to the arbitrary power of a *dominus* or master. The master's power is said to be arbitrary in the sense that it is always open to him to govern his slaves, with impunity, according to his mere *arbitrium*, his own will, and desires. Correspondingly, the condition of slaves is said to be that they are condemned to living *in potestate*, "within the power," and consequently dependent on the will of the master to whom they remain subject at all times (*Digest* 1985, I.6.1, p. 18).

It is this understanding of slavery that we encounter again among the defenders of republican liberty. If we turn, for example, to such early opponents of the Stuart monarchy as John Goodwin in his *Anti-cavalierisme* of 1642, we already come upon a systematic exposition of the theme. What it means to live in "bondage and slavery," Goodwin explains, is to have "lordly" rulers under whom you are required "to live by the lawes of their lusts and pleasures, to be at their arbitterments and wills in all things, to doe and to suffer, to have and to possesse as they shall appoint" (Goodwin 1642: 39). John Locke later provides a celebrated restatement of the same commitment in his chapter on slavery in the *Two Treatises*. To live in servitude, according to Locke's summary, is to live "under an Absolute, Arbitrary, Despotical power"; more specifically, a slave is said to be someone condemned to living in subjection to a Master with "an Arbitrary Power over his Life" (Locke 1988: II.24, p. 285).

If we return to the legal tradition, we find the contrasting concept of the *liber homo* or free-man defined in turn as the antonym of a slave. To be a *liber homo*, according to the *Digest*, is *not* to be *in potestate domini*, within the power of a master. It is to be *suae potestatis*, to be possessed of a power to act according to your own will rather than being obliged to live in dependence on the will of someone else (*Digest* 1985, I.6.4, p. 18). It is consequently a matter of being *sui iuris*, capable of acting as "your own man" and hence "in your own right" (*Digest* 1985, I.6.1, p. 18).

This conception was likewise adopted by the defenders of republican liberty. They do not deny, of course, that the liberty of free-men within civil associations must be regulated if such associations are to survive in security and peace. What it means to be a free-man under such an association is only that your liberty is never curtailed by *arbitrary* power; it is only ever limited by laws to which you have given your explicit consent. They concede that, when you submit to a law, your freedom of action will to that degree be controlled. But they insist that, so long as you give your consent, the law itself can be regarded as an expression of your will, as a result of which you may be said to remain a free-man in obeying it.

It is true that, as a number of royalist writers objected, the giving of consent can hardly be sufficient to ensure that the power so constituted is not of a dominating and hence an enslaving character. Even if you consent to be governed only by elected representatives, and only for limited periods of time, the act of granting your consent will at the same time be the act of submitting to their will. The outcome, as one royalist pamphleteer was to put it in 1642, is to give Parliament "so full an Arbitrary power, that the right and safety of King and People must wholly depend upon their Votes" (*Animadversions* (1642), p. 2). How, then, is government by a sovereign Parliament any less arbitrary than government by a sovereign king?

Few republican writers cared to address these lurking difficulties. Usually they simply assert that the idea of consent can be unproblematically applied to yield the necessary reconciliation between law and liberty. James Harrington, for example, offers a breezy reassurance in his *Oceana* of 1656. To be free under government is "not to be controlled but by the law; and that framed by every private man unto no other end (or they may thank themselves) than to protect the liberty of every private man, which by that means comes to be the liberty of the commonwealth" (Harrington 1992: 20). Provided, in other words, that the laws alone rule, and provided that we ourselves make the laws, then we may be said to be living as free-men in a free state.

It might seem preferable to restate these commitments, as Pettit has done, without invoking the outdated and sexist vocabulary of "free-men" and "free states." Pettit instead proposes that "where I am dominated by another agency, I should be said to be *unfree*" and that "where I am restricted but not dominated – as by a conditioning factor such as an unintended obstacle or a nonarbitrary law – then I should be said to be *nonfree*" (Pettit 2002: 347). A further merit of framing the argument in this way is that it has the effect of highlighting the dramatic implication that, as Pettit presents it, "neither a tax levy, nor even a term of imprisonment, need take away someone's freedom" (Pettit 1997: 56 n. 3).

The problem, however, with Pettit's updating of republican terminology is that his argument has proved to be rather easily misunderstood.

I managed to contribute to the misunderstanding myself when I initially took him to be saying that republican theorists embrace the paradox that it may be possible to render someone free by means of coercing them (Skinner 1998: 83 n.). More seriously, Carter in his contribution to the present volume continues to misunderstand Pettit's position when he takes him to be suggesting that any restrictions imposed on us for our own good ought not to count as instances of interference. He concludes that Pettit must be defending what he describes as a "moralized" account of constraint.

It is certainly true that some early-modern theorists of republican liberty embraced just such an account. John Locke, for example, goes so far as to defend the idea of prerogative rights in strongly moralized terms in his *Two Treatises*. While he allows that rulers who wield such rights may appear to have "some Title to Arbitrary Power," he insists that in this instance such appearances are deceptive. The reason is that "Prerogative is nothing but the Power of doing publick good without a Rule," and consequently escapes the charge of arbitrariness (Locke 1988, II.164, II.166, pp. 377–8; cf. Halldenius 2002: 262–6).

Pettit makes it abundantly clear in his chapter that he has no wish to endorse such a moralized view of constraint. To forestall this misunderstanding, however, it might have been better to cleave to the venerable distinction between enjoying our specific liberties as free-men and enjoying them in a manner compatible with slavery. As we have seen, according to this way of phrasing the argument we remain slaves if we enjoy our liberties only by the grace of someone with arbitrary power; by contrast, we remain free-men if our liberties can be constrained only with our own consent. Citizens who are imprisoned for falling foul of laws to which they have given their consent can therefore be said to retain, even while in prison, their underlying status as free-men, although they have obviously been deprived of one of their civil liberties. The apparent paradox about the compatibility of freedom and imprisonment is thereby resolved, but without offering anything that could be mistaken for a moralized view of constraint.

The essence of the theory I have been sketching can thus be summarized as follows: if you are subject to arbitrary power, then you are a slave; but if you are a slave, then *ex hypothesi* you are no longer in possession of your liberty. We might well feel inclined to object, however, that this is hardly a very illuminating argument. What is it, we still want to know, about the mere fact of your living in subjection to arbitrary power that is supposed to have the effect of taking away your freedom of action?

It is arguable that, in the recent revival of the republican theory, this issue has not always been addressed with sufficient directness. If we return, however, to the leading protagonists of the theory in its heyday, we find them raising and answering the question with a single voice. To have freedom of action, they agree, is to be able to choose between options (or at least alternatives); it is to be able to do or forbear at will, to act according to your own will and desires. Algernon Sidney in his *Discourses* announces the commitment as forthrightly as possible: "liberty solely consists in an independency upon the will of another" (Sidney 1990: 17). Trenchard and Gordon in *Cato's Letters* speak to the same effect: a man in possession of "true and impartial liberty" is someone who is able "to think what he will, and act as he thinks" (Trenchard & Gordon 1995: 429). Richard Price in his *Two Tracts* provides the clearest summary: "to be free is to be guided by one's own will"; it is "to be able to act or forbear from acting, as we think best" (Price 1991: 26, 76).

Given this analysis, it is easy to see why these writers insist that, if you become subject to the arbitrary power of someone else, you thereby forfeit your liberty. The reason is simply that you are no longer able to do or forbear according to your own will and desires. No action of yours can in principle have that character. When you now act, you always do so by the leave and hence with the implicit permission of the master or ruler under whose power you live. As Sidney observes in his *Discourses*, you are only ever able to act by "the grace of the prince, which he may revoke whensoever he pleaseth" (Sidney 1990: 17). But as Sidney has already told us, liberty consists in having an independent will, so that anyone "who can neither dispose of his person nor goods, but enjoys all at the will of his master" must be living in servitude (Sidney 1990: 17).

The nerve of the republican theory can thus be expressed by saying that it disconnects the presence of unfreedom from the imposition of interference. The lack of freedom suffered by slaves is not basically due to their being constrained or interfered with in the exercise of any of their specific choices. Slaves whose choices happen never to fall out of conformity with the will of their masters may be able to act without the least interference. They may therefore appear, paradoxically, to be in full possession of their freedom, since none of their actions will ever be prevented or penalized. Such slaves nevertheless remain wholly bereft of liberty. They remain subject to the will of their masters, unable to act according to their own independent will at any time. They are, in other words, not agents at all. They have no control over their lives, as Harrington puts it, and are consequently forced to live in a state of unending doubt and anxiety as to what may or may not be about to happen to them (Harrington 1992: 20). Trenchard and Gordon, who include in *Cato's Letters* an essay entitled "the Nature and Extent of Liberty," offer a similar account of the slave's predicament. To live in servitude is "to live at the mere mercy of another; and a life of slavery is, to those who can bear it, a continual state of uncertainty and wretchedness" (Trenchard & Gordon 1995: 430).

It is of course true that, should the master decide to remove the slave's uncertainty, then the slave becomes free. A master or ruler with arbitrary and absolute power who agrees to make it strictly impossible for this power ever to be exercised thereby emancipates his subjects from their servitude. So long, however, as such a ruler retains any such power – even if it is never exercised – his subjects remain in the condition of slaves, and thereby deprived of their liberty. It is the mere *potentia* of the ruler that suffices to bring about this result.

The basic claim of the republican theorists is thus that the presence of arbitrary power serves in itself to make us slaves. As they willingly admit, however, it is highly unlikely that anyone could be a slave for long without coming to appreciate the implications of their predicament. As a result, a number of republican writers develop a further argument about the lack of liberty suffered by those condemned to servitude. Suppose, they go on, you come to recognize with full self-consciousness that you have a master who possesses the power to behave toward you, with impunity, in any way he may choose. This awareness will have the effect of imposing further and more specific constraints on your freedom of action. You will now be inclined to shape and adapt your behavior in just such a way as to try to minimize the risk that your master will intervene in your life in a detrimental way.

This argument stands in one respect in strong contrast to the one I have so far been considering. It is no longer the mere presence of arbitrary power that is taken to have the effect of restricting your freedom of action. Rather your reflections on your predicament are said to give rise to these additional constraints. But in another respect the argument is the same as before. There is no implication, that is, that these further restrictions need be due to any interference on the part of your master, nor even any threat of interference. Your further loss of liberty is taken to be wholly the product of your own self-censorship.

By no means every exponent of the republican theory is concerned with this further theme. John Locke, for example, displays almost no interest in what it might feel like to live in subjection to the arbitrary power of someone else (Halldenius 2002: 266). If we turn, however, to the Roman moralists and historians who first articulated the theory, we not only find them much preoccupied with the psychological implications of slavery; we also find their insights much developed by a number of early-modern theorists whose concern was with the value as well as with the meaning of individual liberty.

The Roman writers are interested in two distinct ways in which the experience of servitude can hardly fail to shape and constrain our behavior. One suggestion, originally put forward by Sallust, is that a community living under arbitrary government will find itself languishing for lack of energy and initiative, and restricted above all in its range of economic activities. Among early-modern defenders of republican liberty, Trenchard and Gordon place particular emphasis on this argument in *Cato's Letters*, developing a self-congratulating contrast between the commercial success of free states such as Great Britain and the poverty of arbitrary regimes such as Turkey and France.

The essence of Trenchard and Gordon's argument is that "where there is liberty, there are encouragements to labour, because people labour for themselves: and no one can take from them the acquisitions which they make," whereas "in arbitrary countries, men in trade are every moment liable to be undone" (Trenchard & Gordon 1995: 475). If, under arbitrary government, you accrue a conspicuous degree of wealth, it will always be open to your rulers to filch it from you with impunity. You may even reflect that, the greater your gains, the more likely you are to forfeit them. These anxieties may of course prove needless. But they will be sufficient, Trenchard and Gordon postulate, to act as powerful disincentives. You will be unlikely to think it worthwhile to incur the risks and difficulties attendant on great commercial enterprises. The inevitable consequence is that those living under arbitrary regimes slide into a distinctive state of torpor and sluggishness, cramping and confining their virtuous industriousness until nothing of note in any of the arts or sciences can be expected of them. As Trenchard and Gordon conclude, "slavery, while it continues, being a perpetual awe upon the spirits, depresses them, and sinks natural courage" (Trenchard & Gordon 1995: 431). They quote with relish Paul Ricaut's *Present State of the Ottoman Empire* by way of clinching their argument. "The causes of the decay of arts among the Turks, and of the neglect and want of care in manufacturing and cultivating their lands" arise from the fact that "men, knowing no certain heir, nor who shall succeed them in their labours, contrive only for a few years' enjoyment" (Trenchard & Gordon 1995: 337).

I turn to the other claim put forward by the Roman moralists and historians about the constraining effects of enslavement. This further argument came to be associated in particular with Tacitus, who embodies it in numerous anecdotes scattered through his *Annals* and *Histories*. Reduced to a maxim, his suggestion is that those living in servitude can always be expected to behave with servility. This insight was likewise taken up and developed by the early-modern defenders of republican liberty, and by no one with greater ferocity and eloquence than John Milton in his anti-monarchical tracts, above all his *Readie and Easie Way to Establish a Free Commonwealth* of 1660.

It is important to recognize that what these writers claim to be identifying is a general tendency of the enslaved to act with slavishness. They are not suggesting that those condemned to servitude are strictly obliged to behave with servility in consequence of recognizing that, if they attempt to behave otherwise, they will certainly be penalized or stopped. As we have seen, what the republican theorists take to be distinctive about the predicament of slaves is that there is nothing certain about their situation at all. Should they refuse to act with the deference expected of them, their master may of course respond with lethal vengefulness; but he may on the other hand be amused or impressed, and he may even think it in his interests (as Seneca suggests at one point) to reward such signs of courage and self-confidence (Seneca 1917: XLVII.4, p. 302). The possibility of such a master–slave dialectic was one that profoundly interested the Roman moralists. Tacitus recounts with fascination the story of Clemens, a slave "with a spirit not in the least servile" who succeeded in terrifying the emperor Tiberius with his sheer audacity, while Seneca praises those masters who are willing "to live on familiar terms" with their slaves and treat them "as comrades and humble friends" (Tacitus 1931: II.39, p. 442; Seneca 1917: XLVII.1, pp. 300–2).

As Tacitus frequently insists, however, those living in subjection will always have the strongest motives for playing safe, in consequence of which we can hardly expect from them anything better than abject slavishness. Drawing on Tacitus's authority, John Milton in his *Readie and Easie Way* treats the impending restoration of the English monarchy as a return to just such a condition of servitude, and paints a horrified picture of the servility to come. There are deeply reprehensible forms of conduct, he first observes, that those living in slavery find it almost impossible to avoid. Not knowing what may happen to them, and desperate to avoid the tyrant's rage, they tend to behave in appeasing and ingratiating ways, becoming "a servile crew," engaging in "flatteries and prostrations," displaying "the perpetual bowings and cringings of an abject people" (Milton 1980: 425, 426, 428). At the same time, there are various lines of conduct that they find it almost impossible to pursue. We can never expect from them any "noble words and actions," any willingness to speak truth to power, any readiness to offer frank judgments and be prepared to act on them (Milton 1980: 428).

My own previous discussions of the republican theory of liberty have tended to focus on the different ways in which the experience of servitude may be said to generate these patterns of self-censorship. It is important for me to add, however, that I have mainly emphasized these considerations for polemical purposes. We are frequently told that liberty can be taken away only by acts of overt interference. I have wanted to retort that this is not the case, and that this response can readily be defended by considering the behavior of slaves who become fully aware of their predicament. On the one hand, we can expect them to censor their conduct, and if they do so we can properly describe them as limiting their own freedom of action. But on the other hand, these limitations need not be due to anyone's having interfered with them or even threatened them with interference.

Pettit in his chapter likewise lays his main emphasis on the phenomenon of self-censorship. It now seems to me, however, that both of us have perhaps placed too much weight on this argument. From the perspective of the republican analysis of unfreedom it is of secondary importance, and to single it out may serve to distract attention from the basic conceptual claim that the exponents of the republican theory want to underscore. Perhaps it will be helpful to bring this historical sketch to a close by reiterating what I take to be their central point. They agree that anyone who reflects on their own servitude will probably come to *feel* unfree to act or forbear from acting in certain ways. But what actually *makes* them unfree is the mere fact of living in subjection to arbitrary power. This is what leaves them at the mercy of others, and this is what takes from them the status of free-men and makes them slaves.

III

I am now in a position to consider the bearing of these remarks on the claims that Carter and Kramer have made on behalf of what they describe as the pure negative theory of liberty. While both of them have presented their arguments at considerable length in their recent books, they have also provided helpful paraphrases of their principal conclusions in the present volume, and it will be convenient to refer mainly to these latest statements in responding to their case.

They take as their point of departure an impressively rigorous analysis of the concept of free action. Both reject the standard liberal assumption that one of the principal ways in which it is possible to limit an individual's freedom is by coercing their will, thereby rendering certain choices ineligible. Instead they insist on the hard-edged claim that an individual is unfree to perform a specific action if and only if the action in question is prevented, thereby rendering it impossible of performance (Carter 1999: 219–34; Kramer 2003: 169–84, 245–54). They are thus led to present an analysis of free action reminiscent of the one developed by Hillel Steiner, Michael Taylor, and other contemporary admirers of Hobbes (Steiner 1974–5; Taylor 1982: 142–50). By way of illustrating their analysis, Carter and Kramer both recur to the time-honored example of the highwayman who confronts you with the demand "Your money or your life." They explicitly insist, in Hobbesian vein, that the highwayman is presenting you with a genuine choice. You are free to give up your money, but you are equally free to give up your life. What you are not free to do – what the highwayman's demand prevents you from doing – is to follow the conjoined option of holding on to your cash as well as your life. This is the action that you are now unfree to perform, since the highwayman has rendered it impossible of performance.

It is in the light of this analysis that Carter and Kramer both deny that there is anything distinctive about the republican theory of liberty, and my next task is to try to assess their argument. There is one juncture at which they may appear to be correct in suggesting that Pettit and I have overstated the distinctiveness of the republican case. Not only have we argued that relations of domination and dependence serve in themselves to take away freedom of action; we have also contrasted this commitment with the liberal theory of negative liberty. Kramer is able to quote me as declaring, a little incautiously, that one "key assumption of classical liberalism" is that "force or the coercive threat of it constitute the only forms of constraint that interfere with individual liberty" (Skinner 1998: 84).

This still strikes me as an unimpeachable account of the theory of negative liberty as enunciated by such classical utilitarian writers as William Paley, Jeremy Bentham, and later Henry Sidgwick. As Kramer rightly observes, however, it is not a correct characterization of his own theory of pure negative liberty, according to which your freedom can be limited even in the absence of interference. That this is possible is said to follow from the fact that, as Kramer expresses it, the obstructions that take away freedom may be purely hypothetical in character, since they may only have the effect of removing options from potential choice. As we have seen, Kramer takes this to be the correct way of describing the loss of liberty you suffer when the highwaymen says "Your money or your life." The effect of the threat is to rule out as a potential object of choice the option of disobeying and at the same time preserving your life. Strictly speaking, Kramer ought to have added that the option is ruled out if and only if the highwayman's threat is immediate and unambiguously credible. None the less, his argument may appear sufficient to convict me of overstatement. Although the option of disobeying and preserving your life has been removed, this outcome is not the result of any overt act of interference. The contention, in other words, that freedom can be lost without interference turns out not to be distinctive of the republican tradition after all.

There is room for doubt, however, as to whether Carter and Kramer have satisfactorily characterized their chosen *mise en scène*. They write as if the sole change brought about by the highwayman's intervention in your journey is that an object of hypothetical choice is removed and replaced. But this is to oversimplify your predicament. A further change brought about by the highwayman is that an *existing* object of choice is replaced.[2] Until your journey was interrupted, you were in a position to hold on to your cash as well as your life. But this option has now been replaced by that of being able to hold on to your life only at the expense of handing over your cash. The significance of these considerations is that Kramer's associated contention that the situation is one in which your freedom is reduced, but without any act of interference taking place, appears not to hold good. There *is* an act of interference, for if an option previously available to you has been replaced, some agent must have interfered with sufficient coercive force to replace it.

There is no reason for republicans to reject this way of thinking about how coercion limits freedom of action. Admittedly they do not believe, as liberal theorists are inclined to do, that such acts of coercion represent the fundamental affront to liberty. For republicans, the fundamental affront is always the mere existence of arbitrary power. Nevertheless, they agree that, when someone coerces and thereby bends your will, especially by means of serious and credible threats, such interventions have the direct effect of constraining your patterns of choice, and may therefore be said to constitute a further means of curtailing your freedom to exercise your powers at will.

I want finally to touch on the chief difficulty I find in Carter's and Kramer's case. They repeatedly affirm that the allegedly distinctive characteristics of the republican theory of liberty can be fully accommodated within their own purely negative account. But they are able to uphold this position, it seems to me, only because they have misunderstood the republican theory in two related ways.

Their first misunderstanding is disclosed by their insistence that, if the republican theorists are saying anything coherent about the relationship between domination and loss of liberty, they must be talking in probabilistic terms. Carter maintains that the loss of freedom suffered by slaves depends entirely on the probability that their master will exercise his dominating powers. Kramer agrees that, where the master is almost wholly indulgent, the slave must correspondingly be almost wholly free. Both conclude that, as Kramer writes in his chapter, "to the degree to which the dominating do not interfere, to that degree the freedom of the dominated is unimpaired."

These assertions misunderstand the existential condition of the slave as envisaged by the republican theorists I have discussed. As we have seen, they consider a slave to be someone whose entire behavior is subject to the will of someone else, that of a master or arbitrary ruler at whose mercy they are obliged to live. Slaves are never free, because they are never free of their master's will; their actions are invariably performed by the leave and with the grace of someone else. As a result, a slave's pattern of conduct is nothing other than a reflection of what their master is willing to tolerate. This in turn means that, even if there is almost no probability that such slaves will be subjected to interference in the exercise of their powers, their fundamental condition of servitude remains wholly unaffected. It is the mere fact that their master or ruler has arbitrary powers to intervene that takes away their liberty, not any particular degree of probability that these powers will ever be exercised.

Kramer attempts to counter this argument with his fable of the gentle giant. The political implications of the story are not entirely clear, but perhaps some analogy is intended with the figure of the perfectly virtuous ruler so beloved of early-modern defenders of monarchy. The strength of the gentle giant, as Kramer in his chapter tells the tale, is sufficient to give him complete ascendancy over his community, and he is fully aware of the fact. But we are told that his disposition and inclinations are such that "there is no prospect" of his choosing to impose his will on others. Kramer concludes that to describe the giant "as rendering his contemporaries unfree" is an obvious misrepresentation, for "he is not significantly reducing the overall liberty of anyone else."

One problem here, as any republican will be quick to point out, is that Kramer has not recounted his story with sufficient exactitude. If it is true, as he claims at one stage, that there is *no prospect* of the giant's interfering – if this has somehow been rendered impossible – then a republican will be willing to go even further than Kramer. Kramer says that the giant "is not significantly reducing" the liberty of anyone else, but a republican will want to say that he is not reducing it at all: the community is wholly free, for it is wholly free of the giant's arbitrary power. If on the other hand the freedom of the community remains dependent, as Kramer says at another stage, on the *disposition* and *inclinations* of the giant, then a republican will want to insist that the community is wholly enslaved. If the giant *could* interfere at will and with impunity, then the community remains in his power; and the essence of the republican argument is that living in such a state of subjection is equivalent to living in servitude.

I turn finally to Carter's and Kramer's other misunderstanding of the slave's predicament as described by the republican theorists I have discussed. They assume that the lack of freedom suffered by slaves arises from their continual need to take measures – servile and slavish measures – to ensure that they avoid incurring the ill-will of their masters.

Carter announces this assumption at the outset of his discussion of "resilient non-interference," but it is Kramer who examines it most extensively. As he explains in his chapter, the reason why slaves are not free to engage in non-deferential patterns of behavior is that "somebody who makes use of such freedoms will arouse the ire of the dominant party and will thereby trigger harsh penalties." As a result, the freedom of slaves to behave non-obsequiously "will no longer be exercisable conjunctively" with the freedom to avoid being stopped or penalized. It is "in this manner," Kramer concludes, that "the situation of domination impairs the overall liberty of each dependent person." The lack of freedom suffered by slaves is held to stem, in short, from the fact that "retaliation will be undertaken" if they behave "in any manner that is insufficiently humble or furtive."

It is certainly true, as I have shown, that many republican theorists are deeply interested in what happens when slaves begin to reflect on the implications of their servitude. As will be clear from my historical sketch, however, Kramer gives a misleading impression of the analysis offered by the republican theorists of the predicament in which such slaves are obliged to live. These theorists do not take it to be the case – and nor do they suppose that slaves take it to be the case – that anyone living in servitude *will* be stopped or penalized if they behave in insufficiently humble or furtive ways. Rather they maintain that the situation in which slaves find themselves is that, while they *may* be stopped or penalized, they may be left entirely unconstrained.

Admittedly Kramer may have been misled by some loose talk on my own part in my original formulation of the argument. He is able to quote me as saying that "you *will* find yourself constrained in what you can say and do" as soon as you begin to reflect on your state of dependence (Skinner 1998: 86). As I have subsequently tried to make clear, however, what basically distinguishes the life of slaves according to the republican tradition is that they are condemned to a life of complete uncertainty. They never know what may or may not be about to happen to them. But if this consideration leads them, as it probably will, to act with the servility routinely expected of them, this will not be because they will undoubtedly be stopped or penalized if they behave otherwise. Rather it will be because, in consequence of their basic sense of uncertainty, they feel an understandable disposition to play safe.

The significance of these considerations is that, if we follow Carter's and Kramer's analysis of negative liberty, we shall have to say that slaves in the predicament I have just described are not unfree to behave audaciously. It is not necessarily the case, that is, that they will find it impossible to follow the conjoined option of behaving audaciously and escaping punishment. For it is not certain that their master will stop or penalize them. Perhaps he will, but perhaps he won't. But this is to say that no conjoined options have definitely been rendered impossible of performance. And this in turn is to say that, according to Carter's and Kramer's theory of pure negative liberty, the freedom of such slaves is unimpaired.

According to the republican tradition, by contrast, any slave in the predicament I have been describing is unquestionably unfree. First of all, it is important to recall that republicans, by contrast with pure neg-ative theorists, are not confined to explicating the idea of unfreedom solely in terms of impossibility. They are willing to say that the mere openness of slaves to being stopped or penalized for failing to act with sufficient obsequiousness will tend to constrain their ability to realize even the conditional choices they are able to make, and can therefore be said to count as an additional limitation on their liberty. To which they are willing to add that the observable tendency of slaves to behave slavishly appears to offer strong confirmation of this argument.

The republican theorists are chiefly concerned, however, with the further and deeper sense in which any slave in the predicament I have been describing is unfree. According to the republican tradition, the lack of liberty suffered by slaves is only secondarily due to there being various courses of action they may feel constrained to follow or avoid. To make this consideration primary, as Carter and Kramer have done, is to confuse the existential condition of slavery with the predicament in which slaves find themselves once they begin to reflect on their servi-tude. The basic condition in which slaves find themselves is not that some of their particular actions may be under some degree of pressure or threat; it is that they are condemned to living wholly at the mercy of their master's arbitrary power. As Pettit now wants to put it, they are *under alienating control*, and it is this condition that leaves them bereft of liberty.

The main polemical claim on which Carter and Kramer take their stand is that their pure negative theory fully encompasses the allegedly distinctive features of republican liberty. As I have tried to show, however, between the two lines of argument a gulf remains fixed. According to the republican tradition, the mere existence of arbitrary power, and thus of alienating control, serves to undermine freedom of action. But according to the pure negative theory, the most that can be said about the predicament of someone living in such a state of sub-jection is that certain conjoined options, certain possible objects of choice, will be removed and replaced. To this the republican can offer, as I have shown, two distinct ripostes. One is that, in the situation described by Carter and Kramer, certain *actual* objects of choice are also replaced; the other is that their analysis in any case misses the point about the basic way in which freedom is cancelled by servitude. I conclude that, despite Carter's and Kramer's courteous calls for a rapprochement between the two traditions, and despite their belief that they have man-aged to effect just such a rapprochement, the republican and the pure negative theories of liberty remain stubbornly distinct.

NOTES

1   For commenting on earlier drafts of this chapter I am deeply indebted to Kinch Hoekstra, Susan James, Cécile Laborde, Philip Pettit, and James Tully.
2   I owe this way of formulating the point to Pettit's contribution to the present volume. As he puts it, when laying out his first theorem, "the imposition of a probabilistic or sure-fire burden will replace an option, substituting a burdened counterpart."

BIBLIOGRAPHY

Animadversions upon those notes which the late observator hath published (1642). London.
Carter, Ian (1999). *A Measure of Freedom.* Oxford.
Digest of Justinian (1985). Ed. Theodor Mommsen and Paul Krueger, tr. ed. Alan Watson, 4 vols. Philadelphia.
Goodwin, John (1642). *Anti-Cavalierisme.* London.
Halldenius, Lena (2002). "Locke and the Non-Arbitrary." *European Journal of Political Theory*, 2, 261–79.
Harrington, James (1992). *The Commonwealth of Oceana*, ed. J. G. A. Pocock. Cambridge.
Kramer, Matthew H. (2003). *The Quality of Freedom.* Oxford.
Locke, John (1988). *Two Treatise of Government*, ed. Peter Laslett. Cambridge.
Milton, John (1980). *The Readie and Easie Way to Establish a Free Commonwealth* in *Complete Prose Works of John Milton*, vol. VII, rev. ed., ed. Robert W. Ayers. New Haven, CT, pp. 407–63.
Pettit, Philip (1997). *Republicanism: A Theory of Freedom and Government.* Oxford.

Pettit, Philip (2001). *A Theory of Freedom: From the Psychology to the Politics of Agency.* Oxford.

Pettit, Philip (2002). "Keeping Republican Freedom Simple: On a Difference with Quentin Skinner." *Political Theory*, 30, 339–56.

Price, Richard (1991). *Political Writings*, ed. D. O. Thomas. Cambridge.

Seneca (1917). *Epistulae Morales*, vol. 1, tr. Richard M. Gummere. Cambridge, MA.

Sidney, Algernon (1990). *Discourses Concerning Government*, ed. Thomas G. West. Indianapolis.

Skinner, Quentin (1998). *Liberty Before Liberalism.* Cambridge.

Skinner, Quentin (2002). "A Third Concept of Liberty." *Proceedings of the British Academy*, 117, 237–68.

Steiner, Hillel (1974–5). "Individual Liberty." *Proceedings of the Aristotelian Society*, 75, 33–50.

Tacitus (1931). *The Annals Books I–III*, tr. John Jackson. Cambridge, MA.

Taylor, Michael (1982). *Community, Anarchy and Liberty.* Cambridge.

Trenchard, John & Gordon, Thomas (1995). *Cato's Letters or Essays on Liberty, Civil and Religious, and Other Important Subjects*, ed. Ronald Hamowy, 2 vols. Indianapolis, IN.

Chapter 5
Republican Freedom: Three Axioms, Four Theorems

Philip Pettit

My aim in this essay is to reformulate the republican conception of freedom as non-domination somewhat more formally than I have done before. The account that I offer does not fundamentally depart from that which I have presented elsewhere (Pettit 1997b, 2001, 2007); and, while it may not fit in detail with Quentin Skinner's views, it is certainly in the same ball-park (Skinner 1998; Pettit 2002).[1] The motive for the reformulation is a wish to show how the approach compares with, and scores over, the theory of freedom as non-interference generally but, in particular, the version of that theory that Ian Carter (1999), Matthew Kramer (2003), and others have recently been defending.

The formulation employed uses the notion of control, in particular control over choice, defining liberty as the absence of alien or alienating control on the part of other persons. The notion of being subject to the alien control of others is used to represent the idea of domination. While the language of control is not so salient a part of the traditional republican lexicon as the language of domination or *dominatio* – although it does have a presence there (Pocock 1977) – it may serve better in displaying the connections between liberty and associated notions. The axioms presented in the first section are designed to shape up the concept of alien control so that it serves this purpose effectively.

The broad line of argument is this. Human beings routinely exercise certain forms of control over one another, affecting the probabilities attached to the options they respectively confront. But one variety of control is non-alien, leaving those affected with full freedom of choice, while another is alien or alienating, having a negative impact on freedom of choice. Each form of control can occur with interference, even interference broadly understood, and each form can occur without; thus there may be freedom in the presence or absence of interference, and there may be unfreedom in its presence or absence. Alien control without interference materializes when the controller or associates invigilate the choices of the controlled agent, being ready to interfere should the controlled agent not conform to a desired pattern or should the controller have a change of mind. Non-alien control with interference materializes when things are the other way around: the interferee or associates invigilate the choices of the interferer, being ready to stop or redirect the interference should the interferer not conform to a desired pattern or should the interferee have a change of mind. Invigilation in the sense invoked may occur without awareness on the part of the agent invigilated and may not occasion any inhibition; it involves a virtual form of control in which the invigilator is ready to interfere but only on a need-to-act basis.

The chapter is in three sections. First, I set out three axiomatic assumptions behind the republican definition of liberty as the absence of alien control. Then, using those axioms and some plausible, independent principles, I derive four theorems that define the connection between interference and control: these show how alien control may materialize with interference but also without; and how non-alien control may materialize without interference but also with. At various points in the exposition of axioms and theorems, I respond to some challenges made by Carter and Kramer and then, in the last section, I address their version of freedom as non-interference more directly.

The focus in this chapter is on the freedom of choice, by which I mean the freedom to select one option from among a number of mutually exclusive and jointly exhaustive options; choices just are such structured sets of options.[2] In some ways this focus may be misleading, since the primary interest of republican political theory is in the freedom of the person, not in the freedom of choice. The free person, on the republican understanding, is someone who is systematically protected and empowered against alien control in those choice-types that are deemed significant in social life (Pettit 2006b).[3] Thus the free person will not be someone who manages to avoid alien control in just any choices – including choices harmful to innocent parties – or who only manages to avoid it on an ad hoc basis: say, because of having mafia friends. The free person will avoid alien control in relevant choices and on the right basis.[4] The relevant choices will correspond to the important liberties, however they are understood, and the right basis will be incorporation in a cultural, legal, and political matrix of protection and empowerment.[5]

The republican theory of freedom is distinguished, then, on two separable counts: first, in taking freedom of choice to require the absence of alien control, not just the absence of interference; and second, in taking the freedom of the person to require a systematic sort of protection and empowerment against alien control over selected choices. My earlier presentations of the approach did not distinguish clearly between these different aspects and I am happy to emphasize their separability here. But I focus in this chapter on what alien control means, and on how particular choices may or may not be controlled in an alien way, without addressing the connection with the freedom of the person. That connection remains central to the republican approach, however, and should figure prominently in a fuller account, meriting an independent axiom and generating a richer set of theorems.

The Axioms

The three basic axioms on which the republican conception of liberty relies bear respectively on: the reality of personal choice; the possibility of alien control; and the positionality of alien control.

Axiom 1. *The reality of personal choice*

In order to deliberate about what to do, in the manner that is distinctive of human beings, we have to assume with respect to the options before us in any context that we can take one or we can take another. They are there for us as possibilities that, in the most basic sense possible, are available for choice; they are, quite simply, choosables or enactables. Sometimes, of course, we think of an option, not in the basic terms in which it is so available, but under a richer description that reaches out to include a desired but saliently uncertain consequence; we think of it as hitting the target, for example, rather than just trying to hit the target. But in every case there is an aspect under which each option presents itself to us such that we can think: I can just do that, or I can just refuse to do that; what I do in this choice is up to me. Options are not restricted to basic actions like moving a finger or uttering a sound, which I can intentionally perform without doing anything else as an intentional means of performing them (Hornsby 1980). But they must each be something of which, in context, I can think, and think rightly: this is within my power of choice; this is something I can do.

The axiom of personal choice is the claim that there are many scenarios where we are in a position to make these can-do assumptions and are right to make them: the options we face really are options, so that we can choose or not choose them, at will. I do not offer any defense of the claim here. Doing so would take me far afield, into issues of metaphysics (see Pettit & Smith 1996; Pettit 2001). And in any case a defense is not really necessary, since the axiom is unlikely to be contested amongst moral or political theorists. Such theorists presuppose the possibility of personal choice, as that is understood here, and look at issues that arise in the light of that presupposition.

Before leaving this first axiom, however, it is worth drawing attention to one important aspect of the claim, since it will be relevant later. This is that the notion of being able to choose this or that option, or having the option within one's range of choice, is distinctively agent-centered in character. When we think of an agent from a third person point of view, say as a neural system, or a system of psychological dispositions, or as a sociological type, we will naturally adopt a probabilistic viewpoint – or if we are sure enough of our ground, a deterministic one – assigning different degrees of probability to different options. But none of us can think like that of ourselves or the options before us as we confront a choice and exercise deliberation. In order to be deliberative agents, in order to perform as the makers of decisions, we must set aside the predictive point of view. Predicting decisions is not something we can do as we make the very decisions predicted.[6]

What is true of how we view ourselves as agents holds equally of how we must view others as agents: that is, view them from what we might call the second as distinct from the third person standpoint (Darwall 2006). If we think of others as agents in a certain context of decision, then we have to think of them as having this or that option at their disposal, so that the choice is up to them. We have to think of them in such a way that should they choose to do something that hurts us or hurts another, then we will not view that action in the dispassionate manner of the inquisitive scientist or therapist. As we would contemplate our own ill-doing with a sense of guilt of shame, so under normal circumstances we will have to view theirs with a feeling of resentment or indignation. The theme will be familiar from the tradition of thought that began with Peter Strawson's 1960s paper on "Freedom and Resentment" (Strawson 2003), a way of thinking with which I strongly identify (Pettit & Smith 1996; Pettit 2001).

Axiom 2. The possibility of alien control

The second axiom asserts the possibility of a specific sort of relationship of alien control in which one party may stand toward another, in particular toward someone who faces a choice between certain options. In this relationship the first party will control what the second does, at least to some degree, and control it in an alien way that takes from the personal choice of that agent, jarring with the deliberative can-do assumptions discussed under the first axiom. Suppose that A stands in this relation to B, when B faces a choice between options, x, y, and z. As an alien controller, A will exercise some measure of control over what B does, and this control will mean that with respect to x or y or z, B is no longer able to think, or able to think rightly: I can just do that; the choice is up to me.

In the sense of interest in the current discussion, A will exercise control, alien or non-alien, over B's choice just so far as the following is true.[7] First, A has desires, however implicit, over how B chooses on specific occasions or just in general; at the limit, A may just want to have some impact, no matter in what direction, on B's choices. Second, A acts on these desires, no doubt among others, seeking a certain pattern in B's choices. And, third, A's presence makes a desired difference. Making a difference need not mean making an actual difference, of course. It may just mean making things assume a shape such that the probability of B's taking the desired pattern is raised;[8] more specifically, it is raised beyond the level it would have had in A's absence.[9] The extent to which A's presence and activity increases the probability of B's acting according to the desired pattern will be a measure of the degree of A's control over that pattern.

The control exercised by A may be alien or alienating in any of three broadly different ways. It may impact on B's ability to make a deliberative choice so that the assumption of personal choice is undermined on a general front. Or it may impact on the specific options that fall within the domain of B's choice, in which case there are two sub-possibilities. The control may simply remove one or another option from the set of options faced by B, reducing the total options available, or may seem to remove it. Or it may replace one or another option by a significantly changed option, or seem to replace it by a significantly changed option. An option will be significantly changed – it will count as a different option – so far as it differs in regard to some feature that is valued or disvalued by the agent (Broome 1991: ch. 5; Pettit 1991). Suppose I can choose x in a world where it has a valued or disvalued feature, F, or where there is a probability p that it will lead to a valued or disvalued result, R. Under this criterion of option-identity, you will replace x by a different option, x★, if you do something to affect that feature, F, or the probability of that result, R; more in the last section on this criterion of option-identity.

These varieties of impact – mnemonically, reduction, removal, and replacement – will involve alien or alienating control, since they all undermine the deliberative assumption of personal choice. As we know, this is the assumption that with each option originally on offer the agent, B, is positioned to think, and rightly think: I can do that. If B's ability to choose is reduced, then he or she will not be in a position to think that thought correctly, whether with some or all of the options. If an option is removed, B will not be right to think the thought of that option in particular; and if it seems to be removed, B will not be in an evidential position to think it, whether correctly or incorrectly: the option will not present itself as accessible. Finally, if an option is replaced, B will not be right to think the thought of the option originally confronted; and if it seems to be replaced, B will not be in an evidential position to think it: an option with a significantly different character will present itself at the site of the original option.

Alien control requires a relationship between individuals and individuals, individuals and groups, or groups and groups, in which the controller is aware of the controlled as an agent subject to a suitable form of control. Strictly, the controlled agent, B, need not be aware of the controller, A; B will be controlled, whether or not B registers or feels the control. But A has to be aware of B and of B's susceptibility to intervention; otherwise A would not be in a position to choose to intervene in B's affairs.[10]

The fact that alien control requires this awareness on the part of the controller means that an agent like B may escape the control of a more powerful agent, A, because A is unaware of what he or she can achieve – maybe unaware even of the existence of B. In such a case there is potential alien control but not actual alien control.[11] The case is like that in which there is no actual agent in A's position but it is possible that such an agent might materialize; it is possible, for example, that a number of people might incorporate in order to play a controlling part in relation to another individual or group.

Alien control will be unwelcome to any victim who values having personal choice over independently available options. Alien control compromises such choice, jeopardizing one or more can-do assumptions. A victim of alien control may welcome paternalistic intervention in some cases, of course – an alcoholic may thank you for locking up the booze cupboard – but will not do so on the grounds of thereby retaining personal choice. Alien control is necessarily bad for personal choice but personal choice is not necessarily something that agents may cherish.

Axiom 3. The positionality of alien control

The third axiom, which is quite independent of the other two, asserts that if someone in B's position comes to be able to control what A does, then to that extent A's control over B diminishes, perhaps even disappears. Controlled or countered control is no longer a form of control, as we might say; the expression functions like "fake control" or "pretend control." Or at least adequately controlled control – intuitively, control of degree d that is controlled to at least degree d – is no longer control. Let the resources of mutual control be proportionate in this way, with each party adequately countering the other's control, and they will cancel out, leaving no one in a position of alien control over the other.[12] B may not be able to obtain resources that are quite enough for control of A, of course, but to the extent that B obtains any extra resources, and any degree of counter-control over A, A's control will be decreased.

The thought behind this axiom is the familiar idea that the resources that give one person power or control over another only have such an effect to the extent that they shift the relativities: they change the position of one in relation to the other (Lovett 2001). Alien control is positional. Let the first person enjoy an increase in resources and this will provide no benefit in terms of power or control if the second person enjoys a corresponding increase. The point may originate with Hobbes's (1994: 8.4) observations on the topic: "because the power of one man resisteth and hindereth the effects of the power of another: power simply is no more, but the excess of the power of one above that of another. For equal powers opposed, destroy one another."

The idea embodied in the axiom is intuitive. Suppose that you, B, have a certain choice between x, y, and z. Suppose that I, A, come to be able to exercise some alien control over your choice, making it more probable that you will choose x: I may do this, for example, through removing options y and z, or replacing them with options y★ and z★. And now suppose that, by whatever means, you come to be able to control my options in relation to you, and that you reduce the probability of my taking such steps to the point where the status quo is established. When this happens, you will now be able to think with each option: I can do that. And that means, as in the third axiom, that the control that I at first gained is now lost again; you are no more subject to my control than you were at the beginning. Alien control is a zero-sum commodity; if one gains, another loses. It is a matter of relative position, not of absolute level.

I mentioned in passing that while adequately controlled control will cease to constitute control, less than adequately controlled control will retain a controlling aspect, though in a reduced degree. But there are other complications to put on the page as well. They bring out other ways in which counter-control may be less than fully adequate.

In the paradigm case of counter-control, B can foresee and personally obstruct or inhibit any effort at alien control by A when the intervention is imminent; counter-control means current, personal defense or deterrence. But even when the counter-control is of a suitably high degree, that paradigm case may be varied in either of two ways. It may not be personally implemented but implemented by a deputy who acts on B's express or manifest wishes or by a proxy on whom B relies to act in a way that satisfies those wishes; the proxy will act in that way, not because that is what B wishes, only because such action serves the proxy's own ends (Pettit 2007). And the counter-control may not be currently implemented but implemented by retaliation at a later time, whether by B at a later time or by a deputy or proxy at a later time.

Under either of these scenarios, it is not going to be the case that B at the time of A's intervention can rightly think of the option affected: I-now, alone, can do that. But what is true is that B will at least be able to think: I-now, reinforced by my deputy or proxy, can make it the case that I can do that; or I-over-time can do that sort of thing; or I-over-time, reinforced by my deputy or proxy, can make it the case that I can do that sort of thing. That these propositions are true does not mean that the control suffered by B is controlled or countered in the full, paradigm sense but it does mean that such a stand-off condition is more or less closely approximated.

The Theorems

Theorem 1. Alien control may materialize with interference

I take the notion of interference in an inclusive sense. It covers a variety of intentional or quasi-intentional interventions by one party in the choice of another, where by quasi-intentional interventions I mean the products of negligence in which we would want to hold an agent responsible (Miller 1984). The common feature of the interventions is that, intuitively, they make a negative impact on the choice of the interferee and can be properly attributed to the interferer; they are matters in his or her domain of responsibility. The standard types include the radical manipulation of the choice of the agent, whether by hypnosis, brainwashing, intimidation or any of a range of interventions, but also more common interventions: imposing a sure-fire or probabilistic block on an option or purporting credibly to do so; imposing a sure-fire or probabilistic burden on an option – imposing a cost or penalty – or purporting credibly to do so; or credibly misinforming the agent about the blocks and burdens in place.

The first theorem is the unsurprising observation that one way for A to exercise alien control over B is by interfering with B, whether directly or by means of an associate, such as a deputy or proxy. Interference involves control so far as it serves the desires of the interferer, A, by changing the probabilities associated with the different options before the interferee, B. And that control will be alien so far as the interference practiced undermines B's ability, with one or another option, to think, or think rightly: I can just do that; I can just take that option, as originally presented.

It is not surprising that interference should be able to have such effects and serve the cause of alien control, for the different varieties of interference map closely onto the three broad ways in which alien control may be realized: via reduction of the agent's ability to choose, via the removal or seeming removal of an option, or via the replacement or seeming replacement of an option. Thus, manipulation will reduce the ability of the agent to choose. The imposition of a probabilistic or sure-fire block will remove an option, ensuring that it is no longer something that the agent can just choose at will, and the purported imposition of a block will amount to its seeming removal. The imposition of a probabilistic or sure-fire burden will replace an option, substituting a burdened counterpart, and the purported imposition of a burden will amount to its seeming replacement. And, finally, giving misinformation to an agent about the blocks or burdens in place will make for the seeming removal or the seeming replacement of an option.

Theorem 2. Alien control may materialize without interference

There are two modes of control available in any area, as I have argued elsewhere (Pettit 2001: ch. 2; 2007). While both are modes of actual control, not just modes of potential control, I describe the one as active, the other as virtual. A factor F will actively control for a type of effect E if F is at the causal source of the process that leads to that type of effect. A factor F will virtually control for a type of effect E under weaker conditions. Suppose the effect E is normally occasioned, not by F, but by some other factor, N (for normal), but that in any case where N fails to produce E, F steps into the breach and takes over the productive role. When F steps in like this, it actively controls for the appearance of E. But so far as it is there as a standby cause, ready to intervene on a need-to-act basis, it controls for the appearance of C even when it is not actively in charge. It is a virtual controller of the effect in question.

Whereas interference of the kind discussed under the first theorem is an active way in which an agent, A, may control the choice of a victim, B, it should be clear that A may control what B does without any such interference, whether direct or otherwise. Suppose that A desires that B should generally choose x in the sort of situation considered earlier, being prepared to interfere, where necessary, in order to ensure this pattern of choice. Now imagine that under quite different pressures or incentives B is sometimes independently disposed to display that pattern. A may not have any reason in such a case to interfere in order to ensure the pattern. Doing so might be inefficient, not improving things enough to compensate for the extra effort; or it might be downright ineffective, having the counterproductive effect of inducing defiance in B. So A may stay his or her hand, and be content to let B choose under autonomous pilot; or at least A may be content to assume this position, so long as the pilot guides B in the desired direction. A, as we can say, may invigilate what B does, being ready to interfere but only if this is required.

Does A control B's choice by means of such invigilation? Yes, A certainly does. By being there ready to interfere if necessary, though not interfering as a matter of fact, A is bound to raise the probability of B's x-ing in the case on hand. For in any such case there will always be a small probability attached to B's having a change of mind and becoming disposed not to x. And the readiness of A to interfere in such a case will increase the probability, therefore, of B's actually x-ing. Invigilation is a form of control.

That A acts in this virtually controlling way does not mean that A intentionally controls what B does. Suppose A intends to interfere with B as occasion requires in order to get B to choose according to a certain pattern. Now take the situation where B behaves after the desired fashion, so that A doesn't intentionally interfere. A need not be aware of controlling B in that particular case, perhaps even lacking the concept of control under which it may take a virtual form: that is, lacking the concept of invigilation. And so A need not intentionally control B. What A does is done intentionally, whether this involves interfering or refraining from interference. And what A does entails that A exercises control over B. But still, it does not follow, and it need not be the case, that A intentionally exercises control over B.[13]

As A's virtual control or invigilation need not be intentional, so it need not involve any very explicit surveillance and attention to B's behavior. Consider the case where you drive home from work according to blind habit, and without paying any explicit attention to what you are doing. Does your desire to get home control your action, according to your beliefs about the route? Of course it does, albeit in a more or less virtual way. The behavior is driven by the blind habit but let that habit not take you in the right direction and you will be alerted to the problem and will self-correct, letting your action be actively controlled by your desire to get home and your realization that you are on the wrong road. When A acts with a view to securing a desired pattern of behavior, and when this involves not interfering rather than interfering, that negative behavior may materialize as a matter of default habit, like your behavior in driving home, and yet be controlled by the desire to have B behave to a certain pattern.

When B is subject to the alien control of another, it must be the case, according to our earlier comments, that B's capacity for personal choice is reduced, or that one or more of the options available to B has been removed or replaced, or seems to have been removed or replaced. Which of these conditions is going to be satisfied when A controls B virtually, practicing invigilation but not interference?

If B is unaware of the virtual control exercised by A, say in making it probable that B will choose x, then the difference made by A will be that B will not be in a position to think rightly of y or z: I can just do that. This may be because A is in a position to reduce B's ability to choose, should B go for one of these options. Or it may be because A is prepared to remove such an option, should B be disposed to choose it; in that event, it is clearly going to be false that B can just take the option, or any option like it. Or it may be because A is prepared to replace the option by a burdened counterpart – y★ or z★ – should B become disposed to choose it; in that case too, it will be false that A can take y or take z. Or, finally, it may be because A is able to mislead B on these matters.

All of this will remain true if B becomes aware of the invigilation and virtual control exercised by A and can do nothing about it. But something else will be true in that case as well. Not only will B not be able rightly to think "I can do that" with respect to either y or z. B will not be in an evidential position to think that thought, rightly or otherwise, of y or z. B will recognize, depending on the case, either that no options of the kind are available, or that only y★ and z★ are within reach. Apart from living under the control that goes with being invigilated, B will suffer the inhibition that goes with being consciously invigilated.

B may try as a result of this consciousness to curry favor with A and secure permission to choose one or other alternative, without interference. But the options will not become available on that count as things B can just do. The options available will not strictly be y and z but y-provided-I-keep-A-sweet and z-provided-I-keep-A-sweet; they will be options that vary significantly from the original y and z.

What of the limit case, where A is disposed, as A may be contingently disposed, to let B choose however B wishes? Intuitively, A will still exercise alien control in this situation, since B will only be able to act on his or her wishes, so long as A allows or permits this. But where will the control show up? It will appear in the fact that, again, the options will not be available straightforwardly to B but available only if A remains sweet. Whatever B does will be done *cum permissu*, as used to be said: with the implicit leave or permission of A.[14] And that will affect B's freedom of choice, even if B remains unaware of living under this invigilation.

Theorem 3. Non-alien control may materialize without interference

Non-alien or non-alienating control will occur when one party, A, does indeed control what another party, B, chooses but when the control does not deny B evidential access to the thought "I can do that" with the options independently available, or does not make that thought false. A may act so as to change the probabilities attached to the different options before B — so as to favor the choice of x, for example — but A's action will do nothing to undermine the accessibility or the truth of the can-do assumption that B will naturally make about each of the available options.

In order to see how in general this sort of control is available, two things need to be noted. The first is that human beings are capable of reasoning with themselves about what they should do in any situation of choice rather than just letting their beliefs and desires lead them on. They can slow things down, rehearse the background assumptions they are making, review the pros and cons of the available alternatives, and only decide one way or another in the light of this reflection. That, plausibly, is what deliberation consists in. When people go in for this sort of reasoning with themselves, they are intervening in their own decision-making processes in a way that enhances their personal choice, rather than undermining it. They are giving themselves firmer ground, not only for forming a preference but for knowing what alternatives are available such that, truly, they can think of each: I can do that.

The second thing to note, in the wake of this, is that people can play this same reasoning role, not just with themselves, but with one another. They can lend one another their reason, as it were, playing the role of advisers or collaborators, and helping one another to get clear on the options available in any choice and on the pros and cons of those alternatives. They can act in relation to one another as an *amicus curiae*, a friend of the court. This will show up particularly in the fact that the help provided in such co-reasoning, like the help provided in self-reasoning, leaves the agent in a position to choose as he or she will; the advice or analysis provided may be rejected. Where the agent could rightly have made a can-do assumption prior to receiving counsel, he or she will still be able to endorse that assumption in its wake.

A may exercise a degree of control over B via co-reasoning of this kind, changing the probabilities attached to one or more of the options that are thought to be available.[15] That sort of control will not be alien, however, since it will do nothing to undermine the can-do assumptions associated with personal choice. It will not involve interference, even under the inclusive account of interference given earlier; there will be no blocking or burdening, sure-fire or probabilistic, real or seeming; and there will be no misinformation or manipulation. Or if there is something of this kind, it will not be intentional in the fashion that interference requires.[16]

This is a fairly unsurprising claim, of course, but it supports a congenial line on a controversial issue. This bears on the case where one agent controls what another does by making an offer rather than issuing a threat (Nozick 1969). The line supported is that normal offers or rewards do not make for an alien form of control.

Suppose that A is co-reasoning with B about what B should do, as in the model just given of non-alien control. One of the things that A may usefully point out to B, and do so without exercising alien control, is that the options available, say x, y, and z, can be extended to include the option of choosing x and getting a reward from C for doing so. This will be so if C really wants B to take x, and might be prepared, at least if approached in advance, to promise to reward the choice of that option. But suppose now that what is true of C under this hypothesis is actually true of A, and that A knows this. And suppose that A points out to B that as a matter of fact there is a further option available, apart from x, y, z, neat; this is the option of doing x and receiving a reward from A for doing so. If A's telling B about C was not an instance of alien control, neither can A's telling B about A – thereby effectively making an offer – be an instance of alien control.

This shows that offers, unlike threats, need not involve the alien control of an agent, only control of a non-alien kind. Where the normal threat, being non-refusable by nature, will replace one or more of the options, the regular offer need do nothing of the kind; it leaves x, y, z in place and simply adds a further option, x+: doing x, and accepting a reward (Pettit & Smith 2004). This does not mean that all offers are off the hook. An offer may be non-refusable, in which case it will replace one of the existing options and will represent an alien form of control, however welcome that sort of control may be; not imposing a burden, it will be a non-interfering way of exercising control.[17] Or an option may be a mesmerizing offer that reduces the agent's ability to choose; it may be like the offer of a drink to an alcoholic.[18]

Theorem 4. Non-alien control may materialize with interference

The positionality of alien control means that if B comes to have resources of control over A that match the resources of control over B that A already has, then the resources cancel out and neither exercises alien control over the other; countered control is no longer control. Consider now a case in which A and B do not have alien control over one another, since their resources cancel out, but B does not try to control certain limited forms of interference by A. B exercises counter-control, inhibiting what A does by way of interference, only when A trespasses those limits; B checks A's control, as we say, rather than strictly countering it. This may be a pattern that emerges in the relationship or it may also be a pattern that B explicitly endorses and even announces.

What should we say in such a case? Assume first, as in the paradigm case mentioned earlier, that B foresees every form of interference that A is about to practice, whether within the limits or not, and has the personal ability, there and then, to inhibit it; B invigilates the pattern of A's interference, ready to stop or redirect it if it breaches the limits or ceases to be acceptable. Should we say that the interference practiced by A under those conditions gives A alien control over B? Surely not. Any control that A may seem to exercise over B is controlled completely by B, so that A's interference can be seen as a form of treatment that B, for whatever reason, permits A to impose. The positionality of control means that here, as in the case of the standoff, neither controls the other. Although B will be subject to interference in taking a certain option, it will still be possible and correct for B to think: I can do that. It will be possible for B personally, at any moment, to inhibit A's interference with the option; and that will be a fact that is known by B.

This paradigm case shows how the checking of control, like the straightforward countering, means that actually no alien control materializes. The interferer in this case may be a controller, since the interference may change the probability of what B does in any instance. But the interferer will not be an alien controller who undermines the deliberative can-do assumptions. The interference practiced implements a non-alien form of control, as in the possibility registered by the fourth theorem.

But what now of the sorts of departure from the paradigm case that we mentioned earlier? What of the case where the interference is invigilated and checked, not by B, but by a deputy or proxy? And what of the case where it is not checked at the time of the invigilated interference but only by virtue of some later form of retaliation?

In each of these cases, and of course in the case where both variations occur at once, the strict can-do assumptions are false. But still, the cases approximate one in which they remain true. The agent will be able to impose a counter against the interference currently allowed, whether by redirecting the deputy or proxy, or by acting at a later time to undo the permission given. And so, with the option affected by interference, the agent will be able to think, and think rightly: I-now, reinforced by my deputy or proxy, can make it the case that I can do that; or I-over-time can do that sort of thing; or I-over-time, reinforced by my deputy or proxy, can do that sort of thing.

The interference that occurs under the adequate or close to adequate checking of the interferee may reasonably be identified with the traditional notion of non-arbitrary interference. Non-arbitrary interference, according to this gloss, is not a moralized notion like legitimate interference. Unlike "legitimate," "non-arbitrary" is not an evaluative term but is defined by reference to whether as a matter of fact the interference is subject to adequate checking. Interference will be non-arbitrary, as I have put it elsewhere (Pettit 2001, 2006a), to the extent that, being checked, it is forced to track the avowed or avowal-ready interests of the interferee; and this, regardless of whether or not those interests are true or real or valid, by some independent moral criterion. Thus there is no substance to the claim that the republican theory of freedom I favor is moralized, allowing interference just so long as that interference is morally acceptable; being non-arbitrary may make interference morally acceptable but it is not defined by such acceptability.[19]

The view that non-arbitrary interference does not affect liberty – liberty in the sense of the absence of alien control – is entirely sensible, as the fourth theorem makes clear. Controversy enters only at a point that our discussion does not reach. This is where republicans hold that the interference of a government that is suitably invigilated and

Table 5.1: The four theorems

	With interference	Without interference
Alien control of choice ⇒	Uncountered interference	Uncountered invigilation; the non-refusable offer.
Non-alien control ⇒	Checked interference	Co-reasoning control; the regular offer.
No control of either sort ⇒	Countered interference	Countered invigilation; no tempting offers.

checked by the constitutional people – assuming that the people are organized to serve as a suitable proxy for each individual citizen – is to that extent non-arbitrary (Pettit 2007). The claim is that government will restrict the options available to individuals but, so far as it is invigilated and controlled by the quasi-corporate people, it will not exemplify the domination or alien control of individuals.[20] I do not discuss or try to defend that claim here.

The upshot of these four theorems is nicely summarized in table 5.1, where the two varieties of alien control and of non-alien control are distinguished. Within the table, countered control is broken down into countered interference – typically, a standoff in mutual threats – and countered invigilation: a standoff in the capacity of two or more parties to interfere with one another. The case of no-control is also introduced in the table, on lines implied by the foregoing discussion.

Against the New Version of Liberty as Non-interference

Interference as option-removal

Despite important differences in other respects, Ian Carter (1999) and Matthew Kramer (2003) join in proposing a new version of liberty as non-interference, according to which liberty is inversely related, in my terminology, to the removal of options from the space of choice.[21] Building on the work of Hillel Steiner (1994), they take interference to be the antithesis of liberty and they equate interference with removing an option from an agent and thereby rendering the choice of that option impossible.

Their main thesis, then, is the negative claim that freedom of choice is not affected by anything other than removal of an option. I interfere with you and impact on your freedom only when I block you from doing something; I do not have any impact on your freedom to choose between various options just by coercively threatening, for example, to punish your choice of one or another alternative.

The new theory introduces a positive claim to complement and balance that negative thesis. This is that even when an action I take does not make it impossible for you to choose some actual option, it may make it impossible for you to choose a related potential option. You now have the option of keeping your money or not. I do not remove either of those options, so the line goes, when I make the highway-man's threat, demanding your money or your life: strictly, it remains possible for you to keep your money or not to keep your money. But I do remove a different, conjunctive option, which is that of keeping-your-money-and-keeping-your-life. And I do thereby reduce your "overall liberty": not the liberty to decide between the options of keep-ing your money and not keeping your money – those are assumed to remain in place – but the liberty to make a choice where one alternative is the conjunctive option of keeping your money-and-keeping-your-life.

I follow the standard, decision-theoretic view that a choice is a set of mutually exclusive, jointly exhaustive options and that in the con-tingent context of the choice, as emphasized in the first axiom, each option is one that the agent can just choose; it is within his or her power of choice. The account just given of the negative and positive claims of the new theory is set in this framework of concepts, not cast in the terms used by Carter and Kramer themselves. Within this frame-work, the conjunctive option is not an option in the original choice, since that choice was characterized by just two exclusive and exhaus-tive options. Overall liberty is reduced by coercion, then, so far as an option that does not itself appear in the coerced choice is rendered inac-cessible in related possible choices. That is why your freedom to choose between keeping the money and not keeping the money is not affected but your overall freedom – your freedom across potential as well as actual choices – is reduced.[22]

Coercion in regard to an actual choice is not the only way in which conjunctive options are said to be removed and the agent's power of choosing over such options in various potential choices affected. Paying tribute to the recent reworking of republican theory, Carter and Kramer now say that not only may I affect your potential, conjunctive options in making the highwayman's threat; I may have a similar effect on your overall liberty just through manifestly having the power to make various obstructive or punitive interventions in your life. If my power is manifest then when you become aware of my power, you are likely to preempt any negative response on my part by measures of self-censorship and self-ingratiation. In that case I may not make any options you are actually considering unavailable. But I will make it impossible for you to exercise choice over potential, conjunctive options such as doing-x-and-not-living-in-fear-of-me or doing-x-and-not-currying-my-favor.[23]

The republican theory argues that freedom may be reduced by alien control, however, even when this control is not manifest to the controlled party and does not induce inhibition. Do I affect your freedom, according to this new approach, even when it is not manifest that I hold such power and when you do not practice self-abasement? I do, so the line goes, but only in a probabilistic sense. Plausibly, so it is said, it will be more probable that you will come to be aware of the power and be prevented in this same way from taking certain conjunctive options, as it will be more probable – this was true in the earlier case too – that you will suffer direct prevention at my hands.

The master move in the new approach, then, is to start with a clear, well-defined notion of interference, under which it means removing an option; to cast interference in this sense as the only violation of liberty; and then to explain how an agent's overall freedom as non-interference may be reduced or jeopardized by active coercion, by manifest domination, or even by the sort of domination that is not registered by the dominated party.

A problem with the theory

The striking thing about the new theory of freedom as non-interference, as appears when it is translated into the framework of choices and options, is that it ignores the most salient explanation of why coercion and similar initiatives affect the freedom of a choice. This explanation would point out, as we have seen here, that while unchecked coercion does not simply remove any of the options by which a choice is characterized, it does replace one or another option. I change the option of keeping your money when I make my coercive threat, replacing that option by a life-endangering alternative. Thus, you are no longer right to think of the original option: I can do that; things have been changed so that the option is no longer available to you. And given you are aware of the threat I make, you will no longer be able to think, consistently with that awareness, that the original option is one you can still choose. Your personal choice over the original options will have been radically altered and, assuming that you have no check over me, you will be under my alien control.

Defenders of the new theory might argue that on the proper way of individuating the option of keeping your money, that option does remain in place, even when I issue the coercive threat. This response raises the question, then, as to how we should individuate options: that is, individuate those enactable courses of action that we contemplate as available alternatives in any choice we make. The striking thing about the line taken in the new theory is that it implies that options must be individuated so coarsely that no matter what penalty I impose on an option like your keeping your money, no matter how I change it, that option will remain available for choice; it will not count as having been replaced. Worse still, no room appears to be left for the possibility that an option might ever be replaced, no matter how it is changed by the interventions of another. It seems that while others may be said to remove options from someone's choice, rendering them inaccessible, they are incapable of so changing an option, say by imposing a penalty, that they might be said to replace it. Options are individuated on the coarsest possible basis.[24]

I favor a much finer way of individuating options; in particular, a way of individuating options according to which any unchecked penalty imposed by another will change the identity of the option. The line, as I put it earlier, is that if an option is changed in a way that engages your values – whether or not these are the right values, by some independent metric – then it is thereby made into a different option. I may not replace an option before you by constraining things so that you have to do it with your right as distinct from your left hand, assuming that handedness does not matter to you. But I will replace an option before you if I take steps that, by your own lights, make for a different evaluative profile.

This should not be surprising. An option is a possibility that you can realize in a relevant choice; it is a package of probabilistically weighted possible consequences, each with its own attractive or aversive aspect. You may well think that the possibility before you remains the same option, the same enactable package, if I only introduce changes that do not matter to you. But you will certainly think that you now confront a different possibility, if I make changes that do matter: changes that affect the probabilities of various valued or disvalued consequences.

We can do better than appealing to intuition in support of this way of individuating options. A plausible constraint rules that options should be individuated in such a way that all and only intuitive cases of irrationality – say, all and only intuitive cases of intransitive preference – should have to be indicted as cases of irrationality (Broome 1991). That constraint gives considerable support to the principle of option-individuation adopted here. Suppose you are disposed in a choice between a big apple and an orange, to take the apple and give your friend the orange; and in a choice between an orange and a small apple, to take the orange and give your friend the small apple. Will you be intransitive and irrational if you are disposed in a choice between the two apples, to take the small one and give your friend the large? Surely we should say, no; your disposition testifies to your politesse, not to any lack of rationality. A nice feature of our principle of option-individuation, as distinct from any coarser principle, is that it supports this reply. Taking the big apple is rude by anyone's lights when the alternative left for your friend is a small apple; and so it is not the same option as taking the big apple in either of the other cases – it differs from taking the big apple in those other cases in a valued or rather a disvalued property (Pettit 1991).

Summing up this line of thought, then, my main problem with the new theory of freedom as non-interference is that it looks downright bizarre in ignoring the salient explanation for why unchecked coercion may affect freedom of choice: that it replaces one of the agent's options. Why ignore this possibility in favor of an exclusive emphasis on option-removal? Only, it seems, because options are individuated in an implausibly coarse manner.

The issue of probability

In outlining the republican conception I directed attention in passing to how various criticisms from the proponents of the new version of freedom as non-interference can be countered. In conclusion, however, I would like to address one general issue raised. Both Carter and Kramer argue that certain probabilities that should matter in the theory of freedom don't matter enough in my book, or in the republican approach more generally. I think that the approach does dictate a surprising line on probabilities but I see nothing in this line that is a matter for reasonable rejection.

Republicans will naturally be concerned about the probability that someone may gain alien control over others, and will rejoice at any reduction in this probability. That is not in dispute. But it is said that republicans should also be concerned about the probability of someone who enjoys alien control actually interfering with the person controlled, and should rejoice at any reduction in this probability, no matter what the source of the reduction: this, on the grounds that the reduction increases their expected liberty. The criticism made is that I do not recognize this.[25] In particular, I do not see that if someone powerful is endogenously restrained in some measure from actually interfering with others – restrained, say, by a shift of attitudes or habits – then any potential victim of interference is liberated in corresponding measure: the measure, presumably, in which he or she would be liberated if the restraint came from increased protection. The potential victims suffer a loss of freedom, so it is suggested, only in direct proportion to the controller's probability of actually interfering.

There are two very different sorts of natural restraint that might be envisaged in the objection. One would be so radical as to deprive the controller of full agency, making the option of interference effectively unavailable; it would cripple the agent in the manner of a pathology. The other would not have this disabling effect. While prompting the controller to be less harsh, it would still allow access to interference; it would enable the controller still to think, and think rightly: I can do that, I can take that interfering option.

Were the first sort of restraint in place, then that indeed would be grounds for ascribing an increase in liberty to the victims; it would undermine the agency and hence the control of the would-be controller. But the second sort of restraint would not offer a similar prospect of liberation. Under this scenario the controller remains an agent, and an agent who is in a position to interfere or not interfere in an unchecked manner. Even if the probability of the controller's imposing a sanction is reduced, this will not remove the alien control exercised over the victims. They might have reason to take some consolation from the thought that the controller has become more soft-hearted but this cannot be consolation at an increase in their expected freedom. The controller will maintain the profile of a controller across variations in the probabilities assigned and that robust and daunting fact will survive any consolation derivable from the prospect of small mercies.

In order to appreciate this point, consider the distinction between the evil of being subject to someone's alien control and the evil of being actually interfered with. The first evil is characteristically interpersonal, arising only in the context of two agents in relationship to one another, whether individually or in groups. The second evil is not necessarily of this kind, since the block or burden suffered at the hands of another, may be indiscernible from the block or burden that might come about as a result of a natural accident. You may be obstructed by a tree across the road in just the way I may obstruct you; or you may be inhibited by a natural prospect of physical harm in just the way you may be inhibited by a harm I hold out as a threat.

A decrease in the probability of interference at the hands of an alien controller will not remove the specter of alien control, at least if this is due to a non-disabling, endogenous feature of that agent. That interpersonal evil is more or less insensitive to the endogenously based probability of interference; alien control will remain in place so long as the agent can interfere or not interfere, whatever the reduced probabilities of interference that are dictated by the agent's nature. A decrease in the probability of interference will only provide a reason for consolation with respect to the other, natural evil: that which is associated with the sort of interference actually practiced. It will provide some relief from fear of the treatment that is in prospect, at least if the victims are aware of the situation, but it will not reduce the level of alien control and the associated unfreedom.

Relief from fear of interference can be of enormous importance, of course. To be subject to the power of someone with a lash is to suffer the evil of alien control, regardless of the exact probabilities of the lash being applied on this or that occasion, with this or that severity. While you will remain subject to that control so long as the controller can apply the lash, however, it will be a source of substantial consolation to learn that the probabilities of the lash being applied have decreased, say because the controller has fallen in love or discovered religion. The decrease may come about because pardons are more frequently given or because the use of the lash in punishment is made probabilistic, turning on the toss of a coin. But no matter how substantial the consolation on offer, it will not give you or others any reason for thinking that you are now less unfree than you were previously.[26] This has to be a sticking point, as Carter and Kramer see, on the republican conception of freedom. But it is a good and sensible point on which to stick, not the implausible one that their theory makes it out to be.[27]

NOTES

1 I draw only on my own work in the argument of the chapter, and on my single-authored work; the outlines of the republican conception were sketched earlier in Braithwaite and Pettit 1990. I do not presume to speak for Quentin Skinner, though my strong sense is that we are in broad agreement on the nature of the republican conception of freedom; this is reinforced by his congenial contribution to this volume. Nor of course do I presume to speak for any others who endorse a more or less republican way of thinking about freedom. See for example (Honohan 2002; Richardson 2002; Viroli 2002; Maynor 2003).

2 I do not address the claim in Kramer (2003: ch. 3) that freedom in the sense involved here may depend on more than the freedom that is defined in the space of choice or action.

3 I stress later that whether someone is proof against alien control in a given choice is a factual matter, not one involving values, but notice that the identification of those types of choice that are significant for the freedom of a person will naturally involve an evaluative perspective; it will mean identifying the liberties that count. There is a resemblance in this respect between my view and Kramer's (2003: ch. 5) thesis that someone's overall freedom is determined, not just by the extent of particular freedoms, as Carter (1999) thinks, but by also by the positive weighting that is given to these freedoms. But this resemblance is superficial and does not really reduce the gap between our positions.

4 This means that we might identify free choices, not in the broad manner adopted here, but in a narrower, more demanding fashion as those choices in which the freedom of the person – a status or capacity – is exercised. I adopt that line in some other writings. See (Pettit 2003; Pettit 2006a; Pettit 2007).

5 Someone may remain a free person and still suffer alien control on this or that occasion, as when systematic protection fails. Such a breach of the defenses will challenge the person's status as a free person but need not reduce it significantly, especially if that status is vindicated in the apprehension of the offender and in the exaction of suitable amends; on the theory of amends see (Braithwaite and Pettit 1990; Pettit 1997a).

6 A question often arises, however, as to how far we should take a deliberative or a predictive stance on our future self. Professor Procrastinator knows that he often fails to review books he accepts for review. Should he accept for review a book that he thinks is important and that he is uniquely well-placed to bring to general notice? That may depend on whether he looks on the future self that will write or fail to write the review in a deliberative or a predictive way (Jackson & Pargetter 1986).

7   There is a sense in which control can occur without any related desire on the part of the controller: this is the sense in which the weather may control what someone does. But that sense of control is not relevant to freedom in the same manner as control that occurs in the presence of desire. The presence of the desire does not entail, as we shall see in discussing Theorem 2, that control is always intentional.

8   It will make it more probable that B will perform to the desired pattern, of course, in more than the evidential sense of providing extra evidence that B will do so. There will be extra evidence that B will perform to the pattern but that will be due to A's presence, not merely revealed by it. The need for this qualification is ignored in many definitions of what power or control requires, particularly those that invoke the notion of conditional probability in explicating the idea; see for example Dahl 1957. Notice that A may control for B's x-ing without controlling for that result most effectively – that is, without maximizing the relevant probability – or without controlling for it most efficiently: that is, without maximizing A's overall utility.

9   The relevant contrast for determining whether A raises the probability of B's x-ing should be the probability of B's x-ing in the absence of A, not just the probability of B's x-ing in the event of A not taking the action whereby A exercises control. For suppose that B is negatively affected by the fact that A is present in B's life so that no matter what A does, no matter even if A omits to do anything, A's presence reduces the probability that B will x. It would be strange in that case to say that A had control over B in regard to the x-ing. And yet there might be an action available to A such that by taking that action, A would raise the probability of B's x-ing beyond the level it would have had, if A had not taken that action. A has no chance of controlling for the desired pattern in B's behavior in a case like this. Similarly A would have no chance of not controlling for that pattern did it happen that A's presence meant that B was more likely to x, regardless of how A actually acted.

10 If A chooses not to intervene, this may come about without any very explicit consideration of the option of intervention. Suppose I am aware of your being subject to the influence of my intervention, for example, and suppose that did I think you might make a certain choice, I would consider intervening to try and change your mind. In the case where I do not think that you are liable to make that choice and let you be, without giving any explicit thought to intervention, still I can be said to choose not to intervene. More on this later.

11 In Pettit 1997b I use the word 'virtual' instead of 'potential'; as will appear later, I now reserve 'virtual' for a different purpose. Notice that weaker parties in a situation of potential alien control may take self-denying steps in order to ensure that a stronger party does not become aware of their presence or vulnerability. But this does not mean that the stronger is actually exercising alien control, only that such control is possible and even probable, at least in the absence of the precautionary steps.

12 As I have argued elsewhere, A and B may have fewer choices available in which to enjoy their independence, once they have taken all the steps necessary

to protect themselves against each other (Pettit 1997b: ch. 2). Their freedom as non-domination will not be any more compromised than it was prior to either gaining resources of control over the other. But it may be more deeply conditioned.

13 I think that Matthew Kramer is right to say, then, that my position supports the view that freedom may be reduced non-intentionally; he is mistaken, however, to think that I ever suggested otherwise.

14 Notice that there will still be a distinction between A's only having access to such control over B – being a potential controller of B – and A's actually having or exercising control over B. As mentioned earlier, actual control will require A to be aware of B as subject to the effect of his or her interventions.

15 It may also make it clear that an option previously thought to be available is not available. But that is no problem, since it will not remove or replace any option that was actually available.

16 The argument of this paragraph applies equally, of course, to self-reasoning; it is clearly a non-alien form of self-control. But that, as Quentin Skinner has reminded me, raises the interesting question as to whether there is an alien form of self-control. This would have to involve one aspect or part of the person replacing or removing options otherwise available to another, or reducing the other's capacity for deliberative choice. The Freudian superego might be thought to control the ego in that way or the present self, using techniques of precommitment, might be thought to control the future self in that manner. In the traditional image, reason is said to exercise that sort of control over the passions. Since the passions are not the true self, however, but rather a usurper, at least in the usual representation, such control may not be well cast as an alien form of self-control.

17 It seems reasonable to ask why an offer should be made non-refusable, if it is supposed to be welcome to the recipient. One possibility is that however welcome in some respects, the reward in question is not one that the recipient would necessarily accept, if refusal were possible. And in that case the non-refusable offer begins to look like a form of burdening or penalization, and so a species of interference.

18 For these reasons I hope that my picture of offers may not be as 'rosy' as Ian Carter alleges. There is one respect, however, in which it is less than wholly appealing. It makes the insincere offer no more damaging to freedom than the sincere. While the insincere offer does involve misinformation, this is not misinformation that makes for the seeming replacement of any existing option.

19 This criticism is made in Ian Carter's paper, despite the fact that, as he acknowledges, I have insisted on the non-moralistic nature of the concept of non-arbitrariness. His criticism turns on an independent, strictly irrelevant quarrel, to which I allude in the following paragraph, about how far the notion of non-arbitrary interference can be plausibly realized or approximated by state interference in the lives of citizens; this is not a question I discuss here (see Pettit 2007). Another writer who assumes the same line of interpretation is McMahon (2005); for my response see Pettit (2006b). If the concept of non-arbitrariness and hence the concept of freedom are moralized, then that might justify a paternalistic concern for people's

good, regardless of their perception of the good. I am charged with such paternalism by Brennan and Lomasky (2006: 241) who ask a reasonable question – 'how could liberty as non-domination not give ample shelter to paternalism?' – but treat it as rhetorical and ignore everything I or anybody else has said on the topic. Although they focus on Skinner and me, their 'republicanism' is constructed from a range of authors who have little in common other than claiming to criticize one or another version of 'liberalism'; I have no wish to defend the concoction of theses that they put together for their essentially polemical purposes.

20 This claim is implicit in the old adage, republican in inspiration, according to which the price of liberty is eternal vigilance: that is, the sustained invigilation of those in authority.

21 For Kramer (2003), as mentioned earlier, there are factors other than choices of action that are relevant to freedom; and the inverse relation between a person's overall freedom of choice and the removal of options is not straightforward, since some options are taken to be more important than others for overall freedom. But I shall ignore these complications here.

22 Defenders of the new theory put limits on the range of conjunctive options whose elimination reduces an agent's overall liberty. Ian Carter (1999: ch. 7) suggests that I will reduce your overall liberty by imposing a condition, c, on an option y, in a choice between x and y, only if it was previously within your causal power to take y-with-c or y-without-c. Matthew Kramer (2003: ch. 5) thinks that this is too demanding. It may not have been in your power to engage others in conversation or not to engage them in conversation – this is in part up to them – but if I ensure that you will have no interlocutors then, intuitively, I affect your freedom. He argues that an amendment to Carter's line is needed – one that preserves a similar causal element – but does not spell out the detail of his proposal (Kramer 2003: 395–9). What, on Carter's and Kramer's approach, justifies any restriction? According to their theory, it is bad that I lose potential, conjunctive options; and bad for me as a free agent. Why count only the loss of potential and causally accessible options, then, in estimating my overall liberty? If the focus is on potential options, not on the options over which you are actually choosing, then this restriction looks arbitrary. The motivation as distinct from the justification for the restriction is clear, of course. If the loss of any conjunctive, potential option is to count as a reduction of your overall liberty than almost anything I do will reduce your overall liberty. Let me do something that brings about any consequence, C, and I will thereby make it impossible for you to take an option, x, in the absence of C; I will have removed that conjunctive option from your realm of choice.

23 Needless to say, this claim about the grain-of-truth in republican theory, generous though it is, misses the core message of that theory. It fails to register the focus on alien control or domination as the primary danger to freedom.

24 Carter (1999: ch. 7) and Kramer (2003: ch. 5) do have extensive discussions of how actions should be individuated, particularly within the theory of freedom. This, however, is a different topic. A token or particular action is an actual event, where an option is a possibility that an agent is in a position to realize or not.

Actions may be considered as types rather than tokens and while options might be cast as action-types, they are typed on a very distinctive, decisional basis. Options are ex ante types of actions that are characterized by the types they rule out – the other relevant options – and by the types of consequences, and associated probabilities, that they allow. Such an ex ante type of action will vary in identity, intuitively, as it is associated with consequences or probabilities of consequences that differ by reference to the values of the agent.

25 Rightly or wrongly, Quentin Skinner is said to take a different line. On the relation between our views, as of some years ago, see Pettit (2002).

26 It will thereby reduce the content-dependent disvalue of the unfreedom suffered, though not perhaps its content-independent disvalue; on relevant distinctions see Kramer 2003: ch. 3, who draws in turn on Carter 1999.

27 My thanks to Gideon Rosen for a very helpful discussion of this material and to a number of people for remarks on an earlier draft. Brookes Brown, Philipp Koralus, Cecile Laborde, Frank Lovett, John Maynor and Quentin Skinner provided illuminating comments. And Ian Carter and Matthew Kramer did a great service in guarding me against some misconstruals of their views.

REFERENCES

Braithwaite, J. and P. Pettit (1990). *Not Just Deserts: A Republican Theory of Criminal Justice.* Oxford: Oxford University Press.

Brennan, G. and L. Lomasky (2006). "Against Reviving Republicanism." *Politics, Philosophy and Economics*, 5, 221–52.

Broome, J. (1991). *Weighing Goods.* Oxford: Blackwell.

Carter, I. (1999). *A Measure of Freedom.* Oxford: Oxford University press.

Dahl, R. (1957). "The Concept of Power." *Behavioral Science*, 2, 201–15.

Darwall, S. (2006). *The Second-Person Standpoint: Morality, Respect, and Accountability.* Cambridge, MA: Harvard University Press.

Hobbes, T. (1994). *Human Nature and De Corpore Politico: The Elements of Law, Natural and Politic.* Oxford: Oxford University Press.

Honohan, I. (2002). *Civic Republicanism.* London: Routledge.

Hornsby, J. (1980). *Actions.* London: Routledge.

Jackson, F. and R. Pargetter (1986). "Oughts, Options and Actualism." *Philosophical Review*, 95, 233–55.

Kramer, M. H. (2003). *The Quality of Freedom.* Oxford: Oxford University Press.

Lovett, F. N. (2001). "Domination: A Preliminary Analysis." *Monist*, 84, 98–112.

Maynor, J. (2003). *Republicanism in the Modern World.* Cambridge: Polity Press.

McMahon, C. (2005). "The Indeterminacy of Republican Policy." *Philosophy and Public Affairs*, 33, 67–93.

Miller, D. (1984). "Constraints on Freedom." *Ethics*, 94, 66–86.

Nozick, R. (1969). "Coercion." P. S. S. Morgenbesser and M. White (eds.), *Philosophy, Science and Method: Essays in Honor of Ernest Nagel.* New York: St. Martin's Press.

Pettit, P. (1991). "Decision Theory and Folk Psychology." In M. Bacharach and S. Hurley (eds.), *Essays in the foundations of Decision Theory*. Oxford: Blackwell; reprinted in Pettit, *Rules, Reasons, and Norms*. Oxford: Oxford University Press, 2002.

Pettit, P. (1997a). "Republican Theory and Criminal Punishment." *Utilitas*, 9, 59–79.

Pettit, P. (1997b). *Republicanism: A Theory of Freedom and Government*. Oxford: Oxford University Press.

Pettit, P. (2001). *A Theory of Freedom: From the Psychology to the Politics of Agency*. Cambridge and New York: Polity and Oxford University Press.

Pettit, P. (2002). "Keeping Republican Freedom Simple: On a Difference with Quentin Skinner." *Political Theory*, 30(3), 339–56.

Pettit, P. (2003). "Agency-freedom and Option-freedom." *Journal of Theoretical Politics*, 15, 387–403.

Pettit, P. (2006a). "Free Persons and Free Choices." *History of Political Thought*, 27, Special Issue on "Liberty and Sovereignty."

Pettit, P. (2006b). "The Determinacy of Republican Policy: A Reply to McMahon." *Philosophy and Public Affairs*, 34, 275–83.

Pettit, P. (2007). "Joining the Dots." In M. Smith *et al.* (eds.), *Common Minds: Themes from the Philosophy of Philip Pettit*. Oxford: Oxford University Press.

Pettit, P. and M. Smith (1996). "Freedom in Belief and Desire." *Journal of Philosophy*, 93, 429–49; repr. in F. Jackson, P. Pettit and M. Smith, *Mind, Morality and Explanation*. Oxford: Oxford University Press, 2004.

Pettit, P. and M. Smith (2004). "The Truth in Deontology." In R. J. Wallace *et al.* (eds.), *Reason and Value: Themes from the Moral Philosophy of Joseph Raz*. Oxford: Oxford University Press.

Pocock, J. G. A. (ed.) (1977). *The Political Works of James Harrington*. Cambridge: Cambridge University Press.

Richardson, H. (2002). *Democratic Autonomy*. New York: Oxford University Press.

Skinner, Q. (1998). *Liberty before Liberalism*. Cambridge: Cambridge University Press.

Steiner, H. (1994). *An Essay on Rights*. Oxford: Blackwell.

Strawson, P. (2003). "Freedom and Resentment." *Free Will*, 2nd ed., ed. G. Watson. Oxford: Oxford University Press.

Viroli, M. (2002). *Republicanism*. New York: Hill and Wang.

Part II
Republicanism, Democracy, and Citizenship

Chapter 6
Republicanism, National Identity, and Europe

David Miller

In this essay, I want to address the general question: what kind of political community do we need to have if republican politics and republican values are to flourish? But I also address it with reference to a more particular question, namely whether Europe might be, or shortly become, a political community of the right kind. I do so in the wake of a small, but growing, body of writing that argues in favor of "Euro-republicanism" – the idea that republican values can be realized at European, rather than nation-state, level, and that the European Constitution, assuming we are to have one, might be grounded in these values. This would be a significant development in republican thought. But is it a plausible development, or must republicanism remain tied, in the contemporary world, to political communities whose members are held together by stronger bonds than presently exist among citizens of the EU, most notably bonds of national identity?

The general question is not, of course, new. Throughout the history of republican thought, there has been debate about the kind of political community needed to support republican citizenship, focused particularly on the question of *size*. Must republican polities be small, and if so, how small? Early republican thought more or less took for granted the city as the place where republican politics might be practiced. This is particularly clear in Italian republican writers before Machiavelli, and indeed with some qualifications in Machiavelli himself (Viroli 1990). The *civitas* must be a political community held together not just by law and a constitution, but by relationships of friendship and solidarity among the citizens, who shared a common life expressed in ceremonies, festivals, and so forth. It is worth underlining here that the city-republics whose experience these authors were capturing were considerably smaller than cities typically are today. Accurate population estimates are hard to obtain, but most authorities agree that numbers peaked in about 1300 before being sharply reduced by the Black Death. At this point only Milan and Venice had populations exceeding 100,000, and most cities were considerably smaller – Pisa, Padua, and Verona had around 38,000 inhabitants, Pavia and Lucca fewer still (I have used figures from Martines 1986; Chandler 1987 gives significantly lower estimates). Moreover the number of *citizens* was far smaller still – often no more than 10% of the urban population (Jones 1997: ch. 4). Republican institutions like Sienna's General Council, therefore, were composed of men known personally to many of their fellow-citizens. This, then, is the backdrop to early modern accounts of the public virtue expected of republican citizens. Machiavelli's qualifications had to do not with these ideas themselves, but with his acute awareness of the vulnerability of city-republics to external threats – hence his final preference for "the tumultuous but powerful Roman republic over the peaceful but weak republics of Venice and Sparta" (Viroli 1990: 160; Machiavelli 1970: Book 1, ch. 6; Armitage 2002). If expansion was the only way to create a city large and powerful enough to defend itself, then this was the course that must be taken, even at some cost to the quality of civil life.

Leaping forward to eighteenth-century debates about the merits of republicanism, we find the same issue reiterated: republics must be small if they are to generate sufficient civic virtue to function effectively, but they must be expansive if they are to provide their members with sufficient security against external conquests. Montesquieu, whose opinion on this question was influential, put the matter succinctly: "if a republic is small, it is destroyed by a foreign force; if it is large, it is destroyed by an internal vice" (Montesquieu 1989: 131) – the vice in question being corruption, the prevalence of private interests over the public good (for instance rich citizens raiding the public treasury for personal gain). His general verdict, therefore, was that republics could not survive in the contemporary world. But to this he added an important rider, which was later eagerly seized upon by the authors of *The Federalist*, anxious to show that republican government could exist securely in a large territory: a federal republic – a confederation of small units each of which took the form of a self-governing republic – could offer a third alternative that avoided both internal corruption and external weakness, and there were contemporary examples – Holland, Switzerland, and with some qualifications Germany, that deserved on this basis to be described as "eternal republics" (Montesquieu 1989: Book 9, chs. 1–3; Hamilton *et al.* 1948). And he added a further consideration that became important in the ensuing debate about modern republicanism. A federal republic might be more stable than a unitary one, even leaving external threats out of the picture, because the confederation could help to preserve republican institutions in each of the sub-units. If some powerful individual threatened to take over one of the cities or small states inside the confederation, this would alarm other members and encourage them to send forces to resist the would-be autocrat. Equally, if a state appeared liable to collapse through internal corruption, then other members of the confederation would have an incentive to support it.

This argument was taken still further by later writers. Montesquieu had pointed out that one of the causes that might destroy a republic was an excess of democracy – what he called "the spirit of extreme equality" – in which the people were tempted to usurp functions that ought to be undertaken by executive or judicial bodies. In other words, although in a republic the people were sovereign, there should also be a constitutional division of powers that balanced popular sovereignty against other institutions formed on a more selective basis (see also more generally Skinner 1998). The question, then, was how to ensure that democracy remained "regulated," to use Montesquieu's term. Hume, in his elaborately-constructed plan of an ideal commonwealth, sought to show how a federal arrangement could in this sense regulate demo-cracy. He achieved this partly by an indirect system of election for the Senate – the body assigned executive power at federal level – but partly also by allowing each of the sub-units – counties in Hume's scheme – to veto any law passed by one of the others. Hume therefore rejected "the common opinion" that a republic was only feasible in a city or a small territory. On the contrary "although it is more difficult to form a republican government in an extensive country than in a city; there is more facility, when once it is formed, of preserving it steady and uniform, without tumult and faction" (Hume 1985: 527). The problem with small democracies was that they were "turbulent." "For however the people may be separated or divided into small parties, either in their votes or elections; their near habitation in a city will always make the force of popular tides and currents very sensible" (Hume 1985: 528). This thought was echoed by Madison in his famous defense of large republics in *Federalist* number 10. Distinguishing sharply between democracy and republic, Madison argued that pure democracies "have ever been spectacles of turbulence and contention; have ever been found incompatible with personal security, or the rights of property, and have, in general, been as short in their lives as they have been violent in their deaths" (Hamilton *et al.* 1948: 45). The great advantage of a federal republic, therefore, was that it made it near to impossible for a majority faction to form across the republic as a whole: "the influence of factious leaders may kindle a flame within their particular states, but will be unable to spread a general conflagration through the other states" (Hamilton *et al.* 1948: 47). Representatives elected by different constituencies within each state would serve as checks on each other, dampening down the passions that made democracies turbulent.

Even such a very brief survey of republican thought reveals that the question of the preferred *size* of the political community is intimately bound up with a series of other issues that have divided republicans: the relationship between republicanism and democracy; which social divisions help to support republican values, and which tend to undermine them; what role the constitution should play in a well-functioning republic, and so forth. Very schematically, we might say that two models of the republican political community emerge from the survey. According to the first model, the political community should be small, it should be unitary (a person's primary identity should be as a citizen), it should cultivate public virtue among its members, and it should be governed by the popular will. (This wording is I believe preferable to saying that the political community should be democratic, since for many adherents of model 1, "the people" are those with the status of citizens, rather than everybody physically resident in the political community.) According to the second model, the political community should be large, it should be divided into numerous sub-units (cities, provinces or states), it should rely on constitutional checks and balances to create stability and protect liberty, and popular rule should be mediated by representative institutions. These models should not be seen as exclusive of each other: in a writer such as Rousseau, for instance, some elements from the second model find their way into the first.[1] Furthermore, we can see potential weaknesses in each model which may push its advocates some way toward the other: in the case of model 1, concerns about external vulnerability and the dangers of majority tyranny; in the case of model 2, concerns about a decline into oligarchy, and about maintaining public spirit in a large and diverse republic. So it would be a mistake to claim that either model represents the "true" or "authentic" spirit of republicanism. (One might indeed ask why both models can properly be seen as versions of republicanism. The answer is that they hold certain underlying values in common – the value of communal self-government, of civic spirit as the quality that makes self-government possible, and of personal liberty of the particular kind that republican institutions provide.) What we need to be aware of, however, in approaching the particular question of republican values, nations, and Europe, is that republicanism is a church divided along the lines I have sketched, as well as along other dimensions (see for instance the various distinctions between neo-Greek and neo-Roman versions of republicanism in Maynor 2003; Nelson 2004; Pettit 1998; Skinner 1990, 1998).

II

Before turning directly to that question, however, I should like to explore in a little more depth two issues already touched upon whose relevance will soon become apparent, if it is not so already. The first of these is the issue of divisions within the political community: which social cleavages, if any, should republicans welcome, and why? The second is the issue of the constitution: in what sense should a republic also be a constitutional state?

For an answer to the first question, we can turn once again to Machiavelli, who distinguished between two ways in which republics might be divided, with very different consequences. The first was the horizontal division between the common people and the nobility, which we would now describe as a class division. In the *Discourses*, Machiavelli famously attributed Rome's liberty to the conflict between these two classes, which he claimed led to the making of good laws (Machiavelli 1970: Book 1, ch. 4). He argued that there had been a de facto balance of power between the two groups: if the nobles tried to implement an oppressive law, the people would either take to the streets and threaten disorder, or simply refuse to enlist in the army. There was an inevitable clash of interests between those who already possessed wealth and power and those who aspired to possess these things, but for several centuries this conflict was managed in the way just described,

137

until eventually controversy over the Agrarian law brought down the Roman republic (Machiavelli 1970: Book 1, ch. 37).

The second type of division was the vertical division between "factions," to which Machiavelli attributed many of the difficulties encountered by the Florentine republic. As he put it "some divisions harm republics and some divisions benefit them. Those do harm that are accompanied with factions and partisans; those bring benefit that are kept up without factions and without partisans" (Machiavelli 1965: 1336). By factions, Machiavelli meant groups formed on a patron/client basis, where some powerful man would recruit followers by providing them with private benefits – "doing favors to various citizens, defending them from the magistrates, assisting them with money and aiding them in getting undeserved offices" (Machiavelli 1965: 1337). As this list makes clear, Machiavelli's first charge against factions is that they create an incentive for office-holders to use their position not for the public good, but as a way of getting resources to reward their followers. In that simple way, they tend to destroy civic virtue. Moreover corruption spreads among the ordinary citizens too, who begin to believe that they will be better served by factional leaders than by the republic as a whole. But a second charge is that factions are a source of political instability, because unlike class divisions, there is no "natural" way for a political community to divide vertically. A faction that succeeded in winning power, Machiavelli argued, would remain united only so long as its rivals were effective competitors. Once they were seen as a spent force, those in the winning faction would be tempted to split it for their personal advantage.

Overall, then, Machiavelli presents a contrast between two ways in which political communities may be divided internally. On the one hand the divisions may be such that, although conflict between the parties may at times be tumultuous, it ends in compromise and the making of good law. On the other hand, the divisions may be such that they lead to the victory of one side, the handing over of the spoils of office to its partisans, and possibly to the breakdown of the political community itself (for instance the expulsion of the losing faction). In one passage Machiavelli contrasts Rome and Florence along these lines: "in the two cities diverse effects were produced, because the enmities that at the outset existed in Rome between the people and the nobles were ended by debating, those in Florence by fighting; those in Rome were terminated by law, those in Florence by the exile and death of many citizens" (Machiavelli 1965: 1140).

Machiavelli's thoughts on this matter were echoed by later republicans, most notably by Rousseau, who cited one of the passages from Machiavelli I have referred to above in his critique of partial associations in Book II, chapter 3 of the *Social Contract* – the chapter headed "Whether the General Will can Err." Rousseau's claim here is that when factions form, the common interest of their faction displaces the general interest in citizens' minds, and their votes can therefore no longer express the general will. In citing Machiavelli, Rousseau does not say which, if any, divisions he regards as harmless (or indeed as beneficial). We might therefore conclude that for him, unlike Machiavelli, any social division within the political community may potentially give rise to factions, and thus to the loss of civic virtue. This would reflect his preference for model 1 republicanism, the republicanism of the small and tightly bound political community. Despite this difference of emphasis, we can extract a principle common to all republicans from this discussion: social divisions within the political community are harmful to republican values in so far as they give rise to factions, allegiance to which displaces allegiance to the political community as a whole. Successful republics need not be homogenous – they can accommodate conflicts both of interest and of personal value – so long as these differences do not consolidate into rival factions.

The second issue I want to explore is the place of constitutions in republican thought, in particular the question of how far the constitution itself might serve as a source of allegiance and unity in a republican polity. Now here it is important to distinguish two senses of "constitution." First a constitution might refer simply to the way that power is divided up within a political community, for instance to the division between legislative and executive powers, or the division between bodies representing different social groups. Second, a constitution might refer to a formal document that establishes a constitution in the first sense, and perhaps at the same time lays down certain substantive principles of government – a bill of rights, for example. A constitution in this second sense requires also a body charged with adjudicating constitutional disputes; a constitution in the first sense does not (although of course it may be supported by one). Now republicans have always favored constitutions in the first sense: a republican form of government should include a balance of powers, partly because different functions of government are best handled by bodies of different size, partly to allow one power to check the other, and partly to give

139

different sections of the community – particularly different social classes – a stake in government (see Viroli 2002: esp. ch. 1). The details here may vary considerably from author to author, but the general idea of "mixed government" or "the balanced constitution" is a common theme in republican thought.

Matters are different, however, with constitutions in the second sense – written constitutions with specialized bodies charged with their interpretation. These, of course, are a comparatively modern political device, and so we should not expect them to be discussed, whether favorably or unfavorably, in older republican thought. More recently, however, we can find supportive remarks about constitutionalism in republican writing, most notably among those close to what I have called model 2 republicanism. This is obviously true, for example, of the authors of the Federalist papers, and we find a similar position being taken up in Philip Pettit's influential recent book *Republicanism* (Pettit 1997: ch. 6).

Pettit in fact distinguishes three elements of constitutionalism, all of which he claims support his underlying ideal of liberty as non-domination. The first he calls the "empire-of-law" condition, the idea of government according to the rule of law, as a protection against the arbitrary exercise of authority. The second he calls the "dispersion-of-power" condition, the idea of dividing political power among separate bodies with discrete functions, as a way of preventing excessive accumulations of power. The third he calls the "counter-majoritarian" condition, the idea of protecting at least some laws from easy amendment by the majority, through institutions such as "the bicameral division of parliament, the recognition of constitutional constraints on law, and the introduction of a bill of rights" (Pettit 1997: 181).

It is evident that the first two elements distinguished by Pettit do indeed have deep roots in the republican tradition: we have noted this already in the case of the division of powers, and the idea of the rule of law is as much a republican ideal as it is a liberal one. But the third element may give us pause. The counter-majoritarian measures described by Pettit may look more like liberal devices aimed at protecting individuals from encroachment by the state than genuinely republican institutions. For they appear to involve removing certain questions from political debate, and entrusting them instead to a small group of citizens – judges, say – who are assumed to be impartial dispensers of justice according to the principles of the constitution. This cuts against the basic republican tenet that the freedom of the political community must depend in the last resort on the public virtue of the citizens. By proposing that certain fundamental matters – basic rights, for example – should be removed from normal political debate, inscribed in a constitution, and handed over to the judiciary to protect, we appear to express mistrust in ordinary citizens: they cannot be relied upon to have enough public spirit to defend the rights of their fellows (see also Bellamy, ch. 7 this volume).

Now it may be possible to avoid this objection by treating constitutional limits as self-imposed constraints on the part of the majority – in other words defending constitutionalism not on liberal grounds, but on the grounds that it enables democratic politics to work more effectively. In that way we could remove the tension I have identified between republicanism and the third element in Pettit's constitutionalism. Even so, a fundamental point remains. Republicans will almost certainly favor a constitutional state, in some sense. They will regard the constitution, whether formal or informal, as making some contribution to the preservation of republican liberty. But they will not rely on it entirely: they will not suppose that constitutional protections could ever be a sufficient guarantee of freedom. They will understand that the only guarantee, in the last resort, is the willingness of citizens themselves to defend their own freedom, whether from external or internal enemies. And that depends on their principled commitment to each other (since defending freedom is a public good: each individual citizen benefits from the willingness of others to defend freedom whether or not he joins in that enterprise himself). So republicans will not be tempted to think that freedom can be preserved by constitutions alone, no matter how well-constructed.

III

I have so far been investigating what republicans have thought and said about the kind of political community within which republican values can be realized. What have we learnt? First of all, size matters, not in itself, but because of what it entails about relations between citizens within the community, and relations between different communities. Republicans favor small polities because the fact of being in close proximity to one another encourages citizens to identify with the republic and enhances civic virtue; but they are concerned about what might be called "democratic turbulence" – passionate beliefs and feelings sweeping through a small community and leading it to act wrongly or imprudently against minorities within or enemies without. And they have looked for ways to protect cities or small states from the threat of being engulfed by larger powers. Second, a republican community should be unified, but not homogeneous. Some sources of division are natural, and if handled properly do not threaten the underlying commitment of citizens to live together and sort out their differences through debate and legislation; but other divisions give rise to factions that threaten to tear the community apart. In the face of such divisions, republicans need policies to ensure that the primary loyalty of citizens is to their republic itself, not to the particular sub-group to which they belong. Third, a republican polity needs a constitution, in the sense of an established division of political powers and functions, but the republic itself is more than the constitution – in particular, it is more than the formal, written constitution, if one exists. Citizens' primary loyalty is to one another as participants in a political enterprise, and they express this partly through their willingness to defend the republican constitution, but their loyalty is not to the constitution itself – it could survive a collective decision to alter the constitution, for instance.

Against this background, it is easy to understand why, in a world in which city-states were no longer thought to be viable as independent entities, republicans should have come to regard nations as forming the natural locus for republican politics. I have set out the case for connecting nationality and republican citizenship at some length elsewhere, so I shall only offer a brief sketch here, before responding to some counterarguments (Miller 1995, 2000). The salient points are these. First, nations are large-scale communities within which people identify with one another by virtue of their shared history, their common language or other cultural characteristics, and so on – in other words, nationality answers the question "why should I engage politically with this group of people rather than others?" by saying "these are the people you are already bound to by ties of culture and history; these are *your* people, even though you may not have seen or known many of them as individuals." Second, within such communities people acknowledge special responsibilities of mutual aid; they are motivated to sustain and defend those they regard as their compatriots. When this involves political action, they are motivated to play their part in achieving collective goals such as national defense and a social security system. Third, because they share a common identity, and acknowledge special responsibilities, people in national communities are also disposed to trust one another to a greater extent than they are willing to trust outsiders. This matters because republican citizenship depends on trust: people have to believe that those they are engaging with are doing so in good faith – for example, they are committed to finding compromises that everyone can accept, and committed to sticking to decisions that have been reached in this way.

In response to these claims, however, several critics have argued that the political community itself can fulfill these conditions, regardless of whether the people who belong to it form a nation in the cultural-cum-historical sense. In other words, what can bind people together in a way that is sufficient for republican citizenship to function is simply their common commitment to the polity, regarded as a political system, with a constitution, laws and other practices, and so forth. Andrew Mason, for example, draws a distinction between "a sense of belonging to a polity" and "a sense of belonging together," where the former is a matter of identifying with certain institutions and practices. Mason claims that "in principle at least, the citizens of a state could identify with their major institutions and practices, and feel at home in them, without believing that there was any deep reason why they should associate together, of the sort which might be provided by the belief that they shared a history, religion, ethnicity, mother tongue, culture or conception of the good" (Mason 2000: 127). The chief merit of this proposal, the critics maintain, is that it removes any need for cultural assimilation or integration within the political community – which given the multicultural character of almost every state in the contemporary world is a highly desirable result – while at the same time it opens the door to republican citizenship beyond the nation-state, since multinational federations could become political communities in the sense required.

Before looking directly at the idea that identification with the political community itself might take the place of national identity as the basis of republican citizenship, I want to look more closely at the critique of nationality. It has several strands. One, developed by Arash Abizadeh, is that the nationality argument rests on an equivocation between common *identity* and common *culture* (Abizadeh 2002). It slides between the plausible claim that for democratic citizenship to work, citizens must have a "shared affective identity" and the much less plausible claim that they must have a common culture, involving shared beliefs, a common language and so forth. Abizadeh points out that successful multinational democracies such as Canada and Switzerland do indeed depend on a shared affective identity among citizens – a common sentiment of belonging together – but he argues that they lack a common national culture.

It is obviously true, as a general matter, that collective identities can be formed on many bases other than nationality – religion, ethnicity, territory, class, and gender, to name but a few. Nevertheless there has to be some feature that explains why the boundaries of identity should fall here rather than there – why they include these people but exclude those others. Might this feature simply be the fact of association over time – the fact that I have interacted in the past with members of this group, but not with that? It seems to me that interaction alone cannot give rise to a shared sense of identity unless it is also accompanied by other features: a feeling of like-mindedness, for example, or a sense of having participated in some common project which might now be regarded as a source of pride. Suppose we now turn to ask why the Canadians and the Swiss have a shared affective identity. Why do they continue to feel that they belong together? Why don't the German Swiss choose instead to affiliate with the FRD, the French Swiss with the French Republic, and so on? The answer, surely, is that to be Swiss is to be something quite distinctive, even though German Swiss also participate in aspects of German culture such as literature and music, and likewise for the other groups. The distinctive elements are partly political in a narrow sense: the Swiss belief in direct democracy through the cantonal system, the tradition of political neutrality and the citizen militia. They are partly political in a broader cultural/historical sense: folk heroes like William Tell, significant national events like the Rütli Oath of 1291 or the enactment of the Confederal Constitution in 1848.

In other words, it is a mistake to describe culturally divided societies like Canada and Switzerland simply as multinational democracies, full stop. They are better described as societies whose citizens primarily have what I call "nested national identities" – they identify, typically, not only with the nation as a whole, but also with one of its sub-units, which may also be characterized as a nation (this is most obviously true in the case of Quebec within Canada) (Miller 2000: ch. 8). In this respect, societies like these are very different from states containing minority nations who genuinely share nothing other than the fact that they are governed by the same political system – especially where these national groups make competing claims to control the state itself, or some portion of its territory. States of this latter kind illustrate only too clearly that simple co-existence, or interaction, over time cannot by itself give rise to a shared identity such as would make republican citizenship possible, in the absence of cultural convergence of the kind we discover in national communities.

A second, rather different, critique of the nationality argument accepts that something like a shared national identity is necessary for republican citizenship to work, but then goes on to claim that national identities are essentially manufactured items (Weinstock 2001). They are largely the work of states, anxious to ensure that the populations they govern had enough in common – a common language especially – to work together effectively and to dampen down separatist demands. Given this artificial origin, there is no reason to think that effective shared identities cannot be created on a wider scale, other than the fact that means used in the past to forge national identities, often involving the coercive elimination of minority languages, for instance, would not now be acceptable from a liberal democratic perspective. As Weinstock puts it, "if fellow-feeling and community have been created among the initially disparate peoples that were lumped together within the boundaries of modern France or Germany, there is no reason to think that this cannot be achieved at the transnational level" (Weinstock 2001: 58).

In reply to this, three points should be made. The first is that identity-transformation of the kind practiced in the past by would-be nation-states is indeed no longer possible in societies governed by liberal principles. This is not just because the methods employed would now be seen as a violation of the basic rights of the people they were used on, but also because the idea that minority identities are things to be cherished and some extent protected has taken a deep hold. There is no longer any question of forcing Welsh-speakers to convert to English or Basque-speakers to Castilian: on the contrary, the issue is how to prevent these minority languages from dying out. It follows, therefore, that any project of transnational identity-building that was consistent with these principles could not aim to *replace* national or sub-national identities with larger (e.g. European) ones; at most it could attempt to generate new identities alongside existing ones. So here the analogy with traditional nation-building breaks down: why suppose that the new, larger identity, supposing it was successfully created, would become the main political identity of the people involved?

Second, it is wrong to see the older nation-building projects as involving the political unification of people who were previously simply "disparate," as Weinstock suggests. A more accurate description would be to say that they aimed to strengthen the feeling of peoplehood among people who already recognized their cultural and political kinship and thereby increase their loyalty to the state in question. When French radicals at the time of the Revolution began the project of spreading the teaching of the French language, this was not because the inhabitants of Brittany or the Pays d'Oc in no way regarded themselves as French, but because the Revolutionary ideas of popular sovereignty and equality of opportunity could not be realized unless everyone spoke a common language. The German case is different, but equally clear. The sense of common German nationhood preceded the creation of a German state by at least half a century, no doubt in part provoked as a reaction to Napoleon's conquests, but stemming also from a shared language and the cultural commonality that went with it. It may be that national consciousness of this kind was at first primarily an elite phenomenon: the dynamics of nation-building are no doubt complex, but the process depends on the underlying willingness of all the subgroups involved to be integrated, and that in turn on their sense of rightfully belonging together rather than apart.

Third, we can reach the same conclusion from the opposite direction by contemplating those cases in which nation-building has failed, despite strenuous efforts on the part of the state to make it happen. The most obvious examples here are the ex-communist states that were unable to survive the transition to democracy, and broke up shortly thereafter – dramatically and bloodily in the case of Yugoslavia, for example; quietly and peacefully in the case of Czechoslovakia. Given the virtual monopoly on channels of cultural transmission that the preceding states enjoyed, we have to ask why they were unable to convince ordinary Slovenes, Serbs, Croats, etc. to think of themselves primarily as Yugoslavs, and similarly for the other cases. If nations were simply top-down creations, one would think that close on half a century was time enough to make a good start on the nation-building process, if not to complete it. The lesson of these failed states is surely that where people already have separate national identities, especially identities that are defined in part in opposition to one another, it is extremely difficult, if not impossible, to superimpose a common identity that is sufficient to hold them together once coercion is removed and liberal democratic rights are granted.

I conclude, therefore, that the argument for nationality as the basis for citizenship remains robust. If republican citizenship, which in the contemporary world must take the form of democratic citizenship, is to succeed, the political community needs to have the cement that a common national identity provides. The older republican worry about factional divisions within the community retains all its force. There must be something that can hold people together despite differences of class, religion, ethnicity, and so forth, and allow them to cooperate politically. The mere fact of being subject to the same political system is not sufficient. Nor can we assume that a common sense of identity can be manufactured at will. Having said all this, however, we can still ask just how *thick* the identity needs to be to serve the purposes we have uncovered. Need it be as culturally thick as nationality as it is usually understood, or could republicanism be supported by a civic identity less heavily freighted with cultural baggage? In the next section I want to examine an influential proposal of this kind, the idea that national identities might be superseded by "constitutional patriotism."

IV

This proposal is usually associated with its most distinguished advocate, Jürgen Habermas, although others have also written in its defense (Habermas 1996, 1999, 2001a; Cronin 2003; Ingram 1996). Habermas's work is of particular interest here, by virtue of his claim that a European constitutional patriotism might serve as the basis for European-wide republican citizenship. We need, therefore, to look carefully at what "constitutional patriotism" means, and why Habermas believes it could operate at European as well as national level.

Habermas has written at length about the connection between national identity and republican citizenship, and looking backwards in history he is convinced that the social solidarity needed for citizenship and social justice could only be generated in states formed on a national basis. As he puts it at one point, "only a national consciousness, crystallized around the notion of a common ancestry, language, and history, only the consciousness of belonging to 'the same' people, makes subjects into citizens of a single political community – into members who can feel responsible *for one another*" (Habermas 1999: 113). But he also believes that this connection can be, and must be, superseded in the contemporary world, as nation-states are challenged by multi-cultural diversity within, and the forces of globalization without. What, then, can replace national consciousness as a source of political unity that can motivate citizens to engage in democratic politics and promote social justice? Constitutional patriotism is the answer he proposes, but what exactly is this constitution to which loyalty is owed supposed to be?

In its original German formulations, constitutional patriotism meant loyalty to the political institutions of the post-war German state, including its Constitution and the principles laid down therein (Müller 2006). Habermas's understanding appears to be less institutional than this. According to him the loyalty is not to the constitution as such, but to the principles that are embodied in the constitution – principles that are not themselves unique to the society in question, since they are common ground between different republican constitutions, but that are given a specific national interpretation in each society.[2] This interpretation is worked out through political debate among citizens, a debate that is not seen as reaching a definitive conclusion, so the focus of loyalty is not exactly *an* interpretation of constitutional principles, but rather a set of rival interpretations, or what Habermas at one point calls "a common *horizon* of interpretation" (Habermas 1999: 225). Quite how this is meant to unite citizens into a single body remains unclear, and Habermas concedes that "this notion of constitutional patriotism appears to many observers too weak a bond to hold together complex societies" (Habermas 1999: 118). He also notes that constitutional patriotism has an historical dimension: constitutional principles cannot be interpreted except against the particular historical background of the society in question, and disputes about that history feed into the rival interpretations of the principles, as they did in the German case with which Habermas is most familiar (indeed it has been argued that the very idea of constitutional patriotism emerged from the peculiar relationship of Germans to their national history in the post-Holocaust era).

We find, then, that for Habermas constitutional patriotism does not so much mean loyalty to a constitution as a formal document interpreted by a Constitutional Court as loyalty to a political culture with a significant historical dimension to it (involving competing understandings of national history) (Laborde 2002). The constitution itself is regarded as an expression of this political culture, and cannot be understood apart from it. This being so, we might ask how constitutional patriotism differs from familiar forms of nationalism in which the constitution may well feature as a central element in national identity (as it does most obviously in the American case). If constitutional patriotism is supposed to be a "thinner" identity, in what way is it thinner? The answer, for Habermas, appears to be that it eliminates the ethnic elements of national identity that he regards as problematic in contemporary multicultural societies. But in this respect it does not differ from the position often described as "liberal nationalism," which advocates the transformation of ethnically based national identities into identities based on a public culture that is not tied to any one ethnic group. It seems that for Habermas national identities are unavoidably ethnic in character; but it may be asked whether constitutional patriotism can entirely escape from ethnic entanglement. Constitutions, after all, are written in the national language, not in Esperanto; and national histories are chiefly histories of whichever people or peoples have occupied the land for centuries past. To that extent, both liberal nationalism and constitutional patriotism face the same limits: they can seek to free citizen identity from religious and other elements of private culture that inevitably discriminate among citizens, but they cannot eliminate everything that is peculiar to the society – since both sides in the debate agree that loyalty given merely to abstract constitutional principles, liberty, equality, democracy, and so forth, is not sufficient to create the kind of political community that republican politics requires.

If constitutional patriotism as understood by Habermas does draw in this way on what we would normally regard as elements of national identity, how is European constitutional patriotism possible? He appears to rest most weight on the development of a European public sphere, created on the one hand by a Europe-wide civil society of voluntary groups and on the other by a European party system whose members would address European rather than national issues (Habermas 2001a: 102–3; 1999: 153). He accepts that simply enacting a European Constitution in the absence of such a public sphere would not produce a sufficient degree of integration. But this still leaves open the question of the *cultural* basis of a European constitutional patriotism. In virtue of what would Europeans think of themselves as engaged in a common democratic project, rather than as simply competing to exert influence on European institutions? On this Habermas has been tantalizingly brief. He argues, in answer to Dieter Grimm's skeptical essay on the proposed European Constitution (Grimm 1995), that "what unites a nation of citizens, as opposed to a *Volksnation*, is not some primordial substrate but rather an intersubjectively shared context of possible mutual understanding" (Habermas 1999: 159). Formulations such as this seem tantamount to admitting defeat (*possible* mutual understanding is surely something that exists between people everywhere). Later in the same essay he suggests that European integration can base itself "on a common cultural background and the shared historical experience of having happily overcome nationalism" (Habermas 1999: 161). I will leave readers to judge the plausibility of this claim, but for my part it seems that although the peoples of Europe have indeed succeeded to a considerable degree in *taming* (rather than overcoming) nationalism, their common cultural background often has the opposite effect of making them exaggerate the national differences between them that remain – the phenomenon that Michael Ignatieff has called the "narcissism of minor differences" (Ignatieff 1999).

In one of his more recent essays, Habermas attempts to say more about what distinguishes European political culture from others (Habermas 2001b). He argues that European peoples share a commitment to social-democratic values that cuts across party lines, and that contrasts in particular with American market individualism. This, he says, forms the basis of a common project to regulate the global economy and "counterbalance its undesired economic, social, and cultural consequences" which is most effectively pursued at European rather than national level (Habermas 2001b: 12). He refers also to the historically-formed tradition of toleration as a way of coping with religious and other cleavages, and suggests that in modern circumstances this takes the form of a commitment to protect human rights.

How convincing are these arguments? Two points are noteworthy. The first is that the line Habermas draws between social democracy and what he calls the "neo-liberal vision" is really a line that, if it fall anywhere, falls between the US and the rest of the world. The values he cites are also shared by democratic nations everywhere – Canada, New Zealand, and the other Commonwealth countries, for example.

What is distinctive (and needs explaining) is not European exception-alism, but American exceptionalism. Put differently, one might try to base a European identity on the idea of not being American, but if so, "Europe" would have to expand to take in all these other countries too.

The second point is that, when Habermas gestures toward cultural factors that do seem to be more exclusively European, "Europe" has a tendency to shrink toward its original EEC core, with a heavy emphasis on France and Germany (note, for instance, his inclusion of "Roman law and the Napoleonic Code" among the distinctive features of European political culture). The UK is consistently regarded as a deviant case, no mention is made of the newly-admitted states of Eastern Europe, and even Scandinavia is regarded as an obstacle to developing a dis-tinctive European foreign policy. Habermas, in other words, glosses over real differences of economic and political philosophy that have their source in the varied national traditions of European member-states in an attempt to identify a common political culture that is more than simply the standard set of liberal-democratic principles and values. The "Europe" of his imagination turns out to be what is now sometimes called "Old Europe."

In short, constitutional patriotism as a basis for republican citizenship in Europe looks improbable. Not only is there as yet no constitution to serve as a tangible focus of loyalty, but even if one were to be enacted in the face of widespread current skepticism, it seems doubtful that it could draw on the common cultural background that has made it a plausible form of national identity in Germany, for example. Euro-republicans still need to prove that Europe is or could be the kind of political community that can support republican politics. How have they tried to do this?

V

It is obvious that the EU is a highly complex political system with various legislative, executive, administrative, and judicial bodies having different, sometimes overlapping competences, and moreover that these areas of responsibility intersect with those of national governments and their own subsidiary elements. This fact renders its workings quite opaque even to well-informed citizens of the member states. Asked about which European body is responsible for making which decisions, citizens are likely to respond with blank stares, unless they happen to be have been involved in, for example, a case brought before the European Court of Justice. (National parliaments, by contrast, are reasonably well understood as representative institutions responsible for law-making in each state even if citizens are not privy to their inner committee structures, and so forth.) If citizens have no clear sense of how the EU works, this seems to bode ill for an attempt to understand it in republican terms. What Euro-republicans try to do, however, is to make a virtue out of this complexity and argue that Europe has, in effect, a mixed constitution in something like the traditional republican sense. This is backed up by two further claims: first that European institutions, by virtue of the fact that they disperse decision-making power to many different places, help to provide citizens with resilient liberty as understood by Pettit – liberty as non-domination; second, although there is no such thing as a European demos (expect perhaps in a very thin sense), European citizens are none the less engaged in democratic deliberation in a whole range of fora, some formal, others informal, and in that way are actively engaged in determining the future of Europe (Bellamy & Castiglione 2000; Lavdas & Chryssochoou 2006; Friese & Wagner 2002).

If this is to count as a republican view, clearly it must exemplify what I earlier called model 2 republicanism, the version that is friendlier to social divisions and to checks and balances as means to safeguard liberty. Indeed two of its advocates confirm this when they write that "neo-republican approaches need to distance themselves from two important features of classical republicanism: (a) the 'strong' approach to the constitutive role of civic virtues in the good polity, and (b) republican hostility towards 'factions'" (Lavdas & Chryssochoou 2006: 160). The question, however, is whether the picture of the European constitution presented in these writings really draws upon republican values at all, or whether its roots do not lie simply in liberal pluralism. How might its republican credentials be strengthened?

It might be argued that the multi-layered political structure that has evolved in Europe actually provides better protection to citizens against arbitrary political decisions than nation-states could – for example groups that lose in national parliaments can try to win support in the European parliament, and individual citizens can take their cases to the European Courts. But although there might be some merit in this argument in the case of states whose own democratic institutions are deficient – for instance they do not have adequate mechanisms for protecting human rights – it hardly seems to apply to reasonably well-functioning liberal democracies, which is what existing EU states are. Is liberty any better protected in Sweden and Germany than in Norway and Switzerland by virtue of their EU membership? And the very complexity of legal and political processes within the EU introduces arbitrariness of a different kind – for example if some citizens but not others are able to secure rights through the European Courts that national courts are unwilling to give.

Another argument that might be made here is that the EU safeguards democracy within the member states – this argument picking up the older model 2 republican claim that one of the virtues of a large federal republic was its capacity to protect republican institutions in any of its component parts if these should come under threat (for a defense of transnational republicanism along these lines, see Bohman, ch. 8 this volume). Now it is true that the EU has played a positive role in spreading democracy to states whose democratic credentials were suspect by making it a condition of entry that, for instance, all those permanently resident in the state in question should be given the opportunity to acquire citizenship. On the other hand, it has not yet had to face the test of democratic collapse in one of the member-states (something akin to the collapse of the Weimar Republic, for example). What role would the EU be able to play in such circumstances? What kind of intervention would the other member-states agree to undertake? We have no evidence to help us to answer these questions so the argument here must remain speculative. Given the disparate interests and national cultures of the member-states, particularly since enlargement, collective action to safeguard democracy that went beyond ritual gestures might well prove difficult to sustain.

It might be said finally that the EU has enhanced the quality of democratic citizenship for European citizens by providing more channels through which citizens can engage with policy issues (see also Bohman, ch. 8 this volume). But although no doubt some supporting evidence for this proposition could be produced, politics within the EU remains very largely a matter for the elites – bargaining between ministers, administrative collaboration between police forces, immigration officers, environmental agencies, and so forth. This occurs for perfectly good reasons, but it is hardly democratic (or republican). The most persuasive argument here is the one developed by Neil MacCormick, who argues that the republican idea of the mixed constitution combined democratic and aristocratic elements, and that a case can be made for seeing EU politicians and administrators as a kind of meritocratically chosen aristocracy counterbalancing the democratic element, represented here by the European Parliament, and national representatives who have themselves been chosen by democratic means (MacCormick 1997). As MacCormick admits, "this is by no means democracy perfect or democracy complete" (1997: 344). This seems to me a considerable understatement; *at best* the democratic element in the constitution is small and indirect; there is nothing here equivalent to democratic public opinion, or to the Roman people taking to the streets when the Senate tried to impose some measure that they disliked (for a powerful general critique of the idea of Europe-wide democracy, see Greven 2000).

If the EU as presently constituted does not provide a convincing example of model 2 republicanism, still less does it exemplify model 1, the republicanism of virtuous citizens committed to the common good of the republic. There are at present no European citizens in other than a legal sense: no one thinks and acts as though the collective interests of the people of Europe were his or her primary concern. Politics remains overwhelmingly national in character, except where some regional minority or interest group sees an advantage in directing its lobbying activities toward Brussels or Strasbourg. In that sense, Europe is a Europe of factions, partial associations pursuing their own interests and bargaining with one another with little regard for the greater good. For genuine citizenship to come into being, as even Euro-enthusiasts such as Habermas recognize, certain pre-conditions are necessary: a common language of politics, Europe-wide political parties and other associations, public discussion through trans-national media of communication (Habermas 1999: 160–1). Not only are none of these pre-conditions fulfilled at present, but it is hard to see how they could possibly be fulfilled, particularly in an enlarged Europe of 25 or more nations.

Some hopeful Euro-republicans have thought that the enacting of a European constitution might bring about a sea-change in European politics – that a public formed through the process of enactment itself might then continue to exist *as* a public in the aftermath (for a thoughtful discussion of this idea, see Walker 2004). Earlier in this chapter I expressed some skepticism about the role that formal constitutions can play in supporting republican values. On the other hand, it is sometimes true that the making of a constitution has a significance that goes beyond the content of the document that emerges – for example when it coincides with national liberation, or the overthrow of an authoritarian regime. It is clear, however, that the (presently stalled) process of constitution-making in Europe has nothing of that character. It was and remains an elite project that arouses little popular interest, except where it becomes entangled with national politics. The main passion that was awakened by the process of popular consultation was distrust, in some quarters, of the central European institutions. This is not an argument against having a European constitution, which may be necessary for certain purposes, but an expression of severe doubt that such a constitution, if eventually enacted, will succeed in creating a genuine form of European citizenship.

In the end, the question boils down to this: can there be a republic without active citizens committed to pursuing the public good, whether in the course of legislating for themselves or checking a government that is oppressive or has been captured by private interests? And can there be active citizens without a political community held together by a sense of common belonging? Large conglomerates such as the EU are unsuited to republican politics not just because of their size, and the physical gap that separates the central institutions from most citizens, but because they are divided in such a way that citizens' primary loyalties are inevitably directed toward their compatriots, as many empirical studies have shown. Looked at from the center, these divisions are a natural source of "factions," which is why so much European politics takes the form of bargaining between national interests. I have said already that this bargaining is very often necessary, but it is a mistake to try to dress it up in civic terms, as Euro-republicans are wont to do. If we are looking for promising new sites for republican politics in the twenty-first century, we would do better to look again at the cities and the regions, where political dialogue between elected representatives and ordinary citizens is based on a real sense of common identity and common concerns.

ACKNOWLEDGMENTS

I should like to thank Cécile Laborde for her many constructive suggestions that contributed to the writing of this chapter, and Jessica Kimpell for invaluable research assistance.

NOTES

1   I am thinking here particularly of Rousseau's insistence that a legitimate state requires a clear division between legislative and executive powers, or as he puts it between the sovereign and the government. See Rousseau 1997, esp. Book III.

2   This at any rate is Habermas's view in the writings I am considering. For evidence that he had initially thought of constitutional patriotism simply as a loyalty to abstract normative principles before later coming to appreciate its link to particular social and historical contexts, see Markell 2000.

REFERENCES

Abizadeh, A. (2002). "Does Liberal Democracy Presuppose a Cultural Nation?" *American Political Science Review*, 96, 495–509.

Armitage, D. (2002). "Empire and Liberty: A Republican Dilemma." In M. van Gelderen and Q. Skinner (eds.), *Republicanism: A Shared European Heritage*, vol. 2. Cambridge: Cambridge University Press, 29–46.

Bellamy, R. and Castiglione, D. (2000). "Democracy, Sovereignty and the Constitution of the European Union: The Republican Alternative to Liberalism." In Z. Bankowski and A. Scott (eds.), *The European Union and its Order*. Oxford: Blackwell, 169–90.

Chandler, T. (1987). *Four Thousand Years of Urban Growth*. Lewiston/Lampeter: Edwin Mellen Press.

Cronin, C. (2003). "Democracy and Collective Identity: In Defence of Constitutional Patriotism." *European Journal of Philosophy*, 11, 1–28.

Friese, H. and Wagner, P. (2002). "The Nascent Political Philosophy of the European Polity." *Journal of Political Philosophy*, 10, 342–64.

Greven, M. (2000). "Can the European Union Finally Become a Democracy?" In M. Greven and L. Pauly (eds.), *Democracy Beyond the State?* Lanham, MD: Rowman and Littlefield, 35–61.

Grimm, D. (1995). "Does Europe Need a Constitution?" *European Law Journal*, 1, 282–302.

Habermas, J. (1996). "Citizenship and National Identity. Some Reflections on the Future of Europe." In Habermas, *Between Facts and Norms: Contributions to a Discourse Theory of Law and Democracy*. Cambridge: Polity Press, 491–515.

Habermas, J. (1999). *The Inclusion of the Other: Studies in Political Theory*, eds. C. Cronin and P. De Greiff. Cambridge: Polity.

Habermas, J. (2001a). *The Postnational Constellation*. Cambridge: Polity Press.

Habermas, J. (2001b). "Why Europe Needs a Constitution." *New Left Review*, New Series, 11, 5–26.

Hamilton, A., Madison, J. and Jay, J. (1948). *The Federalist: or, The New Constitution*, ed. M. Beloff. Oxford: Blackwell.

Hume, D. (1985). "The Idea of a Perfect Commonwealth." In Hume, *Essays Moral, Political, and Literary*, ed. E. F. Miller. Indianapolis: Liberty Classics, 512–29.

Ignatieff, M. (1999). "Nationalism and the Narcissism of Minor Differences." In R. Beiner (ed.), *Theorizing Nationalism*. Albany, NY: State University of New York Press, 91–102.

Ingram, A. (1996). "Constitutional Patriotism." *Philosophy and Social Criticism*, 22, 1–18.

Jones, P. (1997). *The Italian City-State: From Commune to Signoria*. Oxford: Clarendon Press.

Laborde, C. (2002). "From Constitutional to Civic Patriotism." *British Journal of Political Science*, 32, 591–612.

Lavdas, K. and Chryssochoou, D. (2006). "Public Spheres and Civic Competence in the European Polity: A Case of Liberal Republicanism?" In I. Honohan and J. Jennings (eds.), *Republicanism in Theory and Practice*. London: Routledge, 154–69.

MacCormick, N. (1997). "Democracy, Subsidiarity, and Citizenship in the 'European Commonwealth.'" *Law and Philosophy*, 16, 331–56.

Machiavelli, N. (1965). *The History of Florence*. In Machiavelli, *The Chief Works and Others*, ed. A. Gilbert, vol. 3. Durham, NC: Duke University Press.

Machiavelli, N. (1970). *The Discourses*, ed. B. Crick. Harmondsworth: Penguin.

Markell, P. (2000). "Making Affect Safe for Democracy? On 'Constitutional Patriotism.'" *Political Theory*, 28, 38–63.

Martines, L. (1986). "Italy, Rise of Towns." In J. R. Strayer (ed.), *Dictionary of the Middle Ages*, vol. 7. New York: Charles Scribner's Sons, 12–18.

Mason, A. (2000). *Community, Solidarity and Belonging*. Cambridge: Cambridge University Press.

Maynor, J. (2003). *Republicanism in the Modern World*. Cambridge: Polity.

Miller, D. (1995). *On Nationality*. Oxford: Clarendon Press.

Miller, D. (2000). *Citizenship and National Identity*. Cambridge: Polity Press, 81–96.

Montesquieu (1989). *The Spirit of the Laws*, eds. A. Cohler, B. Miller and H. Stone. Cambridge: Cambridge University Press.

Müller, J. W. (2006). "On the Origins of Constitutional Patriotism." *Contemporary Political Theory*, 5, 278–96.

Nelson, E. (2004). *The Greek Tradition in Republican Thought*. Cambridge: Cambridge University Press.

Pettit, P. (1997). *Republicanism: A Theory of Freedom and Government*. Oxford: Clarendon Press.

Pettit, P. (1998). "Reworking Sandel's Republicanism." *Journal of Philosophy*, 95, 73–96.

Rousseau, J.-J. (1997). *Of the Social Contract*. In Rousseau, *The Social Contract and Other Later Political Writings*, ed. V. Gourevitch. Cambridge: Cambridge University Press.

Skinner, Q. (1990). "Machiavelli's *Discorsi* and the Pre-humanist Origins of Republican Ideas." In G. Bock, Q. Skinner and M. Viroli (eds.), *Machiavelli and Republicanism*. Cambridge: Cambridge University Press, 121–41.

Skinner, Q. (1998). *Liberty before Liberalism*. Cambridge: Cambridge University Press.

David Miller

Viroli, M. (1990). "Machiavelli and the Republican Idea of Politics." In G. Bock, Q. Skinner and M. Viroli (eds.), *Machiavelli and Republicanism*. Cambridge: Cambridge University Press, 143–71.

Viroli, M. (2002). *Republicanism*. New York: Hill and Wang.

Walker, N. (2004). "The Legacy of Europe's Constitutional Moment." *Constellations*, 11, 368–92.

Weinstock, D. (2001). "Prospects for Transnational Citizenship and Democracy." *Ethics and International Affairs*, 15, 53–66.

Chapter 7

Republicanism, Democracy, and Constitutionalism

Richard Bellamy

Republicanism has had an ambiguous relationship with both democracy and constitutionalism (Waldron 2004). On the one hand, republicans of either a "civic humanist" or "neo-Roman" hue have prioritized the importance of self-rule: the first on the intrinsic grounds that it promotes individual self-realization through political participation (Sandel 1996; Taylor 1979: 181), the second on the instrumental grounds that it guards against domination and enshrines our status as equal citizens (Skinner 1986: 246–9; Pettit 1997: 90). On the other hand, republicans of both varieties have worried about factionalism and tyrannous majorities. They have tended to have a rather high-minded view of democracy as public-spirited, rational deliberation on the public good. However, popular government so conceived makes strong demands of citizens, requiring they possess sufficient solidarity not to sacrifice the public good to private advantage. Consequently, they have thought constitutional mechanisms necessary to check self-interest and foster a more public spirited approach (e.g. Taylor 1995: 191–201; Pettit 1997: ch. 6).

As David Miller notes in his chapter, republicans were well aware that the larger and less homogenous the political community, the more such constitutional mechanisms are likely to be necessary (e.g. Madison in Hamilton *et al.* 2003, no. 10). To the extent all modern democracies are much larger and more diverse than the ancient republics, some form of constitutionalism now appears inevitable. Indeed, republicans had noted how class divisions prevailed even within the small city states of ancient Greece and Rome and Renaissance Europe, making certain constitutional arrangements necessary there too (Polybius 1979: Bk. VI; Machiavelli 1960: Bk. I, ch. 4). However, their understanding of constitutions was rather different to the view dominant today. The prevailing understanding of a constitution is as an entrenched written document that sets out the fundamental law of the polity and is upheld by a constitutional court with the power to strike down executive acts and legislation that the court believes conflict with it (Raz 1998a: 153–4). Historically, though, republicans have regarded a constitution as a particular form of government that incorporates certain ways of sharing and balancing power (McIlwain 1958: ch. 2; Maddox 1982). While current constitutional documents standardly incorporate both these views of the constitution by including not only a Bill of Rights but also an outline of the workings of the political system, it is the constitution in the first, legal, sense that most legal and political theorists regard as the "real" constitution, dismissing the second, political, sense as largely "tautological" (Raz 1998a: 153) or "nominal" (Sartori 1962: 861).

Of course, a constitution in the legal sense is very much a recent, late eighteenth-century invention. It could be argued that earlier republicans did not mention it because they were unaware such a thing existed, but that it fits republican needs in contemporary conditions – a point some theorists have supported via a reading of the American Constitution as the original "modern" republican constitution (e.g. Paine 1989: 81, 131; Ackerman 1991: 28–31). After all, article 4, section 4 of the US Constitution affirms "The United States shall guarantee to every state in this Union a Republican form of Government." The first main claim I wish to make in this chapter is that this contention proves mistaken. A constitution in the legal sense goes quite contrary to core republican purposes – indeed, it was not originally a part of the modern republican scheme for the US constitution (Hamilton in Hamilton *et al.* 2003, no. 84). To the extent republicans became reconciled to it, it was as a popular rather than a judicial charter (Kramer 2004). By contrast, though republican ends are best met by the constitutional means encapsulated in the political sense of a constitution, republican views of how these means might be best configured can and does need to be updated. Here, too, the exceptional longevity of the American constitution has prompted some contemporary republican theorists to see the political arrangements advocated there, especially when read through *The Federalist Papers*, as a scheme for modern republican government (e.g. Sunstein 1993: 20–4; Elkin 1996). The US Constitution predates modern democratic politics, though, possibly even blighting its development within that country (Dahl 2002).

This fact leads to this chapter's second main claim. Democracy as it actually exists today – that is, more or less as Joseph Schumpeter described it: namely, as "an institutional arrangement for arriving at political decisions in which individuals acquire the power to decide by means of a competitive struggle for the people's vote" (Schumpeter 1976: 269), with elections and parliamentary decisions being made by majority rule – offers a republican form of government suited to contemporary conditions. It is constitutional in the republican sense of providing appropriate political arrangements for a form of self-rule that avoids arbitrariness and hence domination (Bellamy 2007). Moreover, to codify such a system as part of an entrenched legal constitution, rendering it subject to a form of process-based judicial review (Ely 1980), is not only unnecessary but also subversive of the basic republican aims it serves. The system itself comprises a self-constituting and constitutional form of political constitutionalism.

I proceed to these two conclusions as follows. First, I outline the republican rationale for democratic self-rule, arguing that the neo-Roman account proves far more plausible than the civic humanist. Second, I examine and reject two republican arguments for a written and judicially protected constitution – the first as a means for upholding substantive democratic ends in the manner typical of the first, legal, sense of constitutionalism outlined above, the other as a way of protecting and codifying democratic procedures – a legal version of the second, political, sense of constitutionalism. Finally, I argue that "actually existing democracy" offers a Republican reading of the constitution in the purely political sense that is appropriate for contemporary societies.

Two Republican Rationales for Democracy

Two republican rationales for democracy appear in the literature. One view, associated with Aristotle and often taken up by contemporary communitarians (Sandel 1996: 4, 274; Taylor 1979: 181; Taylor 1995: 141, 200), links democracy with a positive account of liberty as self-mastery. A second view, recently excavated from the "neo-roman" republican tradition by Quentin Skinner (1998: 30–5) and Philip Pettit (1997: 183–205), links democracy with a negative account of liberty as non-domination. On this account, a condition of political equality must obtain if we are to be free from the potential for mastery by others.

This section argues the second offers a much more philosophically coherent and empirically plausible view than the first, with the defense of the constitutionality of actually existing democracy below resting on this second position.

The first view, linking self-rule to liberty as self mastery, is usually associated with participatory theories of democracy. However, it raises the obvious objection of why individuals should regard the public liberty of participation worth the sacrifice of numerous private liberties. To assert, as such theorists are apt to, that political participation – especially of the demanding sort they advocate – is necessary to human self-realization proves highly contentious. In fact, politicians and political junkies apart, most people tend to find more fulfillment in the private sphere. They would rather cultivate their gardens than the public good.

Of course, their capacity to do so depends on a public framework of suitable private rights. Yet, without a highly unlikely complete consensus on what every particular of that public framework should be, there will always be tensions and occasional conflicts between an individual's liberty and the collective agreements that give rise to the public arrangements necessary to secure it. Again, such republican theorists often do claim that direct participation in decision-making produces a more deliberative process in which consensual agreement is more likely. However, even they concede that such directly deliberative forums are implausible mechanisms for making the key decisions in large-scale and complex mass democracies. These highly participatory sorts of deliberative process assume a comparatively small group able to engage in informed, face to face discussions. At best, they operate either at the very local level, as in small town meetings, or as complements to actual decision-making, as with consultative citizen juries, or as the ideal method to be adopted by a small group delegated with the task of decision making yet chosen by other – non-directly-deliberative – means, as with regulative authorities or representatives in the legislature. As a result, citizens will still end up also having to participate in more indirectly democratic processes, for which the link with self-realization proves weak at best.

Meanwhile, even in directly deliberative democratic contexts, deliberation may produce an illusory consensus or frustrate its achievement. Though the need to engage with the arguments of others on an equal basis may overcome prejudice and self-interest so as to compel all to accept the force of the better argument, the convergence experienced by such groups may equally be the product of "groupthink" or persuasive and emotive rhetoric by the most articulate (Janis 1982; Bohman 1996: 27; Gambetta 1998) that may induce weaker parties to concede too much (Amy 1987). Alternatively, deliberation may polarize opinions as much as transforming and unifying them by solidifying the divergent views of opposed groups (Sunstein 2002). Multiplying perspectives can also overload the decision-making process and up transaction costs (Richardson 2002: 77–8).

Finally, plenty of scope exists for what Rawls has called "reasonable disagreement" to persist among the most well-intentioned and best informed deliberators, no matter how long they discuss with each other (Rawls 1993: 55–7). Certain views may simply be contingently or logically incompatible and be backed by different kinds of incommensurable moral claim. The evidence for different positions may be difficult to identify or interpret, with the concepts and theories informing most political views being vague and indeterminate when applied to concrete cases. In these instances, democracy, in the guise of majority voting, has to perform the rather different instrumental function of breaking deadlock by acting as a closure device. However, this task is hard to reconcile with a view of democracy as the extension of individual autonomy because it returns us to the original conflict between public and private liberty.

As a result of these practical difficulties, the link between liberty as self-mastery and democracy is a tenuous one. It could be argued that even under majority rule democracy maximizes autonomy becauseit encourages the greatest possible number of people to live under laws they have chosen (Dahl 1989: 138–9). But this autonomy-based defense acknowledges that for some democracy limits autonomy. Indeed, we shall see how even the members of any majority coalition do not get all that they want but must necessarily compromise with others. So the argument that democracy is an expression of individual autonomy only proves coherent on a somewhat implausible view of positive liberty, in which political participation serves as a vital component to individual self-realization and leads to a consensus on the common good. Unsurprisingly, many have regarded such linkages with suspicion (Berlin 1969: 129–31; Oppenheim 1981: 92; Christiano 1996: ch. 1; Richardson 2002: 58–61). However, these problems can be overcome when democracy gets tied to freedom as non-domination (Skinner 1986).

According to this thesis, freedom depends on not being subject to arbitrary rule. There are two ways democracy might contribute to this goal. It could provide a means for identifying non-arbitrary outputs, or it could offer a process of non-arbitrary inputs (Richardson 2002: chs. 3 and 4). The output based view involves democracy securing results that promote the public good by treating citizens in ways that track their common interests and offer them equal concern and respect. On this account, democracy offers a way to thwart governmental interferences that serve the interests of those with state power, such as a monarch, by preventing them from enacting legislation or promoting policies that are in their interests rather than those of the population as a whole. The input based view, though not insensitive to the desirability of achieving generally beneficial and equitable results, conceives arbitrariness and its avoidance in procedural terms. On this account, the virtues of democracy lie in giving all citizens an equal status in the processes of public decision-making, not in making decisions that secure their equality *per se*. Given that all citizens are autonomous individuals, we need to treat them as political equals and so "recognize everybody with whom we communicate as a potential source of argument and reasonable information" (Weale 1999: 57). From this perspective, democracy promotes liberty not because it fosters self-mastery in some ethical naturalist sense of self-realization, but simply by regarding no citizen as entitled to be the master of another – all are on a par, being potentially rulers and ruled in turn. In what follows, I shall defend the second approach as the most coherent and plausible, with the best democratic and republican credentials.

There are various versions of the outcome view. All raise problems and have dubious democratic credentials. We have already seen the difficulties with one possible version of this argument: namely, that of those direct deliberative theorists who make epistemic claims for democracy as a means to arrive at the best argument. As we saw, these claims prove highly questionable – though I shall defend a weaker account tied to a more realistic account of party democracy below. A different, aggregative version of this thesis – usually criticized by advocates of deliberation – might be a roughly utilitarian argument that democratic voting promotes the collective welfare by securing the greatest happiness of the greatest number (Barry 1979: 176ff.). However, there are notorious problems in aggregating the preferences of individuals into a social preference (Arrow 1968). There is also the difficulty that the utilitarian goals of maximizing total or average welfare can be compatible with sacrificing a few to the greater good of the many, thereby dominating some – potentially even enslaving them – for the benefit of the rest. This possibility serves as the basis for fears of the tyranny of the majority – even if, as we shall see in the final section, this fear proves far less justified than many have assumed.

Some theorists have proposed avoiding this dilemma by insisting on all public decisions being made unanimously, thereby ensuring that no collective measure gets adopted the advantages of which did not outweigh the costs no matter how they might end up being distributed (Buchanan & Tullock 1965: 12, 14; Buchanan & Musgrave 1999: 21). At one level, unanimity might appear to be a very pure form of democracy. However, unless the claims of deliberative theorists are true and democracy promotes a consensus on just outcomes, such counter-majoritarian devices simply create a system of individual vetoes that is biased toward the status quo. Only if we provide for pre-existing base line conditions that involve no domination that favors, either directly or indirectly, private agents or agencies, and which the proposed government action may be directed at removing, will unanimity guard against rather than entrench arbitrary rule (Rae 1969, 1975). The unanimity requirement also overlooks one of the central dilemmas of pluralism alluded to earlier when discussing deliberative views – the impossibility, given the problems of incompatibility and incommensurability, of accommodating all worthwhile values and interests in a single social world.

Finally, some theorists have followed Rousseau and seen democracy as a method for producing "the general will" rather than the "will of all" (Rousseau 1973: 185). Whereas the latter, being the product of self-interest and factionalism, could give rise to the tyranny of the majority, the former allegedly produces decisions that treat all as equals by serving their common interests. Certainly, a public good, like the environment, can appear to have this structure, at least in principle (Barry 1967: 119–23). If, for example, citizens consider when voting what it would be like should a given piece of self-serving polluting behavior, such as being able to drive their car in the inner city at rush hour, be generally adopted, then it would probably lose its attraction as a collective as opposed to a purely personal option. By contrast, promoting clean air offers a general benefit that can be enjoyed equally by all. Even so, as Rousseau conceded, to reach such happy results it will almost

certainly be necessary to screen out quite a lot of potentially conflicting considerations of the kind any full account of such decisions
invariably raise, and assume a background of rough social equality that
excludes free riding (Barry 1967: 123–6).

On the whole, the generality requirement rules out either too little
or too much to be a reliable and non-contestable way of identifying
the common good. For example, generality often serves as a formal
criterion for the rule of law. The idea is to ensure laws apply equally
to all and are not aimed at persecuting particular individuals. The difficulty
is that rules can be general in form and still discriminate against groups,
such as Jews in Nazi Germany. Yet, sometimes discrimination is
warranted because there can be relevant differences that mean some
people may need to be treated differently in certain circumstances. As
a result, more substantive versions of the generality requirement, that
try to tackle the problem with formal accounts by explicitly ruling out
discrimination against particular groups, go too far. Thus, libertarians
have seen generality as an alternative to the unanimity view as a way
of preventing collectively financed programs that benefit some rather
than others (Buchanan & Congleton 1998: 44). However, this would
exclude measures where equal treatment may require discrimination, such
as special access arrangements for the disabled or maternity leave
for women. Moreover, it would be wrong to regard such policies as
self-interested moves on the part of these groups – many able bodied
or male citizens respectively would support these measures because
they thought them just and certainly generalizable in form (Richardson
2002: 45–7).

Democracy, therefore, cannot provide a fail safe method for identifying non-arbitrary outputs that track the interests of each individual.
Indeed, all attempts to define the public interest in an appropriately
egalitarian sense face insurmountable problems of practical rationality
(Christiano 1996: 64–6). Not only are people's interests constantly
evolving, but they also apply different normative criteria to their
evaluation. On the one hand, social activity is so complex and open,
that it is hard to predict the impact of any policy, however well
intentioned. On the other hand, our assessments are both conflicting
and incommensurable. Any metric that tries to sift this information
will be arbitrary. Attempts to avoid this problem by blocking almost
any collective decision by insisting on unanimity or strict generality are
themselves just as arbitrary, there being no more grounds for believing

the status quo – which they favor – as preferable to any other collective policy.

We seem faced with an impasse. All but anarchists accept some collective policies are necessary for social life to go well, yet we seem confronted by an insurmountable problem in deciding which ones truly are in the collective interest. As Albert Weale (1999: 8–13) and Jeremy Waldron (1999: 107–13) have argued, this situation of needing collective decisions while, because of the limitations of human reasoning, reasonably disagreeing as to what these should be, form "the circumstances of politics". The process based view of democracy enters here. For, though we cannot identify whether outcomes are non-arbitrary with certainty, we can have a non-arbitrary process for their selection and contestation. The role of the democratic process in these circumstances is less to generate outcomes we agree *with*, though it can help in that regard by improving the degree to which government decisions are informed by and responsive to popular concerns, and more to produce outcomes that all can agree *to*, on the grounds they have been fairly and legitimately arrived at.

For a process to be consistent with both the "circumstances of politics" and non-domination, it must meet the following two criteria. First, citizens will need to feel that no difference of status exists between them and other decision-makers, including those they may choose as their delegates. Decision making cannot be the preserve of supposedly "superior" sorts of people. Second, the reason the views of some citizens may count for less than those of others in the actual decision cannot be because some people hold the "right" view and others the "wrong" one. The democratic process of voting meets these criteria in a fairly straightforward way. A defining characteristic of a democratic vote is that each person counts for one and none for more than one. In elections for local or national legislatures, all citizens are treated equally in this respect – including members of the currently incumbent government. The reason that the legislature favors certain peoples' views more than others is because more people have voted for a given party's representatives than for those of other parties. Such aggregative accounts of democratic voting are sometimes criticized as mechanical or "statistical" (Dworkin 1996: 364), and liable to produce majority tyranny – a concern to which I return in the final section. But whatever the supposed failings of democratic decision-making, this very mechanical aspect of democracy has a decided advantage in the context of disagreement. It allows those on the losing side to hold on to their integrity. They can feel their views have been treated with as much respect as those on the winning side, counting equally with theirs in the vote, and that the winners are not thereby "right", so that they are "wrong", but merely the current majority. That position has been regarded as paradoxical (Wollheim 1969: 84). Yet, any real world, and hence fallible, decision procedure involves accepting some distinction between the legitimacy of the process and one's view of the result (Waldron 1999: 246). After all, a court may also produce results litigants or observers disagree with, but will be accepted none the less because it satisfies procedural norms of due process. The distinctiveness of the democratic process lies in its non-dominating character. For it involves accepting one's own view as just one among others – even if one feels passion-ately about it, because others feel just as passionately on the other side. Democratic citizens must step back from their own preferred views and acknowledge that equal concern and respect are owed to their fellows as bearers of alternative views. It is only if we possess some such detach-ment that we can live on equal (non-dominating) terms in circumstances of political disagreement by finding workable ways to agree even though we disagree.

Below I shall argue that the most common way of organizing the democratic process in modern societies – as a competitive election between parties for a majority of the people's votes – is constitutional in the polit-ical sense, albeit without the need of any formal legal codification within a written constitution. That is, it offers a political system that provides reasonable protection for the constitutional goods of rights and the rule of law. However, before doing so, I want to look at two republican arguments for a legal conception of the constitution – the first as a mech-anism for protecting ideally democratic outcomes, the second as a means for democratic procedures.

Republicanism and Substantive Legal Constitutionalism

Philip Pettit offers a prominent example of a republican argument for a substantive view of constitutions as securing non-arbitrary outcomes. He maintains that arbitrary rule, and hence domination, arises when no guarantees exist to ensure that governmental and other power holders "track the common recognizable interests" of those affected

(Pettit 1997: 56, 184; 2000: 107). For only the pursuit of such genuine public interests can treat all with equal concern and respect. He suggests that a process of rights-based judicial review, supplemented by various contestatory democratic mechanisms, offers the most appropriate means to achieve this goal. If we see rights as protecting the basic common interests of all individuals, judges as the impartial arbitrators of this structural framework able to ensure all power holders abide by these standards, and popular contestatory mechanisms as a final safeguard to make sure all follow the rules of the game, then we would seem secure from arbitrary rule (Pettit 1997: ch. 6).

The success of this argument involves us being able to come up with an objective account of "common recognizable interests" and our accepting the legitimacy of a constitutional court as their best guardian. Yet both these elements are doubtful. Pettit attempts to get round the worry that one might be deferring simply to some individual's or group's view of common interests by imagining they have emerged from a hypothetical democratic process. A "common interest", he writes, is one supported by "cooperatively avowable considerations" – that is "considerations such that were the population holding discussions about what it ought to cooperate in collectively providing, then they could not be dismissed as irrelevant" (Pettit 2000: 108). If autonomy is regarded as being able to choose on the basis of reasons, then – so the argument goes – we can surely model a description of the public interest that is non-arbitrary if it is based on reasons none could reject, and so treats all equally as autonomous agents.

This thesis substitutes an idealized apolitical democratic process, of the kind deliberative democrats tend to advocate, for real democratic politics. No doubt, hypothetical reasoners who are suitably abstracted from their core commitments in some way might be able to reach such a consensual agreement. However, that begs the question of the uncontroversial character of these abstractions. All such attempts, be it Habermas's "Ideal Speech Situation" (Habermas 1990) or Rawls's "Original Position" (Rawls 1971: ch. 3), rest on disputable assumptions about human nature and social causality that reflect the conclusions their advocates seek to generate from them. As Henry Richardson has remarked, in real politics the reasons none can reject is likely to be an empty set (Richardson 2002: 53). Within pluralist societies, the range of core values held by individuals is so wide, and the task of identifying the policies needed to implement them or the consequences that flow from so doing so complex and contested, that almost any proposed reason is likely to conflict with that of someone else.

Unless the constitution can claim to be based on terms none could reasonably reject, and judges can be said to be faithful interpreters of its prescriptions, then judicial review of legislation can only claim legitimacy as non-dominating if it has similar procedural credentials to democracy and can meet the two criteria given in the previous section for acceptable collective decision-making in circumstances of political disagreement. It is unclear that it can. Judges do seem to be claiming a different status to ordinary citizens. After all, their role as constitutional guardians is often justified in terms of their being a check on irrational, self-interested or plain myopic populist sentiments (e.g. Sunstein 1994: 16–18). Yet it is uncertain what grounds these claims. True, they rarely allege superior moral wisdom to ordinary citizens. Their credentials lie in their legal expertise as upholders of the constitution. However, we have now seen the constitution cannot be viewed as an objective fount of moral and political wisdom. Even if it could, we know judges and legal scholars more generally differ on how any given constitution should be interpreted and its implications for particular cases. Moreover, their divisions are often as much ideological and moral as legal, even if they feel obliged to treat them as disagreements about the nature of the law rather than politics and morality.

Far from being above democracy, multimember courts typically resolve their not uncommon disagreements by the very democratic procedures they claim to supersede: majority vote. Yet, the citizen is entitled then to ask why his or her views have counted for less than those of the nine or so figures on the bench. By contrast to elected politicians, judges have no incentives to heed the views of their fellow citizens. The winning majority on the court is simply imposing its opinion over everyone else's because of their status as constitutional court justices. They do have to give reasons for their decision, but citizens and their political representatives have reasons too, and the latter must defend them in the legislature, before the media and in elections. Meanwhile, judicial reasoning is rarely uncontested or immune to reasonable disagreement even among legal experts. Indeed, the reasons behind a given judgment may be disputed by a significant minority on the court itself.

Of course, courts claim to offer a fair and impartial process, where all are treated as equals. But when it comes to the making of decisions about our collective life, they lack the intrinsic fairness and impartiality of the democratic process – that of treating each person's views equally. For a start, litigation is a costly and time consuming business, with constitutional courts perforce having to be highly selective as to which cases they hear. When they do so, the case is presented as a dispute between two litigants and the only persons and arguments with standing have to relate to the points of law that have been raised by those concerned. Such legalism is vital in what one might call the "normal" judicial process, being intimately linked to the rule of law in the formal sense of rule by known and consistently interpreted laws. But it is inappropriate for determining the bearing of fundamental political principles on the collective life of the community. In this sort of decision, the limits imposed by the legal process risk excluding important considerations in ways that may be arbitrary so far as the general issues raised by a case are concerned. Restricted access to and standing before the court, certainly means not all potentially relevant concerns have an equally fair chance of being presented. Meanwhile, it is ultimately judges' views that count. They may be counted equally, but they are more equal than all the other citizens with an interest in the decision. Given their freedom to interpret the law in diverse and inconsistent ways, according to the moral, ideological and legal positions they hold, with no more authority than any other legal interpreter apart from the mere fact that they are in a position to impose their opinion, their rule cannot be other than arbitrary and hence dominating.

Almost in recognition of this fact, many arguments for improving the legitimacy of judicial review turn on making the judges subject to some form of idealized democratic process of selection, such as having them mirror the racial and gender balance of the wider community. However, there can be no guarantee that such artificial attempts to produce a microcosm of society will reflect the same balance of opinions as would result from all citizens having an equal voice. At best, it will amount to a rough approximation that involves the selectors and those selected deciding which issues are most salient for particular groups of people, with many of these groupings being somewhat arbitrary categorizations so far as their diverse membership is concerned. Such apolitical schemes also remove the key mechanism possessed by electors for ensuring the elected respond to their evolving concerns – the capacity to remove them from office should they fail.

Does the possibility of contestation get around these difficulties? Not in the form Pettit envisages it. He has distinguished what he calls "authorial" from "editorial" democracy (Pettit 2000, 2005). The former suggests the people in some way propose public policies, while the latter simply allows them to ensure rulers adhere to publicly declared rules and standards. Thus, editorial democracy might be satisfied by having some sort of statutory watchdog, such as an Ombudsman, to whom citizens could appeal. Yet, this account assumes that the constitutional rules are uncontroversially in the public interest and a consensus exists as to their meaning – the trouble lies with the odd rogue judge or mistaken judgment. However, the difficulty lies deeper than this. The problem is that we disagree about both rules and judgments. In which case, we need a process of the kind described above that treats all views as deserving equal respect in the authorizing, if not literally in the authorship, of the decision.

If we had good constitutional rules and virtuous and sagacious judges to enforce them, then arguably the domination of arbitrary rule might be overcome. Whereas the Enlightened Despot is enlightened only at his or her pleasure, the good laws bind the upright and wise judges. Of course, even such paragons might have the odd off day – hence the need for a negative, contestatory check on their actions. However, we can now see such prudential guarantees are insufficient, for this proposal rests on very dubious foundations. We simply do not have fail safe ways of ascertaining whether the laws are good and the judges have the requisite expertise, for there is no outcome based process for doing so.

Republicanism and Procedural Legal Constitutionalism

At this point, a process-based version of legal constitutions comes into play, which advocates that the purpose of written and justiciable constitutions should be to uphold democratic procedures rather than to determine what the results of such procedures should be (Ely 1980). For it will be objected that none of the above rules out the need to have a constitution that ensures that the democratic process is itself fair and open. Indeed, some republican theorists, such as Frank Michelman

(1988, 1989) and Cass Sunstein (1988), have made a concern with the constitutionalization of such matters as voting rights and campaign finance the touch stone of a republican approach to legal constitutionalism. However, a major difficulty exists with a procedural approach: namely, that when policies are reviewed on procedural grounds, such review either proves vacuous or involves a hypothetical account of what policy ought to have been adopted in ideal procedural circumstances. In other words, it turns into the outcome or results-based substantive approach (Dworkin 1986a: 57–69). Some theorists have concluded that nothing distinctive can be said about procedures, therefore. Whatever the problems, we simply have no choice but to defend certain outcomes as desirable and attempt to secure them in as efficient a way as possible (Raz 1998b: 45–6).

If true, this would make a procedural form of republican constitutionalism of any kind a non-starter. However, this argument moves too fast, for several distinctively procedural issues remain. Indeed, even the outcome approach begs the resolution of certain procedural considerations. Why is this? For a start, it will be impossible to specify all outcomes in advance and detail the most suitable procedures for each of them. Rather, it will be necessary to guide institutional design by certain general considerations about how given procedures are likely to work in reaching their conclusions – their capacity to canvass all relevant views, to sift the evidence in an impartial manner, to be decisive and so on. Even if we assume no potential disagreement about outcomes, at least some of these issues will have to be settled in relative ignorance of the particular outcomes we might want to secure. Of course, once we factor in disagreement, then the need to abstract even further from specific outcomes and focus on notions of procedural equity, efficiency and effectiveness becomes even greater.

Second, precisely because we cannot specify all the outcomes in advance, and so have to merely propose procedures likely to produce good results, whatever procedures we choose will almost certainly throw up a bad outcome at some time or other. In these circumstances, we will have to give the legitimacy of the procedures an independent normative weight with regard to outcomes. This will be true even if we hand such questions to a constitutional court. Of course, that does not mean we need accept the outcome as the right one. But we will still have to accept the prevailing procedure as the legitimate means for overturning it.

Finally, we have seen the avoidance of domination gives us a reason to prefer procedures that instantiate a right to participate over those that do not. From this perspective, even if judges could be relied on to reach good outcomes when deciding constitutional questions, it would be procedurally illegitimate for them to do so. As we saw, this would be so not just for prudential or instrumental reasons, but for intrinsic ones relating to equality of respect.

These considerations get round a further objection from theorists of the substantive view. They point out that even if we do not necessarily disagree about procedures for the same reasons as we disagree about outcomes, as some accounts make it appear, we nevertheless can disagree just as fervently about procedures as we do about outcomes. After all, different procedural concerns underlie arguments for different voting arrangements, prioritizing parliamentary or presidential systems, the merits and demerits of unicameralism as opposed to bicameralism, and so on. Bur if our disagreements on procedures are on all fours with those about outcomes, then, these critics argue, why not pass on to the interesting topic straight away (Raz 1998b: 47). However, we can now see we have no choice but to prioritize procedures over outcomes because we have no way of knowing what all these last will be (Waldron 2006: 1345–6). We have to settle our disagreements over the former at least in part as a way for deciding future disagreements about the latter. Though outcome considerations will be relevant to the design of procedures, these will need to be general rather than specific. To the extent they raise distinct issues concerning the legitimacy of the process, then the avoidance of domination points clearly toward those that allow citizens views to be counted on an equal basis.

These arguments might seem to be compatible with a constitution that explicitly enshrines only procedures. For example, the Australian constitution contains no bill of rights. It merely describes the machinery of federal decision-making, outlining the processes to be used and the competences of the different levels of government. Although a standing temptation exists to read rights into such a procedural constitution and employ them for the judicial review of legislation, that can – and for long periods has been – resisted. Meanwhile, a procedural legal constitutionalist might maintain that having some fixed account of procedures is necessary to prevent an otherwise infinite regress. For, if we prioritize procedures, then which procedures do we employ to select the procedures, and so on? (Michelman 1997: 162–5;

Richardson 2002: 67). Some procedure will be needed to set up the preferred procedure, which will itself be contentious in certain aspects. Yet, this problem will bedevil the writing of the constitution itself. Seeing the constitution as the product of constitutional politics will not get around the problem. Some republican theorists, such as Michelman and (when in republican mode) Habermas, get tempted back into a hypothetical "ideal" procedure to resolve this issue. In different ways, they argue that democracy itself assumes certain norms. However, we saw how such "substantive" proceduralism proves purely circular. The "method" used to ground the approved political rights builds those rights into its very design. As such, from the perspective of those who hold alternative views, it will appear arbitrary.

We simply have to grasp this procedural nettle and start from some-where – be that the "already existing" political system, or – in the case of new regimes emerging from war or revolution – with whatever arrangements can be cobbled together to get the process of designing a regime off to a start. But having done so, the very fact that disagreements about process will be ongoing argues against constitutionalizing these procedures. Rather, they must be left open so we may rebuild the ship at sea – employing, as we must, the prevailing procedures to renew and reform those self-same procedures. Some legal constitutionalists fear such arrangements will be self-serving and risk being highly unstable. They claim a role for the courts as neutral third party arbitrators in such areas. However, as *Bush v. Gore* (531 US 98) revealed all too clearly, judges have just as much an interest in the outcome of elections as other citizens – possibly more, since the likely impact on their institution of a given politician coming to power is more direct and predictable than it is for most people. Meanwhile, the evidence of the US Supreme Court suggests courts to be highly reluctant to act in this area and remove the abuses most of these republican procedural constitutional-ists correctly identify in the American political system. That record of judicial inaction compares unfavorably with the slow, incremental yet profound and progressive constitutional reforms achieved by normal political processes in Britain and New Zealand, say. So there would appear to be no overwhelming empirical objections to disturb the basic nor-mative case for a thorough-going democratic proceduralism that goes all the way down.

It should be noted that this argument for the democratic process as self-constituting is also at variance with treating a procedural constitution as the product of periodic moments of democratic constitutional politics that bind the normal political process in between (e.g. as Ackerman 1991 proposes). First, the qualities said to distinguish constitutional from normal democratic politics reflect a version of the idealized model of deliberative democracy criticized above. The aim is to ensure the constitution can only be changed when proponents of reform can command a near consensus by restricting amendments to super majorities. Such a consensus, it is argued, is only likely to emerge when citizens drop self-interested concerns and focus only on the public welfare. We have seen, though, how the epistemic claims for democracy as a producer of good outcomes are limited. As the eighteenth amendment to the US Constitution, prohibiting the sale of alcohol, revealed, moral super majoritarianism can have disastrous consequences. However, if the main virtue of democracy is procedural, offering fairness in deciding between competing views, then that is impugned by limiting democratic decisions on constitutional matters to special occasions involving a higher than normal majority. The effect of such arrangements is to unfairly weight the decision toward maintenance of the status quo (Rae 1975). To do so is arbitrary and a source of domination if there is no good reason to believe most amendments will tend to detract from rather than add to the existing constitution. In fact, the likely result is the privileging of the already privileged. Second, in between democratic constitutional moments citizens will be subject to the dominating and arbitrary rule of judges as analyzed above, who will have a superior position to them as interpreters of the constitution. Thus, the republican concern with non-domination means we must see normal democratic politics as constitutive. I now turn to exploring how far it is also constitutional.

The Democratic Constitution

As I noted above, constitutions in the political sense are sometimes dismissed as a mere description of the political system (e.g. Raz 1998a: 153). In that case, any political system – even dictatorships – could be said to possess a constitution. To avoid this fate, a political process must be said to foster certain sorts of constitutional good if it is to be designated as being in and of itself a constitution. In particular, it must constrain power from being wielded in ways that do not consult the rights and interests of citizens, on the one hand, or fail to treat them in an equitable fashion, as equal under the law, on the other. However, as I noted above, the long shadow of the American constitution has also influenced the ways republicans think about these processual issues. For example, Pettit's two criteria for such mechanisms, what he terms the counter-majoritarian and the dispersal of power conditions (Pettit 1997: 173, 177–83), both reflect the ways the pioneering American "modern" republicans, such as Madison, allegedly conceived of the separation of powers and the federal division of power (see Madison in Hamilton *et al.* 2003, no. 10, p. 51, and Dahl 1957: ch. 1, though Dahl has acknowledged Madison later changed his mind, Dahl 2002: 36–7, and see Madison in Hamilton *et al.* 2003, no. 58, p. 286 and the discussion in McGann 2004: 57–8). Such devices have come to be seen as necessary constitutional checks on democracy and the potential for "majority tyranny". In fact, though, their origins predate the development of mass democratic systems and rest on erroneous notions of the nature of democratic societies and decision making.

The classic republican doctrine of the "mixed constitution" assumed the division of society into different classes with distinct interests: namely, the people, the aristocracy, and the monarchy (Bellamy 1996: 440–2). The crux was to achieve a balance between these three groups. The majority in this context referred to the largest group – that of the common people. Later republicans attempted to apply this thinking to a formally classless society. These early theorists of popular democracy continued to fear the propertyless had distinct interests from the rest of the population and might use their electoral muscle to redistribute resources from the rich to the poor. A related worry concerned various self-interested factions who might exploit populist policies to obtain power and pursue their own ends. They advocated counter-majoritarian measures – which mainly involved reworking the older ways of dispersing power – to guard against these possibilities.

The separation of power between different branches of government was an adaptation of the "mixed constitution" and the attempt to balance the interests of different social groups (Bellamy 1996: 442–7). It was supposed to prevent either the majority group in the legislature or a populist executive being in a position to enact laws in their own interest. Bicameralism offered a further check, with the second chamber supposedly representing both longer term interests and, within a federal system, those of different regions. Yet, a prime effect of such mechanisms has been to multiply veto points and produce *imbalances* that favor vested interests and privileged positions. As such, they have invariably had a regressive impact. For example, in the US it enabled the state and federal courts to strike down some 150 pieces of labor legislation between 1885 and 1935 of an analogous kind to those passed by western democracies free from such constraints over roughly the same period (Waldron 1999: 288). Change only came when chronic economic depression and war allowed a hugely popular President with a large legislative majority to overcome judicial and other barriers to social reform.

Of course, opponents of such social legislation rarely argue on self-interested grounds. Rather, they contend they are upholding the property rights necessary for a dynamic economic system that it is in the public interest to keep. Hence the need to give these rights constitutional protection against myopic majoritarian calls for redistribution. However, proponents of social justice mount a similarly principled case that also appeals to arguments for economic efficiency, and seek likewise to constitutionalize social rights. Such debates are a prime source of "reasonable disagreement" in contemporary politics – indeed, the ideological divide between Left and Right provides the principal political cleavage in most democracies (Klingermann, Hofferbert & Budge 1994). The enduring character of this division arises to a large degree from genuine difficulties in specifying what a commitment to liberty and equality actually entails in terms either of social arrangements or particular policy recommendations. Views on both tend to be subject to a certain amount of guesswork and constant updating in the light of experience and evolving circumstances (Gallie 1956). Constitutionalizing either position simply biases the debate toward the dominant view of the time, usually that of the then hegemonic groups, by constraining the opportunities for critique and the equal consideration of interests.

By contrast, we have seen how a prime rationale of democracy lies in its enshrining political equality by providing fair procedures whereby such disagreements can be resolved. That this is also a constitutional process arises from the way it incorporates the old notion of balance in a new and dynamic form, so that affected individuals are moved to abide by the classical injunction of "hearing the other side" that lies at the heart of procedural accounts of justice (Hampshire 1999: 21). This requirement calls for the weighing of the arguments for and against any policy, and the attempt to balance them in the decision. It also involves opportunities to contest and improve policies should they fail to be implemented correctly, have unanticipated consequences – including failure, or cease to be appropriate due to changed circumstances. Finally, it renders rulers accountable and responsive to the ruled, preventing them seeing themselves as a class apart with distinct interests of their own. These qualities offer a procedural approach to showing individuals equal concern and respect.

All three senses of balance are present in majority voting in elections between competing parties. This mechanism promotes the equal weighing of arguments in order to show equal respect, produces balanced decisions that demonstrate equal concern, and involves counter-balances that offer possibilities for opposition and review, thereby providing incentives for responsive and improved decision-making on the part of politicians. Let's take each in turn.

I have already remarked how one person, one vote respects people as equals. In May's terms, it is anonymous, neutral, and positively responsive as well as decisive (May 1952). However, notorious problems potentially arise with three or more options (Arrow 1968). As Arrow and his followers have shown, in these circumstances any social ordering of individual preferences, not least majority rule, is likely to be arbitrary. Yet, though logically possible, cycles and the resulting problems of instability, incoherence or manipulation turn out to be rare (Mackie 2003). The range of options considered by both the electorate and legislatures is considerably fewer than the multifarious rankings people might offer of the total range of policy issues. Instead, they choose between a small number of party programs. Parties and the ideological traditions they represent have the effect of socializing voters so that their preferences resemble each other sufficiently for cycles to be unusual and eliminable by relatively simple decision rules that help voters select the package of policies containing their most favored options. In this respect, the aggregative phase of elections is always prefaced by a deliberative phase. While this deliberation may not produce consensus, it can shape preferences sufficiently to curtail the set of rankings the final decision procedure has to deal with by weeding out purely self-interested preferences and forcing large bodies of very different groups of citizens to produce an agreed agenda that reflects certain general normative commitments (Miller 1992; Dryzek & List 2003). And though voting systems may produce different results, the choice between them need not be regarded as arbitrary – all the realistic contenders can make legitimate claims to fairness and possess well known advantages and disadvantages that make them suited to different social circumstances (Mackie 2003).

It might be objected that these effects result from elites controlling party agendas, making them instruments of domination (Bachrach 1967). Yet party programs have been shown to alter over time in ways frequently at variance with the interests of entrenched social and economic groups. To a remarkable degree, election campaigns determine policy, with party discipline rendering politicians far more like electoral delegates than trustees (Klingermann, Hofferbert & Budge 1994). Party competition also plays a key role in the production of balanced decisions. To win elections, parties have to bring together broad coalitions of opinions and interests within a general program of government. Even under PR systems, where incentives may exist for parties to appeal to fairly narrow constituencies, they need to render their programs compatible with potential coalition partners to have a chance of entering government. In each of these cases, majorities are built through the search for mutually acceptable compromises that attempt to accommodate a number of different views within a single complex position (Bellamy 1999: ch. 5). Such compromises are sometimes criticized as unprincipled and incoherent (Dworkin 1986b: 178–9), encouraging "pork barrel politics" in which voters get bought off according to their ability to influence the outcome rather than the merits of their case. Despite a system of free and equal votes, some votes can count for more than others if they bring campaigning resources, are "deciding" votes, or can ease the implementation of a given policy. However, different political resources tend to be distributed around different sections of the community (Dahl 1989: Part 5), while their relative importance and who holds them differs according to the policy. Democratic societies are also invariably characterized by at least some cross-cutting cleavages that bind different groups together on different issues. Many of these bonds relate not to interests in the narrow economic sense, but shared values. After all, the purely self-interested voter would not bother going to the polls (Brennan & Lomasky 1993).

These features of democratic politics create inducements to practice reciprocity and so support solidarity and trust between citizens. Aptly described as mid-way between self-interested bargaining and ethical universalism (Gutmann & Thompson 1996: ch. 2), reciprocity involves an attempt to accommodate others within some shareable package of policies. This attempt at mutual accommodation does not produce a synthesis or a consensus, since it contains many elements those involved would reject if taken in isolation. Rather, it responds to the different weights voters place on particular policies or dimensions of a problem – either allowing trade-offs to emerge, or obliging those involved to adopt a mutual second best when too many aspects are in conflict (Bellamy 1999: ch. 4; Richardson 2002: ch. 11). In sum, the best is not made the enemy of the good. So, those opposed on both public spending and foreign policy, but ranking their importance differently, can accept a package that gives each what they value most. Likewise, civil partnership can offer an acceptable second best to opponents and proponents of gay marriage.

In circumstances of reasonable disagreement, such compromises recognize the rights of others to have their views treated with equal concern as well as respect. They legitimately reflect the balance of opinion within society (Bellamy 1999: ch. 4). Naturally, some groups may still feel excluded or dissatisfied, while the balance between them can alter as interests and ideals evolve with social change. The counterbalances of party competition come in here. The presence of permanent opposition and regular electoral contests means that governments will need to respond to policy failures and alterations in the public mood brought about by new developments. The willingness of parties to alter their policies is often seen as evidence of their unprincipled nature and the basically self-interested motives of politicians and citizens alike. However, this picture of parties cynically changing their spots to court short term popularity is belied by the reality. Leap-frogging is remarkably rare, not least because they and their core support retain certain key ideological commitments to which changes in policy have to be adapted (Klingermann, Hofferbert & Budge 1994). Nevertheless, that parties see themselves as holding distinctive rather than diametrically opposed views renders competition effective, producing convergence on the median voter, which is generally the Condorcet winner (Ordeshook 1986: 245–57). It also provides protection for minorities. Because an electoral majority is built from minorities and is prone to cycling coalitions, a ruling group will do well not to rely on a minimal winning coalition and to exclude other groups completely – thereby reducing the possibility of such cycles. In this respect, majority rule protects minorities. Either a currently excluded minority has a

181

good chance of being part of a future winning coalition, or – for that very reason – is likely not be entirely excluded by any winning coalition keen to retain its long term power (McGann 2004: 56, 71).

By contrast, the separation of powers removes (in the case of courts) or weakens (in the case of elected second chambers) such incentives, for the various branches of government can hardly be viewed as competing in the requisite sense (Brennan & Hamlin 1994). The ability of courts particularly to isolate themselves from public pressure is often seen as an advantage. But it can lead to blame shifting as responsibility gets divided, with each branch seeking to attribute the political and financial costs of their decisions to one or more of the others. Federal arrangements can often have similar drawbacks. These divisions also favor immobilism, advantage ideologically concentrated over more dispersed majorities, even allowing extremes to muster strategic blocking points, and far from protecting minorities, as Guinier (1994) believes, can lead to their complete exclusion (McGann 2004).

Of course, the more polarized social divisions are, the harder it will be for such mechanisms to work. The danger of majority domination increases in societies deeply divided on ethnic, religious or linguistic lines. In these conditions, democratic arrangements generally require measures to secure minority influence. Strictly speaking, many of these need not be considered as anti-majoritarian. Enhancing proportionality simply represents a fairer way of calculating the majority than plurality systems, say, while greater regional autonomy for territorially concentrated minorities merely devolves decision making over certain policies to a different majority. Thus, many of the systems Lijphart (1984) famously characterized as "consensual" democracies are really "majoritarian" rather than "plurality" democracies, with such countries as the Netherlands and Sweden that have majority rule legislatures and few checks and balances performing notably better with regard to minority inclusiveness to countries such as the United States that institutionalize supermajoritarian rule (Dahl 1989: 189–90). Indeed, where it proves necessary to go beyond proportionality by giving minorities a veto or an equal or much inflated role in executive power or federal law making, the danger arises that the checks and balances arising from party competition get eroded. The elites of the different social segments gain an interest in stressing the particular divisions they reflect over other differences or any shared concerns, with debates about the organization of government undermining accountability for its conduct (Barry

1975). However, a legal constitution is unlikely to counter such tendencies. It will either reproduce them, its legitimacy depending on the degree to which the court and constitution reflect the main political divisions, or it will rightly or wrongly become identified with the dominant elite who have the greatest interest in preserving unity (Dahl 1989: 190–1).

What about "discreet and insular minorities?" As Mark Tushnet counsels, "we have to distinguish between *mere* losers and minorities who lose because they cannot protect themselves in politics" (Tushnet 1999: 159). Within most democracies, the number of minorities incapable of allying with others to secure a degree of political influence is very small. However, there are undeniably certain groups, such as asylum seekers or the Roma, who have little or no ability to engage in politics. In such cases, the necessity for legal constitutional protection might appear undeniable. Even here, though, three caveats are in order. First, such protection will only be necessary if it is assumed that: *a*) such minorities are at risk from widespread prejudice from a majority of the population and their elected representatives, and *b*) the judiciary are free from such prejudices. However, most defenders of legal constitutionalism accept it is unlikely to have much effect unless the rights it enshrines express a common ideology of the population about the way their society should be governed – that these rights are the "people's law", not just "lawyers' law" (Raz 1998a: 154). As the example of Nazi Germany reveals, widespread popular prejudices against a minority are likely to be shared by a significant proportion of the ruling elite, including the legal establishment, and where they are not the judiciary is unlikely to be able to withstand sustained popular and governmental pressure (Ely 1980: 181; Dahl 1989: 173). So judicial review will only afford protection where there is a temporary lapse from commonly acknowledged standards. Such cases – which need to be balanced against those where the judiciary may similarly fall short – do not offer a basis for a general defense of strong judicial review. Yet, it may be difficult to distinguish the exceptional case, where it may be legitimate and beneficial for the judiciary to intervene, from the standard cases where it is not.

Second, as I noted, when the judiciary do intervene they do so in limited ways. Courts naturally view even constitutional questions from the narrow perspective of legality and formal instances of discrimination or unfairness. As a result, their judgments risk being either too narrow or too broad (Tushnet 1999: 160–3). They either capture only clear *ultra vires* instances of executive or administrative discretion, or treat all attempts to distinguish between categories of individual as potentially discriminatory. Meanwhile, informal – largely structural – exclusions arising from unequal access to various kinds of resource can rarely be addressed, since these do not fit the traditional legal model of compensatory justice. Moreover, structural injustice usually requires redistributive measures that courts can only tackle through general regulatory measures. As the example of bussing in the United States reveals, such instruments can be too crude – failing to consider knock on effects for other related forms of public expenditure, on say health or housing (Sunstein 1993: 147–9).

Finally, judicial foreclosure can impair or distort political mobilization, yet is rarely successful in its absence. The key "liberal" US Supreme Court decisions of the 1960s to which most contemporary legal constitutionalists refer, such as *Roe v. Wade* and *Brown v. Board of Education*, all reflected emerging national majorities. For example, liberal legislation in most states meant that well before *Roe* some 600,000 lawful abortions were performed a year (Sunstein 1993: 147). The narrow terms in which *Roe* was decided had the negative effect of "privatizing" abortion rather than treating it as a social issue requiring public funds (Glendon 1991: 58–60). It has also centered political activity on capturing the court rather than engaging with the arguments of others. By contrast, the extensive moral discussion in the UK Commons of the Medical Termination of Pregnancy Bill, that occupies some 100 pages in Hansard, compares favourably with the couple of paragraphs of principled, as opposed to legal, argument in *Roe*. In particular, it led opponents to acknowledge the respectful hearing given to their views, which went some way to reconciling them to the decision. Indeed, the eventual policy includes numerous forms of principled "compromise" to accommodate a range of moral concerns, including the evolving status of the fetus (Waldron 2006: 1346–7). Likewise, the civil rights movement had far more impact than *Brown*. Ten years after this landmark decision no more than 1.2 percent of black children attended desegregated schools in the Southern states (Sunstein 1993: 146–7). Desegregation only truly gained momentum following the passage by large majorities in Congress of the Civil Rights Act and the Voting Rights Act in 1964 and 1965.

In sum, even where legal constitutionalism appears strongest, it is only as effective as the democratic constitution can make it. Only democracy can galvanize popular support around a measure by reassuring citizens of its fairness by balancing it against other considerations and indicating that a degree of reciprocity underlies measures that may be costly for them. In the United States, labor legislation, the New Deal, environmental reforms, deregulation, gender equality have all been products of democratic politics, effecting constitutional change more than any isolated Court decision. Indeed, they were often passed against judicial opposition. Likewise, in Britain the Representation of the People's Acts of 1918 and 1928 were enacted against judicial hostility, while such measures as the National Assistance Act 1948 and the Sex Discrimination Act 1975 were legislative not judicial initiatives.

Conclusion

This chapter has defended "actually existing democracy" as an effective constitutive and constitutional mechanism. Yet, even a sympathetic reader might wonder if this defense of the republican credentials of modern democratic politics against eighteenth-century constitutionalism comes a little late, when the "owl of Minerva" has well and truly flown by. Though vibrant in the nineteenth and twentieth centuries, party politics is now in a sorry state (Mair 2006). Trust in politicians and parties is at an all-time low in most advanced democracies, with party membership and voter turn out in steady decline, albeit haltingly and with variations between countries. Quite apart from the shortcomings of the actors involved, these mechanisms are also felt to be ill-suited to securing effective and equitable government in today's complex and globalizing societies. The electorate is too vast and diverse, the problems too technical, the scale of government too large for citizens to be able effectively to relate to each other, the tasks of politics or the institutions and persons assigned to tackle them.

I have two observations to make on this pessimistic scenario. First, the criticisms of non-majoritarian democratic mechanisms still stand. Advocates of the ever more prominent use of non-majoritarian forms of delegated governance habitually defend them against charges of arbitrariness by emphasizing their deliberative decision-making character, on the one hand, and their subjection to rights-based judicial review, on the other (e.g. Majone 1998). But if both these mechanisms are themselves potential sources of arbitrary rule, then the danger may actually have been deepened rather than lessened. Second, the only legitimate and effective way to ensure all citizens are treated with equal concern and respect is to have procedures that provide them with equal power to make their rulers responsive and accountable to their rights and interests. In sum, democracy may have to be remade to suit new conditions but it cannot be abandoned.

ACKNOWLEDGMENTS

I am grateful to Cécile Laborde for her suggestions for and on this chapter. Early drafts were delivered to the LSE Political Theory seminar and as a Keynote Lecture at a conference on "Constitutional Values" organized by the Academia Sinica in Taiwan. I wish to thank participants at both events for their helpful comments, particularly Rodney Barker, John Charvet, Paul Kelly, Christian List, and Anne Phillips, at the first, and Carl Shaw and Ying-wen Tsai, at the second.

REFERENCES

Ackerman, B. (1991). *We the People: Foundations*. Cambridge, MA: Harvard University Press.

Amy, D. (1987). *The Politics of Environmental Mediation*. New York: Columbia University Press.

Arrow, K. (1968). *Social Choice and Individual Values*, 2nd ed. New Haven: Yale University Press.

Bachrach, P. (1967). *The Theory of Democratic Elitism*. Boston: Little, Brown.

Barry, B. (1967). "The Public Interest." In A. Quinton (ed.), *Political Philosophy*. Oxford: Oxford University Press, pp. 112–26.

Barry, B. (1979). "Is Democracy Special?" In P. Laslett and J. W. Fishkin (eds.), *Philosophy, Politics and Society*. Fifth Series. New Haven: Yale University Press, pp. 155–96.

Barry, B. (1975). "Political Accomodation and Consociational Democracy." *British Journal of Political Science*, 5, 477–505.

Bellamy, R. (1996). "The Political Form of the Constitution: The Separation of Powers, Rights and Representative Democracy", *Political Studies*, 44, 436–56.

Bellamy, R. (1999). *Liberalism and Pluralism: Towards a Politics of Compromise*. London: Routledge.

Bellamy, R. (2007). *Political Constitutionalism: A Republican Defence of the Constitutionality of Democracy*. Cambridge: Cambridge University Press.

Berlin, I. (1969). *Four Essays on Liberty*. Oxford: Oxford University Press.

Bohman, J. (1996). *Public Deliberation: Pluralism, Complexity and Democracy*. Cambridge, MA: MIT Press.

Brennan, G. and Hamlin, A. (1994). "A Revisionist View of the Separation of Powers." *Journal of Theoretical Politics*, 6, 345–68.

Brennan, G. and Lomasky, L. (1993). *Democracy and Decision*. Cambridge: Cambridge University Press.

Buchanan, J. M. and Congleton, R. D. (1998). *Politics by Principle, Not Interest*. Cambridge: Cambridge University Press.

Buchanan, J. M. and Musgrave, R. A. (1999). *Public Finance and Public Choice: Two Contrasting Visions of the State*. Cambridge, MA: MIT Press.

Buchanan, J. M. and Tullock, G. (1965). *The Calculus of Consent: Logical Foundations of Constitutional Democracy*. Anne Arbor: University of Michigan Press.

Christiano, T. (1996). *The Rule of the Many: Fundamental Issues in Democratic Theory*. Boulder, CO: Westview Press.

Dahl, R. A. (1957). *A Preface to Democratic Theory*. Chicago: University of Chicago Press.

Dahl, R. A. (1989). *Democracy and Its Critics*. New Haven: Yale University Press.

Dahl, R. A. (2002). *How Democratic is the American Constitution?* New Haven: Yale University Press.

Dryzek, J. and List, C. (2003). "Social Theory and Deliberative Democracy: A Reconciliation." *British Journal of Political Science*, 33, 1–28.

Dworkin, R. (1986a). *A Matter of Principle*. Oxford: Clarendon Press.

Dworkin, R (1986b). *Law's Empire*. London: Fontana.

Dworkin, R. (1996). *Freedom's Law: The Moral Reading of the American Constitution*. Oxford: Oxford University Press.

Elkin, S. (1996). "Madison and After: The American Model of Political Constitutionalism." In R. Bellamy and D. Castiglione (eds.), *Constitutionalism in Transformation: European and Theoretical Perspectives*. Oxford: Blackwell, pp. 180–93.

Ely, J. H. (1980). *Democracy and Distrust: A Theory of Judicial Review*. Cambridge, MA: Harvard University Press.

Gallie, W. B. (1956). "Liberal Morality and Socialist Morality." In P. Laslett (ed.), *Philosophy, Politics and Society*. Oxford: Blackwell, pp. 116–33.

Gambetta, D. (1998). "Claro": An Essay on Discursive Machismo." In J. Elster (ed.), *Deliberative Democracy*. Cambridge: Cambridge University Press.

Glendon, M. A. (1991). *Rights Talk: The Impoverishment of Political Discourse*. New York: The Free Press.

Guinier, L. (1994). *The Tyranny of the Majority: Fundamental Fairness in Representative Democracy*. New York: The Free Press.

Gutmann, A. and Thompson, D. (1996). *Democracy and Disagreement*. Cambridge, MA: Harvard University Press.

Habermas, J. (1990). "Discourse Ethics: Notes on a Programe of Philosophical Justification." In J. Habermas, *Moral Consciousness and Communicative Action*. Cambridge: Polity Press, pp. 43–115.

Hamilton, A., Madison, J., and Jay, J. (2003). *The Federalist with Letters of "Brutus"*, ed. T. Ball. Cambridge: Cambridge University Press.

Hampshire, S. (1999). *Justice is Conflict*. London: Duckworth.

Janis, I. L. (1982). *Groupthink*. Boston: Houghton Mifflin.

Klingermann, H.-D., Hofferbert, R. I. and Budge, I. (1994). *Parties, Policies and Democracy*. Boulder, CO: Westview Press.

Kramer, L. (2004). *The People Themselves: Popular Constitutionalism and Judicial Review*. New York: Oxford University Press.

Lijphart, A. (1984). *Democracies: Patterns of Majoritarian and Consensus Government in Twenty-One Countries*. New Haven: Yale University Press.

Machiavelli, N. (1960). *Discorsi sopra la prima deca di Tito Livio*. In N. Machiavelli, *Il principe e discorsi*, ed. S. Bertelli. Milan: Feltrinelli.

Mackie, G. (2003). *Democracy Defended*. Cambridge: Cambridge University Press.

Mair, P. (2006). *Polity-Scepticism, Party Failings and the Challenge to European Democracy*. Uhlenbeck Lecture 24, NIAS, Wassenaar.

Majone, G. (1998). "Europe's Democratic Deficit: The Question of Standards." *European Law Jounral*, 4, 5–28.

May, K. (1952). "A Set of Independent, Necessary and Sufficient Conditions for Simple Majority Decision." *Econometrica*, 10, 680–4.

McIlwain, C. H. (1958). *Constitutionalism: Ancient and Modern*, rev. ed. New York: Great Seal Books.

Maddox, G. (1982). "A Note on the Meaning of 'Constitution.'" *American Political Science Review*, 76, 80–9.

McGann, A. J. (2004). "The Tyranny of the Supermajority: How Majority Rule Protects Minorities." *Journal of Theoretical Politics*, 16, 53–77.

Michelman, F. (1988). "Law's Republic." *Yale Law Journal*, 97, 1493–1537

Michelman, F. (1989). "Conceptions of Democracy in American Constitutional Argument: Voting Rights." *Florida Law Review*, 41, 443–90.

Michelman, F. (1997). "How Can the People Ever Make the Laws? A Critique of Deliberative Democracy." In J. Bohman and W. Rehg (eds.), *Deliberative Democracy: Essays on Reasons and Politics*. Cambridge: MIT Press, pp. 145–71.

Miller, D. (1992). "Deliberative Democracy and Social Choice." *Political Studies*, 40, 54–67

Oppenheim, F. (1981). *Political Concepts: A Reconstruction*. Oxford: Blackwell.

Ordeshook, P. C. (1986). *Game Theory and Political Theory*. Cambridge: Cambridge University Press.

Paine, T. (1989). "The Rights of Man, Part I." In *Political Writings*, ed. B Kuklick. Cambridge: Cambridge University Press.

Pettit, P. (1997). *Republicanism: A Theory of Freedom and Government*. Oxford: Oxford University Press.

Pettit, P. (2000). "Democracy: Electoral and Contestatory." In I. Shapiro and S. Macedo (eds.), *Designing Democratic Institutions*. New York: New York University Press.

Pettit, P. (2005). "Two Dimensional Democracy, National and International." IILJ Working Paper 2005/8. (History and Theory of International Law Series.)

Polybius (1979). *The Rise of the Roman Empire*, tr. I Scott-Kilvert. Harmondsworth: Penguin.

Rae, D. (1969). "Decision-Rules and Individual Values in Constitutional Choice." *American Political Science Review*, 63, 40–56.

Rae, D. (1075). "The Limits of Consensual Decision." *American Political Science Review*, 69, 1270–94.

Rawls, J. (1971). *A Theory of Justice*. Oxford: Oxford University Press.

Rawls, J. (1993). *Political Liberalism*. New York: Columbia University Press.

Raz, J. (1998a). "On the Authority and Interpretation of Constitutions." In L. Alexander (ed.), *Constitutionalism: Philosophical Foundations*. Cambridge: Cambridge University Press, pp. 152–93.

Raz, J. (1998b). "Disagreement in Politics." *American Journal of Jurisprudence*, 43, 25–52.

Richardson, H. (2002). *Democratic Autonomy: Public Reasoning about the Ends of Policy*. Oxford: Oxford University Press.

Rousseau, J.-J. (1973). *The Social Contract and Discourses*, tr. G. D. H. Cole. London: Dent.

Sandel, M. (1996). *Democracy's Discontent: America in Search of a Public Philosophy*. Cambridge, MA: Harvard University Press.

Sartori, G. (1962). "Constitutionalism: A Preliminary Discussion." *American Political Science Review*, 56, 853–64.

Schumpeter, J. A. (1976). *Capitalism, Socialism and Democracy*. London: Unwin.

Skinner, Q. (1986). "The Paradoxes of Political Liberty." In S. M. McMurrin (ed.), *The Tanner Lectures on Human Values*, vol. VII. Cambridge: Cambridge University Press, pp. 225–50.

Skinner, Q. (1998). *Liberty Before Liberalism*. Cambridge: Cambridge University Press.

Sunstein, C. R. (1988). "Beyond the Republican Revival." *Yale Law Journal*, 97, 1548–58.

Sunstein, C. R. (1993). *The Partial Constitution*. Cambridge, MA: Harvard University Press.

Sunstein, C. R. (1994). "Approaching Democracy: A New Legal Order for Eastern Europe – Constitutionalism and Secession." In C. Brown (ed.), *Political Restructuring in Europe*. London: Routledge.

Sunstein, C. R. (2002). "The Law of Group Polarization." *Journal of Political Philosophy*, 10, 175–95.

Taylor, C. (1979). "What's Wrong with Negative Liberty." In A. Ryan (ed.), *The Idea of Freedom*. Oxford: Oxford University Press, pp. 175–93.

Taylor, C. (1995). *Philosophical Arguments*. Cambridge, MA: Harvard University Press.

Tushnet, M. (1999). *Taking the Constitution Away from the Courts*. Princeton: Princeton University Press.

Waldron, J. (1999). *Law and Disagreement*. Oxford: Oxford University Press.

Waldron, J. (2004). "Judicial Review and Republican Government." In C. Wolfe (ed.), *That Eminent Tribunal: Judicial Supremacy and the Constitution*. Princeton: Princeton University Press, pp. 159–80.

Waldron, J. (2006). "The Core Case against Judicial Review." *The Yale Law Journal*, 115 (2006), 1346–1406.

Weale, A. (1999). *Democracy*. Basingstoke: Macmillan.

Wollheim, R. (1969). "A Paradox in the Theory of Democracy." In P. Laslett and W. G. Runciman (eds.), *Philosophy, Politics and Society*. Second Series. Oxford: Blackwell.

Chapter 8

Nondomination and Transnational Democracy

James Bohman

By reintroducing the important ideal of freedom as nondomination, the republican tradition has significantly altered the landscape of political philosophy. Despite the fruitfulness of this new vocabulary, many basic republican concepts related to it remain relatively underdeveloped. Following the republican adage that "to be free is to be a citizen of a free state," many republicans have assumed for too long that their commitments are inimical to cosmopolitanism, perhaps because of the long association between cosmopolitanism and liberalism. While it is now widely recognized that liberalism has both a cosmopolitan and a nationalist form, a similar conceptual space for republican cosmopolitanism remains unoccupied, even though many Enlightenment defenders of republicanism in the eighteenth century were clearly cosmopolitans. My purpose here is to develop a republican form of cosmopolitanism in contrast with both the thin liberal conception of rights and the thick civic republican conception of membership within a bounded political community. I contend that neither is sufficient to establish the robust nondomination that is possible only on the condition of common liberty.

An obvious way to develop this transnational dimension is through a stronger linkage of nondomination to democratic citizenship. This democratic conception of nondomination could in turn establish the obligation to form a republic of humanity, insofar as just such a political community is required in order to realize nondomination. Indeed, even if fellow citizens within a free state could be said to enjoy nondomination in relation to each other, this status cannot be fully attributed to them so long as they stand in relations of domination to other political communities. A republic of republics is necessary to check the tendencies of democratic republics to establish *imperium* over nonrepublican and technologically less developed communities. Such mastery of others not only denies them the status of humanity that establishes political obligations across communities; it also makes it impossible for the citizens of imperially expansive republics to enjoy secure nondomination at home. It is just this historical tendency that moved Enlightenment republicans from Diderot to Kant to oppose European colonial empires not only for their grave injustices but also as destructive of the common liberty of humanity.

Given the republican emphasis on nondomination, it would be odd indeed for republicans not to be concerned with international politics or to think that relations across communities are causally inert and engender only moral obligations of beneficence. Although no longer the anarchical state of nature, the international system is the location for many forms of domination by powerful state and private actors (Bohman 2004). For example, multinational corporations can exercise *dominum* in the absence of legal norms sufficient to establish justice as regularity that applies across communities, sometimes taken to establish the need for stronger states (Slaughter 2005; Miller, ch. 6 this volume). In the era of globalization, however, new principal/agent relations have created new forms of unaccountable authority as extensions of state authority. War remains a means by which states solve international conflicts, and failed states are unable to check civil wars that spill across borders. The conception of sovereignty tied to freedom as noninterference cannot offer any normatively acceptable solutions to these problems. Yet contemporary republicanism, if it is more directly informed by this anticolonial and cosmopolitan legacy, could offer just such normative resources.

My argument has four steps. First, I show that the version of republicanism that has fueled the current revival is historically incomplete. As historians such as Anthony Pagden and Sankar Muthu have pointed out, a striking feature of the later history of republican thought is its shift away from the modern European state toward a transnational form of community that would be an alternative to colonial empires. In this way, the experience of colonialism deeply transformed the earlier seventeenth and eighteenth century "Commonwealthman" tradition. While much favored by Philip Pettit and others, the legacy of this particular republican tradition has long been marked by its elitism (Pettit 1997; Skinner 1998). Indeed, what is distinctive about later transnational

191

republicanism is the way in which the rejection of European colonialism led to a much stronger distinction between ancient and modern political forms. This objection to "antiquated political forms" included ancient republics as well as monarchies and empires and led to a significant revision of the ideal of nondomination among anticolonial republicans. Second, I develop a distinctly normative conception in its place, according to which nondomination is secure only if one's normative statuses and powers – including one's political memberships – cannot be changed arbitrarily. Third, on the basis of this normative conception of nondomination, basic rights can be taken to be just those normative statuses and powers that are sufficient to secure nondomination. Fourth and finally, I argue that human rights can be given a republican political twist by conceiving them as elaborating the most basic membership status: membership in the human political community. The import of human rights so understood can best be seen by considering the fate of those whom Arendt called "stateless" persons, those who for various reasons lack the standing to make claims on any political community and whose domination is not simply that of slaves. Moreover, if republicans are also committed to democracy, this commitment brings with it the extension of a "democratic minimum," the core of which is the normative power to initiate deliberation that is the basis of common liberty and nondomination.

In order to secure common liberty, a human political community or republic of humanity must be established, for many of the same reasons why republicans have always thought that federal forms should be established. Instead of extolling the virtues of bounded political communities such as Rousseau's Corsica, modern republicans should once again defend transnational political community as an alternative to the tyranny of empire and the renewed willingness of states to engage in war.

Transnational Republicanism: The Enlightenment Opposition to Colonial Empire

The particular political conception of justice that I am defending has now been articulated sufficiently to give it a name: "republican cosmopolitanism." Contrary to the dominant "civic republican" interpretation, republicanism is neither inherently anticosmopolitan nor inseparable from the nation state, and this holds despite the classic republican adage that "to be free is to be a citizen of a free state." As Pettit has shown, the Commonwealthman tradition typically thought of those who possess such liberty as "a people" while also accepting representative government as the primary means by which civil liberty can be secured (Pettit 1997: 29). Such an account, in which the political subjects of republican freedom are peoples, is often thought to be opposed to cosmopolitanism. Like an empire, a world state, it is claimed, would be a "soulless despotism" too distant to be responsive. My aim here is to show that such arguments for bounded communities and peoples as the proper subject of civil liberty are based on contingent historical facts rather than necessary conditions. Rather than a product of ties of common sentiment, communal identification is a product of reciprocal freedom, a shared "measure of nondomination that comes with being a fully incorporated member" (Pettit 1997: 260). This justification does not establish that the identification with any particular community needs to be *exclusive*, since there may be many ways in which such freedom is shared with others.

Critics of liberal democracy, including civic republicans and participatory democrats, think that even the national context is too large for robust democracy. These views often inspire criticisms of globalization as undermining democratic self-determination and as increasing the scope of nondemocratic political authority typical of international institutions. Republican cosmopolitans, including anticolonial English republicans such as Richard Price, turn these democratically motivated arguments around and argue that political rights aimed at freedom from domination supply the normative warrant for democracy beyond the state that is generally lacking in more liberal versions of political cosmopolitanism. Indeed, the "despotic" world state and "bloated" cosmopolis that is the subject of republican criticism is not a political community at all but an undifferentiated empire. Building on the republican arguments for modern institutions such as representative bodies, Enlightenment republicans proposed the political form of a peaceful federation to be the signal institutional innovation of modern republicanism that had finally transcended the limits of all ancient models (Pagden 1995; Muthu 2003).

This democratic form of cosmopolitanism is not a recent innovation. As opposed to the sovereignty of the people in either its Lockean or Rousseauian versions, there is an alternative democratic tradition that recognizes the importance not only of a plurality of democratic forms but also the necessity of transnational institutions in order to overcome modern colonialism as the spur to European globalization. Indeed, many thinkers have used republican ideas to argue for a kind of transnational federalism as the alternative to colonial resurgence of the antiquated political institutions of Empire. For many republicans (including Price, Diderot, and Turgot, among others), federalism had the dispersion of power necessary to overcome the domination of colonies by the center (Pagden 1995: 200). Given that the transnational political problem to be solved was (and remains) domination, these republicans rejected the idea that the size of the polity was the decisive consideration. Indeed, neither hypothetical nor real contractualism based on counterfactual agreement or actual consent is enough to overcome the potential for domination built into sovereignty as hierarchical authority, and colonialism was built upon claims to territory as an extension of sovereignty. But with the emergence of *imperium* abroad, *dominum* within the state inevitably reasserted itself as the metropolitan center sought to control the colonial periphery by escalating its authority and coercive power. As a result, anticolonial republicans argued that the imperial form of European globalization undermined republican checks upon sovereign power at home and abroad. They concluded that the extension of republican institutions beyond the state was the only solution. From Diderot to Kant to Madison, a transnational federation is the solution to the European *imperium*.

In this way, the fundamental experience that informs Enlightenment republicans is their repudiation of two inadequate forms of global political integration: not only did they reject the emergence of a religious community of humanity under the "universal monarchy" of the Christian ruler; but they also rejected the transformation of political community into Empires based on the colonial domination of non-European peoples. The political integration of humanity was a necessary means to avoid the great ills and injustices of colonial domination. The alternative to empire is not the division of the world into autonomous peoples, but rather the creation of federations based on interlocking and self-enhancing relationships between various levels of republican institutions, including ones crossing state boundaries. In this way, the commitment to check *dominium* within the state through institutional differentiation provided the basis for arguments to extend this mechanism to check the state's *imperium* abroad. One consequence for the conquering nation is that the control exercised over its new subjects quickly extends to its own citizens (Pitts 2005). Given such negative feedback relations, the solution is found in large-scale, interactive and more differentiated institutional structures that enhance common liberty across political communities.

The difference between Commonwealthman and Enlightenment republicans is that the latter recognized that extended empires ultimately undermine the constitutional provision of various powers for citizens. Since constitutions apply only to specific communities, they are no longer sufficient to enable "the agent to prevent great ills from happening to them" (Pettit 1997: 69), of which I would include the great evils of modern warfare. The mutual benefits of commerce or the amity among republics was thought to be the source of peace. But it became clear as colonial policy impacted the conduct of government at home that what is required for peace was not just the rule of law, but rather active citizenship and responsive institutions. This means that what is important is not just that citizens have a recognized and shared status, but that decision-making powers are embedded in democratic institutions, so that agents acquire the normative role of citizens and the freedoms and powers that membership provides become the means by which to avoid the ills of war, conquest and economic exploitation. One way in which these ills can be resisted within communities is for citizens to oppose having such obligations of service and taxes imposed upon them, and thus to make executive powers the subject of public debate.

Charles Tilly has argued that warfare has historically been an important mechanism for the introduction of social rights, as the state became more and more dependent on the willingness of its citizens to accept the obligations of military service (Tilly 1990). Republicans took the emergence of modern warfare as evidence for the lack of political rights, especially as conquest emerged at the same time as the means to acquire and control colonial territories. Once the institutional mechanisms of war-making shifted from representative bodies toward much less accountable administrative and executive functions and thus undermined the balance of institutional powers within republics, the capacity of citizens democratically to reject the obligations related to war and preparations for war became greatly reduced. Constitutional provisions alone proved inadequate when security demanded suspending and limiting civil freedoms and entitlements. Such limitations on civil liberties are no less true now than in the eighteenth century, when

195

monarchs sought to censor newspapers and trade journals from publishing information regarding the situation in the colonies (Habermas 1998: 49). Thus, Enlightenment republicans saw a clear negative feedback relationship between the expansion of centralized and executive powers in the international arena and the active powers of citizenship even within the borders of the free state. Indeed, modern warfare shows repeatedly how the relationship between empowered citizenry and international peace has in fact been systematically severed.

The Enlightenment republican critique of the imperial tendencies of states has enormous practical significance for the institutional design of any contemporary republic (Bohman 2007). It suggests that if citizens are to have the means by which to prevent the great evils of war and colonial expansion, then they should demand an international system of institutions that would afford such protections and limit the imperial ambitions of their own states. If we take such modern republican arguments seriously, we need to modify some deep assumptions about the proper location for democracy and the exercise of the powers of citizenship. One possibility is that some supranational institutions must exist if democratic states are to become more rather than less democratic and expand the public space of common liberty even within their borders.

A good starting point arguing for at least some such institutions is the republican analogy between the justifications for federations and for transnational institutions. One of the great benefits of federal arrangements is their ability to deal with questions of complexity and size. Furthermore, contrary to the state demand for exclusive sovereignty and the monopoly of certain powers, federal institutions are based upon an anti-domination principle that Pettit calls the "dispersion of power condition" (Pettit 1997: 177–80) to counteract the tendency toward the centralization of state power. The republican defense of federations and the dispersal of powers across different institutional levels, deliberative bodies, and various offices can be consistently extended transnationally for the sake of realizing freedom from domination. In this way, the dispersion of power condition is best seen as historically variable. Given that some executive powers of the state have already been delegated to international bodies such as the World Trade Organization and to transnational bodies such as NAFTA adjudication boards, the dispersion of power condition has a new range of application.

Reinterpreting Nondomination: Status, Powers, and Citizenship

Much of the debate generated about Pettit's form of republicanism has centered on the fact that his definition of domination is modal: it is the dominator's *potential* "capacity to interfere" on an arbitrary basis in the choices of another. Pettit includes among these capacities "financial clout, political authority, social connections, communal standing, informational access, ideological positions, cultural legitimation and the like" (Pettit 1997: 52). But the capacity to interfere is not a necessary condition for domination, precisely because such a capacity can be exercised by a "nonmastering interferer" (Pettit 1997: 55), such as a government that acts in accordance to the rule of law and also "tracks" the opinions and interests of those who are interfered with. In order for me to avoid domination I must enjoy a "secure and resilient form of noninterference," and thus "be in a position where no one has that power of arbitrary interference and I am correspondingly powerful" (Pettit 1997: 69). These powers derive from the status of being a citizen.

Many critics have pointed out that this conception of domination is overly broad (Friedman, ch. 10 this volume). While correct with respect to the role of the will of the dominator, this criticism overlooks the important sense in which Pettit's concept of nondomination is essentially a membership or status term, which makes the person powerful, or more precisely in possession of "the power to prevent certain ills from happening" (Pettit 1997: 69). Given the myriad sources of potential domination, agents must be very powerful indeed. Previously, Pettit had defined this power of the agent negatively as an "antipower." In this section, I want to recover this neglected conception by making use of the empirical linkage between nondomination and the active powers of citizenship (rather than constitutionally secured status alone) to offer a revision of the basic conception of nondomination. This conception goes beyond the distinction between arbitrary and nonarbitrary interference to see citizenship in terms of normative powers, specifically, the capacity of citizens jointly to create and modify their own obligations and duties rather than having them imposed upon them.

The distinctions between arbitrary and nonarbitrary interference cannot be determined simply by reference to the interests or the wills of the affected parties. Arbitrariness as a predicate makes sense only given the normative background of rights, duties, roles, and institutions that actors take for granted in their social action (including various legal and political rights). For this reason, Henry Richardson has criticized Pettit's republicanism for giving a "nonnormative definition of domination" that concedes too much to liberal non-interference. Richardson argues instead that domination and nondomination are inherently normative notions, and that "the purported exercise of a normative power – the power to modify the rights and duties of others – is essential to the idea of domination" (Richardson 2002: 34). Domination is thus not just the capacity to interfere arbitrarily in another's life, but also the capacity to employ a distinctly normative power that operates against this institutionalized background of normative expectations; it is thus the ability to impose obligations and duties on others arbitrarily. The key here is then to recast the important term "arbitrary" in terms of the use of normative powers.

What is it to use normative powers with respect to obligations, duties and statuses arbitrarily? If we follow Richardson here, it would seem that instances of domination must somehow violate norms and statuses or the expectations that norms and statuses produce. This still leaves domination as the exercise of an arbitrary will rather than as the arbitrary exercise of a normative power (Bohman 2007: ch. 2). Thus, dominators stand in some normative relation to the dominated, as father, or king, or colonial administrator and in these cases exercise the normative power of authority to impose rights and duties, indeed to change the normative statuses of the dominated arbitrarily. This would certainly be tyrannical. However, the "rational" administrator may well decide impartially to impose new duties for the sake of the common good and may even act in conformity with general legal rules that are publicly known. Would this still be domination?

According to this normative account, domination does not require that a power be used arbitrarily in the sense of being a violation of a rule or norm of a practice or even a settled expectation. Rather, domination is the use of normative powers without recourse or remedy for the dominated person. In light of this requirement, Pettit argues that "a suitable legal regime" (Pettit 1997: 35) is necessary for nondomination in the sense that this normative status and its powers do not depend on the good will of others. The stability of normative expectations, or justice as regularity in Rawls's terms, is too weak to capture the intensity of an agent's nondomination. Instead, the normative powers of citizenship are necessary, precisely as the power to shape the content of one's political obligations democratically.

With respect to the content of particular obligations, the requisite sort of political freedom might then be reconceived as a form of anti-power. According to Pettit, antipower is "the capacity to command noninterference as a power" (Pettit 1996: 589). As in the case of domination, Pettit's emphasis on the will leaves out the essential normative features of antipower: rather than the capacity to control others and resist having obligations imposed by another's will, antipower must be the power over the content of one's obligations and statuses. That is, the most basic normative power of citizenship is the positive and creative power to interpret, shape and reform those very normative powers possessed by agents who seek to impose obligations and duties on others without allowing themselves to be addressed by others. Understood normatively, nondomination is thus tied to the exercise of *communicative* freedom, an active power that must be included among those powers necessary to establish and secure free social relationships in which obligations and statuses are not simply imposed by one party or bearer of an institutional role. Instead of appealing to existing social norms and institutions, the public use of communicative freedom makes it possible to use existing norms to give content to their mutual obligations and even to create new norms through joint deliberation.

In this way, specifically normative powers regulate social relationships and powers not merely by constraining them by rules or norms, but also by making creatures with social and natural powers able to change these same norms and rules. In no other role or location than as citizens in democratic institutions do members of modern societies exercise their normative powers of imposing obligations and changing statuses. Certainly, other forms of authority exist in modern societies that also make it possible for these statuses and obligations to change without the popular influence or discursive control of citizens. Democracy itself is then the joint exercise of these powers and capacities, so that they are not under the control of any given individual or group of citizens. Such powers must be redefined jointly and creatively when the circumstances of domination change. The powers that citizens have over their own obligations and over the scope of these normative powers are central achievements of democratic institutions in securing nondomination.

We can now return to the issue of the dispersal of power in multiple levels as a means to achieve robust nondomination. Some have argued that deliberative legitimacy is local, rising to no higher level than that of the nation state (Dahl 1999; Kymlicka 1999; Miller 1995). Properly organized with dispersed power, however, large and numerous units also have deliberative advantages. At least some existing practices of the European Union (EU) employ institutional structures of cooperation to take advantage of the dispersal of power and deliberation in multi-leveled and polycentric polities. Contrary to classical modern sovereignty, republican cosmopolitan institutions ought to further separate powers by disaggregating state monopolies and functions into a variety of institutional levels and locations as well as by disaggregating centralized transnational powers and redistributing them to citizens, thereby opening them up to their deliberation. One clear instance of how such institutions might promote further democratization can be found in the institutionalization of human rights in the European Convention for the Protection of Human Rights and the recent EU Charter of Rights.

What is the purpose of this new layer of human rights enforcement beyond that already provided by the constitutions of member states? Along with the supranational European Court of Human Rights that grants rights of individual petition independently of the EU, there are (at least in the juridical dimension) multiple new institutions and memberships that can be invoked when making claims about human rights. Such overlapping differentiated and polyarchical structures permit greater realization of these rights and their claims against domination, as citizens exercise the various entitlements gained from their overlapping memberships. This feature of the EU can be generalized in two ways. One way is to see how the institutional design and practices of the EU could be used to promote this fundamental normative power, the power that is basic to the right to have rights. The EU could do so by providing a variety of locations and sites for deliberation in which publics interact with each other and with institutional authorities. This division of powers could not be exclusively territorial, however, or else it would be indistinguishable from a large nation state. The second way to promote deliberation follows from these features. In order that citizens not have obligations imposed by deliberators at other institutional sites, citizens will have to have the capacity to initiate deliberation at multiple levels. The exercise of such normative powers requires robust interaction across such levels and institutional locations in which interested publics can raise issues of common concern. This same understanding of nondomination suggests that unless such normative powers are extended to all human beings, the power that is exercised in any particular institution is ultimately democratically arbitrary. In this case, citizens become dominators of other citizens.

The Republic of Humanity

In the previous section I recounted how anticolonial republicans argued that a transnational federal structure was needed to overcome the negative feedback relationship by which empires abroad undermined liberty at home. This cosmopolitan commitment led republicans such as Fletcher to argue that "mankind would be best preserved from the convolutions of misery if instead of framing laws for a single society," free governments would do so with the common interests of their neighbors and humanity in mind. A republican transnational trope employed by Madison and Kant as well as Fletcher is the ideal of the Achaean league of cities, a federation of distinct cities that was not "one vicious and ungovernable city" (Pagden 1995: 188). As Kant put it, such a federation would not be one in which every state could "expect to be able to derive its security and rights from its own power and its own legal judgment, but rather solely from this great federation (*Foedus Amphictyonum*)" (Kant 1970: 47). Just as we had the obligation "to leave the state of nature and create a civil condition," so too Kant argues that we have the obligation to create a cosmopolitan civil condition. In this section I argue that the obligation to create such a federation is an obligation to humanity that is best fulfilled in the joint commitment to democracy and human rights. This obligation demands that at least some institutions that create the civic condition (the status and powers of citizenship) be global in scope.

The concept of humanity has played a central role in the development of human rights and humanitarian law, as is particularly evident in the important concept of "crimes against humanity." As many have noted, humanity has at least two senses. Bernard Williams, for example, remarks that it is a name "not merely for a species but for a quality" (Williams 1995: 88). The distinction here is between humanity as the human species or empirical aggregate of all human beings, and humanity as a moral quality that makes us human. This moral quality might be called "humanness" and has been given various interpretations, such as human dignity, rational nature, and so on, that might supply the basis for the attribution of rights. Rather than accept the usual distinction exemplified by Williams, I offer a third and more republican conception that combines features of both: *humanity as the human political community*. It is first and foremost an interpretation of humanity in terms of a moral property: the status of membership in a political community. Yet, rather than appealing to a specific moral property or status, membership in this community has the advantage of including the full range of human capabilities. It also captures humanity in Williams's aggregative sense, since this particular status is membership in a fully inclusive political community. In the absence of various institutions, humanity in this political sense may not yet be fully realized, but humanity has direct practical significance.

In her *Eichmann in Jerusalem* and in various exchanges with Jaspers concerning the Nuremberg trials, Arendt emphasizes the dual difference between *Menschlichkeit* and *Menschheit*, between "humanness" and "humanity" (Arendt & Jaspers 1993: 413). When Kant in his moral philosophy asks us to "respect the humanity of another," he is referring to the former rather than the latter, that is, to *moral* demands of respect owed to persons with their own intrinsic ends or, to use Rawls's phrase, as self-originating sources of claims. "A human being regarded as a *person*, that is as the subject of a morally practical reason . . . possesses a *dignity* . . . by which he demands *respect* for himself from all other rational beings in the world" (Kant 1996: 553). Dignity is the specific object of humanness, a certain moral *status* that implies an authority demanded for oneself by reciprocally and freely recognizing it in others. Humanity is thus tied to the rational capacity to be a source of value or self-originating source of claims (Korgaard 1996; Darwall 2005). Notice then that there is a double ambiguity here: not just between humanity and humanness, but between humanity as tied to a normative capacity to set ends and make claims, and humanity as a normative status that can be rightly demanded from every other free person even when it is not recognized.

We might call humanity as a capacity tied to freedom first-personal, while humanity as a status is second-personal. It is second-personal in that it is a normative status realized in relations with others who also have the same status of membership in a community of interaction. This is the status term invoked by the republican idea that citizens have no master, and can live on their own terms without fear and look each other in the eye, or as Milton put it, "to walk the streets with other men, to be spoken to freely, familiarly, without adoration." These republican phrases signify what it means to achieve the freedom intrinsic to such relationships without domination – the relations among free persons mediated by the status of membership in a political community that are expressed in the republican adage "to be free is to be the citizen of a free community." Only in relation to humanity in this sense do democracy and political rights have intrinsic value. This intrinsic value is present not just in cases of bearers of human rights living in a fully realized democratic political community, but also in the case of the rightless person who lacks all of these statuses and powers and had his or her human status violated.

What aspect of humanity is at stake in such violations? This question provides the opening for a republican interpretation. As Arendt notes, humanness in the first-personal sense does not capture the notion of crimes against humanity, even if basic human dignity has been violated; it is rather the second-personal normative status that has been violated when people are made rightless and stateless by organized and systematic acts of violence. With this concept we move beyond the standard republican contrast between master and slave with its suggestion that what is at stake is a matter of subordination to the will of a master. Instead, it is the arbitrary loss of humanity, the capability to have a status as such. People who seek justice after having lost their membership in some particular political community, whether through acts of violence such as genocide or through explicit acts of denationalization, may appeal to this status of humanity. The calamity of the rightless is not that such people are deprived of life, liberty and the pursuit of happiness, but "that they no longer belong to any community whatsoever" (Arendt 1973: 297). In other words, humanity is at stake because rightless persons have not only lost a specific membership with specific powers, but they have also lost their human status, their standing necessary to demand respect from others. We may then think of freedom from domination as a kind of right to membership, a right to the statuses and powers that make our freedom secure and allow us to be free to avoid the ills and evils that result from the loss of such a status.

Here the republican argument for transnationalism has its greatest force. In the case of *human* rights the community that is addressed is not the same as the one in which the violated person has *de facto* membership, but rather the human community as such (Bohman 2007: ch. 3). The right of membership in this community is thus basic because it is this most fundamental normative status that is implied by having human rights (which include various directly political rights). It is then the most basic normative power to resist the loss of this status in cases of tyranny and domination that at the same time creates the community of humanity. But we cannot make such a claim without political institutions to support a community that is addressed by those who have had their basic statuses violated. While any particular set of institutions can act on behalf of humanity, at least some transnational institutions are necessary to secure this most basic form of nondomination. In the case of the international system, none are secure in their nondomination. If some are dominated, then all may be dominated under the right circumstances. The only way to realize nondomination is through common liberty, and in this case such freedom from domination requires that all are free, and not merely as a result of the power exercised within and by a particular, arbitrary community.

In the absence of world government, many have objected that humanity cannot be taken to be a political community, a people, a *demos*, or even a collective entity. Indeed, David Luban has recently objected that "to call humanity – humankind – a party of interest is not to regard humanity as a political community but as a set of human individuals" (Luban 2004: 137). But more importantly, the issue here is what constitutes a political community, and Luban has a very narrow functional criterion: "only political communities promulgate law, and for this reason humanity is not a political community" (p. 126). For humanity to be the party of interest, however, does not require any particular legislative act that makes it so. Rather, humanity is a complex property consisting of a range of capabilities that we have in common with others to the extent that we are free. The human rights regime and its institutions thus constitute humanity in the political sense, in the absence of which human rights would best be thought of as merely moral rather than political obligations. This would mean that in the absence of civil authority and laws, putatively rightless and stateless persons could, in Locke's memorable phrase, only "appeal to heaven."

Having *human* rights of membership then comes with the normative power to have rights: the power to make claims upon all those who also have human rights (and to be responsive to their claims), and thus upon humanity or the human political community on whose recognition these rights depends. This makes sense of Arendt's elliptical phrase, "the right to have rights." Furthermore, international law recognizes a very similar set of claims in "the right to nationality" as a political right that is the basis of rights of asylum seekers and refugees. The right to nationality is thus not a mere right to protection; it is not just a right not to have one's membership arbitrarily taken away, but the right to have a status that makes the exercise of normative powers possible regardless of one's *de facto* nationality. While it does not yet refer to any actual political community as such, this right to membership is no longer a matter of national sovereignty or the arbitrary choice of some political community whether to grant such a status. Instead, it is the status necessary for a shared common liberty with all others with whom we interact and thus best realized in many different institutional locations. If appropriately organized, membership in such an inclusive political community could turn rights claims into statuses and powers. To the extent that they are based upon commonly exercised normative powers and freedoms, democracies have special commitments to humanity.

Democratic Obligations to Humanity

In the age of empire, nondomination cannot be realized and secured by each republic on its own. Such a claim to secure freedom ultimately refers to humanity as the horizon of this obligation precisely because no dominating community can ever secure the nondomination of its members. Bounded political communities must exercise the normative powers that secure nondomination in common with other such communities and thus create a common civil condition with them. I want now to expand this argument from the commitment to the ideal of freedom as nondomination to a similar set of obligations that come from the ideal of democracy and its entailments. The core of this argument is related to the republican claims that I considered above. Democracy may fail to establish common liberty by establishing liberty for some at the price of the domination of others, such as in the rule of citizens or of majorities over noncitizens and minorities. In order to have full democratic legitimacy, states must extend certain minimal statuses and powers to all persons, giving democracies special obligations to establish the republic of humanity even within their borders.

The minimum power necessary to meet the threshold of democratic nondomination – what I call "the democratic minimum" – requires more of legitimate authority than that it simply grants the permission to be consulted. The inadequacy of consultation without empowerment can best be elucidated not through the classical republican contrast between citizens and slaves (who lack liberty as such), but rather between citizens and rightless persons (who lack common liberty held with others). Unlike such rightless persons, citizens have the shared ability to initiate deliberation; this entails the ability not just to have officials or rulers respond to their interests, but also to set the items on an agenda and thus to be secure in their freedom from domination. As Arendt put it: "Beginning, before it becomes an historical event, is the supreme human capacity; politically, it is identical with human freedom" (Arendt 2000: 479). This capacity marks the specific democratic contrast between citizen and slave, between having distinctively political rights that entail normative powers to do certain things and the inability to participate effectively in the absence of such powers. As Isaiah Berlin noted, this is true even if the master is an enlightened, liberal-minded despot or Rousseauian lawgiver who may permit a large measure of personal freedom. Since whatever freedoms are granted to the slave (or to an elite), she remains dominated and thus lacks any intrinsic normative authority (or powers) even over herself; at best, she may only respond to the initiatives of others. But to be entirely rightless, and thus to have no status whatsoever, is not to lack the ability to contest or resist changes in normative status, but rather to lack the genuine ability to begin. This political status is precisely what democratic citizens have and is thus the minimum for their powers to be truly democratic.

Consider two alternative accounts, one based on the powers of citizens to deliberate and the other based on the power of citizens to hold those who deliberate accountable. Pettit sees the basic achievement of democracy in the latter terms, as the capacity of citizens to hold accountable those who actually deliberate and set the agenda. Hence, democratic representative assemblies have legitimate authority because they are epistemically better able to "track" the public good of citizens than officials (Pettit 1997: 88). Domination, however, is not merely due to epistemic failures, but is more a matter of who is entitled to offer interpretations of the public good. Nor should nondomination be regarded as a primary good (Pettit 1997: 91), but as a capability that is a constitutive feature of effective deliberation. Walzer is correct in arguing that rights of membership are basic; or, as he puts it, they are "the first social good" to be distributed, and thus the basis for the recognition of further entitlements and of participation in social life (Walzer 1983: 50). However, to think about nondomination as a good to be distributed is misleading; membership is itself defined in terms of the basic freedoms that it enables, the most basic with respect to freedom manifested in common deliberation. Thus, we can see non-domination as a fundamental condition for participation in projects that are common only to the extent that, *qua* member, one can influence the terms of cooperation with others and not simply be ruled by them. Most of all, this conception of accountability presupposes rather than defines the statuses and powers that citizens must have in order to avoid domination.

This argument still leaves open the question of how it is that citizens exercise the democratic minimum. According to Pettit, repub-lican institutions must be constructed in such a way that as a matter of fact the policies and laws that they produce will "track" the common good. In order that such institutions do not produce domination, non-mastering interference for the sake of realizing the common good is nonarbitrary to the extent that it takes into account the interests and opinions of citizens from their own point of view (Pettit 1997: 88). But how will this be possible? Here Pettit develops something akin to the democratic minimum, since tracking requires that citizens have a certain shared power: the power to engage in effective contestation. Citizens are accordingly free from domination only if they are "able effectively to contest any interference" that does not answer to their relevant interests and ideas (Pettit 1997: 185). But is contestation what makes nondomination possible?

According to Pettit, in order to be "effective," contestation must occur within deliberative institutions, in which public decisions are respon-sive to reasons because they are made in a "deliberative way" (Pettit 1997: 185). Pettit's analysis seems to have it exactly backward, since he embraces deliberative democracy precisely only insofar as it makes decisions contestable. If citizens' intrinsic power to contest decisions depends on their more basic power to participate in deliberation effectively, then it follows that contestation is based on the even more fundamental power to *initiate* new deliberation. Otherwise, they will be merely consulted, and thus unable to introduce new points of view and new relevant interests and opinions. For this reason, this deliberative capacity is constitutive of, and not merely instrumental to, nondomination. This shift from contestation to deliberation requires rethinking the idea of nondomination in terms of normative powers rather than as freedom from arbitrary interference, since normative powers are only truly such on the condition that all may exercise them in common.

Furthermore, the consequentialist justifications offered by Pettit for a minimal contestatory democracy are unconvincing. Since democracy enacts basic political rights, it is intrinsically justified to the extent that it is constitutive of human political rights and nondomination, and not merely because it is the best means to attain these goals. As constitutive of nondomination, the initiation of deliberation is thus generative of political power in a way in which contestation and *post hoc* disapproval are not. When faced with cases of injustice, it is this dynamic and creative interaction between freedom of initiation and democratic accountability that makes it possible for citizens to make their democracies more just and more accountable. While one might number this capacity among the democratic powers, contestation that gets any institutional response must take the form of deliberation addressed to a public of citizens. Even more specifically, such institutions must be organized to respond not just to citizens' reasons, but also to their deliberative initiatives. Many institutional actors are quite powerful but lack the fundamental normative power of initiation (even if they are not slaves). While judges, for example, may refuse to hear particular cases, they cannot initiate them and instead must rely on citizens to do so. Indeed, judges lack final control over the agenda precisely on the republican grounds that they do not dominate citizens. The same argument would apply both to other citizens of the same republic whose deliberation becomes authoritative and to the citizens and officials of other republics whose normative powers could undermine the condition of common liberty. At the very least, this means that if a democracy is to avoid domination, then it must hold open the possibility that its current boundaries and membership, the scope of those whose political rights create obligations, remains open.

It is precisely by fixing such boundaries that democracies become dominators. In order to develop the virtues of this particular republican account, the democratic threshold of "freedom as the capacity to begin" can be further operationalized in two ways: first, in terms of the capacity of citizens to amend the basic normative framework, that is, the power to change the ways in which rights and duties are assigned; and second, in terms of the capacity of citizens to set an item on an open agenda, and thus to initiate joint, public deliberation. Robust nondomination cannot then be limited to the constituted powers as they are currently distributed within a particular community. Without such an openness to the deliberation of others, it remains possible for a political community that merely tracks the interests of its own members to be a dominator of other republics and thus to arbitrarily exercise its normative powers so as to purport to be able to impose obligations upon other citizens.

Humanity emerges within constituted democracies in the struggles over status and membership, most often in claims made by those who might be called quasi-members or denizens – persons who *de facto* have the dependent status that Kant called "mere auxiliaries to the republic." The role of humanity is in these cases to function as the addressee of claims to justice that may be answered by a larger or a future democratic community. Here we might look to the European Union as providing an example of the ways in which a transnational order can promote democratization and resist arbitrary democratic closure. How does the EU embody the perspective of humanity in its constitutional practices concerning human rights? As a transnational polity, the EU has begun to address the domination of citizens over noncitizens by providing the legal basis on which "guest workers" and cultural minorities may challenge state policies. It is clear that with respect to these gaps in human rights between citizens and noncitizens, the EU has been a catalyst for democratization, fulfilling the democratic minimum for the first time for many residents of Europe who are not citizens of any member state. Indeed, it might be thought that these rights are matters for individual states to decide (perhaps as a task for the principle of subsidiarity). However, the European Convention on Human Rights entitles foreigners without nationality in any EU member state to appeal to the European Human Rights Court and the EU Court of Justice for the ongoing juridical recognition of their rights, creating adjudicative institutions that build upon the constitutional traditions of member states, even as they are extended to noncitizens. Nondomination is more robust simply in virtue of EU citizens having multiple ways and intersecting locations in which claims to common liberty can be effectively realized. EU-level institutions can thus serve to make these states more democratic (Weiler 1998). The extension of human rights in the EU to even noncitizens without naturalization shows the advantages of having multiple pathways for realizing human rights in differentiated institutions that incorporate the perspective of humanity. As based in common liberty, such institutions are neither countermajoritarian nor antidemocratic, but the means by which current arrangements are tested for democratic arbitrariness.

This account of democratic obligations to humanity is complementary to transnational federalism insofar as it adds to the specific statuses and powers necessary for transnational nondomination. If we include among them powers that are part of the democratic minimum, then the transnational political community that is responsive to human rights claims must be democratic to some degree. Such claims obligate democratic communities to act on behalf of humanity, to regard their political community as part of the human political community. Once the right to have rights is enriched by the democratic minimum, the claims of others create potentially stronger obligations owed to all bearers of human rights. We cannot ignore these claims without becoming dominators and thereby undermining the conditions for democracy and common liberty. Democratic communities that honor the democratic minimum for all do not merely act for the benefit of humanity; they also *constitute* the human community as the basis of common liberty that all share. Indeed, such international institutions generate the sort of feedback relations that enable rather than limit democracy within states, precisely by making it more difficult for states to promote security by undermining common liberty.

On this basis we can now conclude this argument from human rights to a republic of humanity. The basic freedoms are justified negatively and positively as the necessary conditions for avoiding great harms such as domination and destitution on the one hand and for living a worthwhile human life on the other. For both, membership in humanity, understood as the right to have rights, is thus the most basic of human freedoms. For an initial clarification of this idea we can do no better than to quote from the *Universal Declaration of Human Rights*: "Everyone is entitled to a social and international order in which the rights and freedoms set forth in this Declaration can be fully realized" (*UDHR*, article 28). Having *human* rights of membership of this sort comes with the normative power or right to have rights: the power to make claims upon all those who also have human rights (and to be responsive to their claims), and thus to make claims of justice to humanity or to the human political community on whose recognition these rights depend. For this reason, the obligations of humanity exceed the list of crimes against humanity as recognized by the International Criminal Court, especially with regard to the statuses that ought to be assigned to all persons as bearers of human rights. But the normative statuses of persons as members of the human political community must also bring with it the constitutive capacity to shape and govern those institutions, and this requires the further development of democracy within the international system. This burden does not necessarily have to be carried by a global political system on the model of a state, but should rather be one that distributes rights and responsibilities on many different mutually reinforcing levels.

This fundamental right to an institutional order that realizes rights as normative powers demands that we rethink the exclusively juridical understanding of rights that informs the current human rights regime and much philosophical thinking as well. Habermas, for example, claims that "rights are juridical by their very nature" (Habermas 1998: 190). At the same time, this criticism should not lead us to be skeptical about human rights as such, but only about the prospects for realizing them simply through protective and coercive legal institutions that fix their content independent of any political process. Operating without a rich institutional background of political institutions, such coercive mechanisms could well become a source of domination and may well violate human rights by enforcing them in the absence of this background of constitutive political activity. This has led Richard Bellamy to reject the assumption of liberal constitutionalism that rights provide the stable and fixed framework for politics, and instead argue for a "political constitutionalism," in which citizenship operates "as the right to have rights rather than as a given set of rights" (Bellamy 2001: 16). The current human rights regime reflects the juridical conceptions of its postwar founding generation, who sought coercive institutions to protect those whose rights have been violated. This protective and juridical conception leaves unresolved the difficult political problem of implementing human rights without increasing domination. If deliberative capabilities are necessary in order that the very institutions that protect human rights do not impose duties arbitrarily, then they must also be exercised in those same international political institutions that establish the right to have rights.

If a political constitution is only a necessary but not sufficient condition for nondomination, what more can be said about the institutional order of the human political community? Rather than in a single, bounded community, freedom as nondomination can best be realized in a highly differentiated, decentered polity with a commitment to common liberty. On normative grounds, many of the core commitments of constitutional democracy are inherently universalistic and thus cosmopolitan; on institutional grounds, humanity can best be realized in a complexly interconnected and overlapping deliberative and polyarchic structure. Such a polity will realize nondomination robustly not merely in individual states, but in an overall institutional structure that includes at least some global institutions that do not regard current boundaries and memberships as fixed for the purposes of common liberty. As the anticolonial republicans have pointed out, the structural consequences of extending rights solely to bounded political communities is self-defeating for democracy and leads unavoidably to democracies becoming dominators. We see this today in the rise of neocolonialism by democracies such as the United States. As in previous forms of colonialism, the neocolonial power imposes its preferred normative order upon the colonized, now "democracy" instead of the benefits of "civilization." As in the case of Napoleonic republican imperialism, such an instrumental justification of establishing democracy elsewhere uses contradictory means of domination to achieve the end of democratization, a means that severs any linkage between democracy and peace. In the absence of broader and transnational institutions to disperse their powers and achieve common liberty, bounded democratic communities will remain potential dominators abroad and at home. This instrumentalization of human rights and democracy thus subverts them as ends and closes off existing possibilities for realizing them by more appropriate means.

Anti-imperialist republicans have long pointed out how *imperium* abroad leads to the heightening of executive and police powers, and recently in many democratic states this tendency has once again undermined the constructive democratic powers of citizens while enhancing the instrumental powers of the state to employ coercive means over their citizens. This development requires a cosmopolitan republican response that diffuses such power at many different institutional locations and in that way promotes nondomination. The conditions that make this generalization robust are internal to democratic practices and may now be disappearing, as fear and the need for security replace supposedly rational interests in peace.

If we are to continue the democratic project at least in part because of its connection to the ideals of peace and to the moral obligation to end pointless human suffering, it is best to see that democracy's capacity to do so is a contingent historical fact and a fragile achievement. The same is true of its relation to bounded political communities generally that face the constant challenge of interacting with each other without sacrificing their democratic character. The European Union examples show that robust interconnections between democracies at local, national and transnational levels can help to create and entrench the conditions for democratization. Now these include the conflict between those who are privileged citizens of the zone of the democratic peace and those who lack access to international normative powers and are potentially dominated by the protective apparatus of warlike democratic states and their coercive legal institutions. The new circumstances of neocolonialism now demand transnational institutions that disperse power across borders so as to enhance the common liberty of humanity.

Conclusion

One of the great merits of Pettit's particular interpretation of freedom as nondomination is that it is neutral with regard to issues related to the size of the political community. Pettit argues, for example, that both foreign policy and the use of force internationally have direct implications for the capacity of a political community to sustain its commitment to the nondomination of its citizens. Since *Republicanism*, he has developed a two-dimensional account of democracy as contestatory and electoral that is applicable to state and international settings (Pettit 2000). I have argued that the development of the republican tradition ties the commitment to nondomination to the ideal of a republic of humanity, so that basic republican principles require transnational and even global institutions, given the circumstances of modern, complex and globalizing societies.

While my argument is internal to the republican tradition, it is clear that it also demands the revision of certain basic republican concepts. First, it requires that we rethink the conception of nondomination itself, so as to join it more closely with the ways in which citizenship and freedom are linked not just to status but also to the exercise of normative powers. Second, this account asks us to rethink how it is that citizenship makes us secure from domination. Membership in a single political community is insufficient for robust nondomination. In order to be secure, such normative powers need to be distributed across institutional levels and across communities, including transnational institutions and the political community of humanity. Finally, these arguments suggest that the form of democracy that does not produce the domination of citizens over noncitizens is one in which the democratic minimum is realized in the common liberty of humanity. The goal of my argument has been the same as that of the first transnational republicans, who saw the deep connection between the ideals of transnationalism and freedom as nondomination.

This insistence on humanity as a political community may seem to underestimate the significance of other forms of community that might be attributed to humanity. For example, humanity must also be a moral community, the Kingdom of Ends. Such a form of community is important, since it establishes obligations to individuals and concern about their life chances that ought to constrain our moral statuses and powers, which must be consistent with our moral obligations to humanity. Such moral demands may also be thought to lead more directly to humanity as a legal rather than a political community, in which human rights are taken to be juridical statuses that are realized institutionally in the legal protection and recognition offered by institutions such as the International Criminal Court and in the social goods provided by the UNHCR. While these institutions act on behalf of humanity as a party of interest in cases of the gross violation of human rights, there are clear limitations on the extent to which legal enforcement and protections, however important, can disperse power or realize robust nondomination and common liberty. This requires a transnational political constitution and transnational powers of citizenship.

Understood as having republican aims, the human rights regime opens up a space for an emerging transnational political community to the extent that the content of rights and the form of their implementation may be put up to democratic deliberation. Such a global civil rights movement would serve not only to begin the process of forming a human political community, but it could also test the myriad possibilities for implementing and interpreting human rights (locally and globally) and would itself reflexively model essential features of publics and institutions that aim at this end. At the same time, this movement should not only aim at creating juridical institutions alone, however important they may be in checking tyranny. The normative powers exercised in such democratic institutions require that such a community realize human rights in overlapping and iterated ways, and that robust nondomination now requires membership in many different interacting and inter-related political communities, which together constitute the republic of humanity.

BIBLIOGRAPHY

Arendt, H. (1973). *The Origins of Totalitarianism*. New York: Harcourt Brace.

Arendt, H. (2000). "What is Freedom?" In P. Behr ed. *The Portable Arendt* (pp. 438–62). New York: Putnam.

Arendt, H. and K. Jaspers (1993). *The Hannah Arendt and Karl Jaspers Correspondence*. New York: Harcourt Brace.

Bellamy, R. (2001)."Constitutive Citizenship versus Constitutional Rights: Reflections on the EU Charter and the Human Rights Act." In T. Campbell, K. D. Ewing, and A. Tomkins (eds.), *Sceptical Essays on Human Rights* (pp. 16–39). Oxford: Oxford University Press.

Bohman, J. (2004). "Republican Cosmopolitanism." *The Journal of Political Philosophy*, 12(3), 336–52.

Bohman, J. (2007). *Democracy Across Borders: From Demos to Demoi*. Cambridge, MA: MIT Press.

Dahl, R. (1999). "Can International Organizations Be Democratic? A Skeptic's View." In C. Hacker-Cordon and I. Shapiro (eds.), *Democracy's Edges* (pp. 19–37). Cambridge: Cambridge University Press.

Darwall, S. (2005). "Fichte and the Second-Person Standpoint." *International Yearbook for German Idealism*, 3, 91–113.

Habermas, J. (1998). *The Inclusion of the Other*. Cambridge, MA: MIT Press.

Kant, I. (1970). *Political Writings*, tr. and ed. R. Nisbett. Cambridge: Cambridge University Press.

Kant, I. (1996). *Practical Philosophy*, tr. and ed. Mary J. Gregor. Cambridge: Cambridge University Press.

Korsgaard, C. (1996). *Creating the Kingdom of Ends*. Cambridge: Cambridge University Press.

Kymlicka, W. (1999). "Citizenship in an Era of Globalization." In C. Hacker-Cordon and I. Shapiro (eds.), *Democracy's Edges* (pp. 112–27). Cambridge: Cambridge University Press.

Luban, D. (2004). "A Theory of Crimes Against Humanity." *Yale Journal of International Law*, 29, 85–167.

May, L. (2005). *Crimes Against Humanity*. Cambridge: Cambridge University Press.

Miller, D. (1995). *On Nationality*. Oxford: Oxford University Press.

Muthu, S. (2003). *Enlightenment Against Empire*. Princeton: Princeton University Press.

Pagden, A. (1995). *Lords of All of the World*. New Haven: Yale University Press.

Pettit, P. (1997). *Republicanism: A Theory of Government*. Oxford: Oxford University Press.

Pettit, P. (2000). "Democracy, Electoral and Contestatory." In I. Shapiro and S. Macedo (eds.), *Designing Democratic Institutions* (pp. 105–47). New York: New York University Press.

Pitts, J. (2004). *A Turn to Empire: The Rise of Imperial Liberalism in Britain and France* Princeton: Princeton University Press.

Richardson, H. (2002). *Democratic Autonomy*. Oxford: Oxford University Press.

Slaughter, S. (2005). *Liberty Beyond Neoliberalism*. London: Palgrave.

Tilly, C. (1990). *Coercion, Capital and European States*. London: Blackwell.

Walzer, M. (1983). *Spheres of Justice*. New York: Basic Books.

Weiler, J. H. (1998). "An 'Ever Closer Union' in Need of a Human Rights Policy." *European Journal of International Law*, 9, 658–723.

Williams, B. (1995). *Making Sense of Humanity*. Cambridge: Cambridge University Press.

Part III
Republicanism, Rights, and Domination

Chapter 9

Republican Punishment: Consequentialist or Retributivist?

Richard Dagger

May a republican be a retributivist? Not according to John Braithwaite and Philip Pettit, the authors of *Not Just Deserts: A Republican Theory of Criminal Justice*. Republicanism and retributivism are rivals, in their view, and republicanism is in two ways superior to the retributive "idea that criminals should be punished because they deserve it."[1] First, republicanism is more comprehensive, offering a systemic approach to criminal justice in general that "does not focus exclusively on punishment in the way that retributivism does . . ." (*NJD*: 157). And it is better, second, even with regard to punishment itself, for the "answers provided by retributivists" to the questions the practice of punishment raises "are manifestly less satisfactory than the republican responses. Republican theory defeats retributivism even on the home ground of retributivism" (*NJD*: 157).

Are Braithwaite and Pettit right? Their book is certainly an important contribution both to republican theory and to long-standing debates on the point and practice of punishment, but I do not think they have made their case against retributivism. In particular, Braithwaite and Pettit fail to prove that a republican must be a consequentialist rather than a retributivist. Republicanism may well be more comprehensive than retributivism, as Braithwaite and Pettit claim, but that leaves open the possibility that a republican theory of criminal justice may take a retributive stand on punishment. Not only may republicans be retributivists, then, but retributivists may be republicans – a possibility that ought to hearten anyone who hopes to see the republican revival of recent years extend its reach.

To show that republicans *may* be retributivists is not, of course, to show that they *should* be. Nevertheless, I shall argue that republicans *should* take a broadly retributive stance with regard to punishment. Indeed, Pettit himself seems to have moved in this direction as he has developed, in response to criticisms of *Not Just Deserts*, a theory that centers on "punishment as rectification" rather than "the *maximization* of the dominion of individual people."[2] As a result, his republican theory of punishment bears a remarkable resemblance to the communicative theory that Antony Duff has elaborated in such works as *Trials and Punishments* and *Punishment, Communication, and Community*. This resemblance is noteworthy because Duff is both a retributivist and a critic of consequentialist theories of punishment. Moreover, Duff's communicative account of punishment as "a species of secular penance" (2001: 106) is, in my view, quite powerful. Taken together, these points suggest not only that republicans may be retributivists but that they may lay claim to a particularly powerful form of retributivism. And that is why republicans should be retributivists.

Such, in brief, is my argument. Before proceeding, however, it is necessary first to say something about its key terms. With regard to 'republicanism,' I shall follow Margaret Jane Radin's brief but expansive definition of a republican as someone who is dedicated "to the flourishing of citizens in a community by means of their self-government" (1993: 159). The "flourishing of citizens" I take to include living free from domination, in accordance with Pettit's arguments in *Republicanism* (Pettit 1997a), but I also believe that it has a broader civic dimension, in keeping with the traditional republican emphasis on civic virtue and self-government. I take the citizen, then, to be a *public* person – that is, someone who need not believe that a life devoted to politics is the best of all ways of life, but who does acknowledge that self-government requires attention to public concerns and considerations.

Coming to Terms with Punishment

When subjected to the scrutiny of lawyers and philosophers, punishment proves to be one of those familiar concepts that is surprisingly difficult to define. For present purposes, fortunately, it is not necessary to confront these difficulties. Duff has set out a concise definition of punishment that most philosophers will regard, I believe, as a good foundation for the discussion of how punishment is to be – if it can be – justified. Moreover, this is a definition that Braithwaite and Pettit can accept.[3] We shall proceed, therefore, with Duff's definition of legal punishment as "typically, something intended to be burdensome or painful, imposed on a (supposed) offender for a (supposed) offense by someone with (supposedly) the authority to do so; and . . . typically intended to express or communicate censure" (2001: xiv–xv).

Of the remaining terms that require explication, 'consequentialism' and 'retributivism,' the former is the less troublesome. Consequentialism is the doctrine that an act or institution is right, just, or proper if it produces consequences better than, or at least as good as, those that any other act or institution could produce in the same circumstances. Consequentialists thus believe that what justifies punishment is its ability to produce desirable consequences, which is to say that they take a forward-looking approach to justification. To be sure, consequentialists differ among themselves in a number of ways. Some want consequences only to count in the general justification of punishment as an institution (e.g., Hart 1968), or perhaps in the justification of particular forms of punishment, while others would apply the test of consequences to individual cases – insisting, for instance, that a guilty person should go free if no good will come of punishing him or that an innocent person should be punished if it will serve the greater good to do so (e.g., Smart 1973). Consequentialists also disagree as to the kinds of consequences they would like to achieve and avoid. There is general agreement that deterring and preventing crime are desirable consequences, but why these are desirable is a matter of dispute. For Jeremy Bentham and the classical utilitarians, the ultimate aim is happiness or pleasure. For other consequentialists, the justification of punishment rests on its ability to promote some good other than utility or happiness – notably, for our purposes, the good that Braithwaite and Pettit call 'dominion.' Whatever the good may be, though, consequentialists see its promotion or maximization as the justifying point of punishment.

Retributivism, by contrast, is usually understood to be a backward-looking approach that is more concerned with doing what is right or just than with promoting any kind of good. How to determine what is right or just – and how much concern, if any, to devote to promoting the good – are problems that have led to many varieties of retributivism. This variety is what makes it a more troublesome term than consequentialism. Retributivists often appeal to desert, but not all do;

and what they mean by 'desert' varies considerably. In 1979 John Cottingham distinguished nine different, if occasionally overlapping, varieties of retributivism. Since then, other varieties have been discovered, among them negative, positive, and permissive retributivism, to use J. L. Mackie's terms (1985: 207–8), and Jeffrie Murphy's distinction between grievance and character retributivism (1998: esp. 68).

Fortunately, again, it is not necessary to survey these forms here, let alone determine which is best, for Braithwaite and Pettit's understanding of retributivism is much the same as Duff's. For Braithwaite and Pettit, retributivism is "the idea that criminals should be punished because they deserve it" (*NJD*: 2); for Duff, it is the conviction that "punishment can be justified only as being deserved" (2001: 3). What divides Braithwaite and Pettit from Duff, then, is not the way they conceive of retributivism but the value they attach to it. For Braithwaite and Pettit retributivism is the wrong side, for Duff the right, in the debate between consequentialists and retributivists that has long dominated philosophical discussions of punishment. In the end, as I have already suggested, Pettit's theory of punishment and Duff's are remarkably similar. That is not, however, the end that Braithwaite and Pettit set out to reach.

Braithwaite and Pettit's Consequentialist Republicanism

To say that Braithwaite and Pettit take consequentialism to be the right side in the consequentialist-retributive debate is in a way misleading, for they believe that their *republican* theory of criminal justice is superior not only to retributivism but also to other consequentialist theories. On the one hand, they claim that republicanism avoids the problems besetting retributivism, such as the difficulty of justifying the institution of punishment without appealing to deterrence or crime prevention or some other good consequence that a system of legal punishment supposedly promotes (*NJD*: esp. 157–66). On the other hand, they also hold that republicanism avoids the problems plaguing such consequentialist theories as utilitarianism and "preventionism," especially the problem of securing the rights of the innocent: for "it seems perfectly possible that on occasion the penalization of an innocent person will promise to maximize overall happiness in the calculations of the zealous agent of the system" (*NJD*: 52).

The question, then, is what makes republicanism immune to the problems of other consequentialist theories; and the answer Braithwaite and Pettit supply is *dominion*. What makes republicanism special, in their view, is the good – dominion, or "freedom in the social sense of full citizenship" (*NJD*: vii) – that republicans aim to promote or maximize. What makes dominion special, in turn, is that "it is part of the very concept of having dominion . . . that a person cannot enjoy dominion fully if she perceives or suspects that the agents of the state, or indeed any other powers in the land, will be unscrupulous in respecting her rights" (*NJD*: 76). Dominion is thus the hinge on which Braithwaite and Pettit's theory hangs, and we must look more closely at this concept before we can assess their argument.

The argument from dominion

Braithwaite and Pettit conceive of dominion as a form of negative liberty. As such, it "involves, roughly, the absence of interference by others . . . ," and it is to be distinguished from autonomy and other forms of positive liberty, which involve something more than the mere absence of interference – something such as "the absence of physical inability, psychological incapacity, personal ignorance, or something of that kind . . ." (*NJD*: 55). Dominion differs from other forms of negative liberty, however, in that it is a specifically republican conception of liberty. Because the republican view presumes a holistic rather than an atomistic conception of society, republican liberty is not so much a matter of being left alone as it is "the condition of citizenship in a free society, a condition under which each is properly safeguarded by the law against the predations of others" (*NJD*: 57). To enjoy dominion is therefore to enjoy a social standing or status – that of the citizen – that depends upon the recognition of others and the rule of law; for "the bearer of dominion has control in a certain area, being free from the interference of others, but has that control in virtue of the recognition of others and the protection of the law" (*NJD*: 60).

Dominion is clearly a concept with implications extending well beyond considerations of crime and punishment. Crime, however, will certainly be a central concern of anyone who wishes to promote or maximize dominion, as Braithwaite and Pettit do. On their account, crime constitutes an "invasion of dominion" in the form of an assault on one's "person" (as in murder or rape), "province" (as in kidnap or harassment), or "property" (as in burglary or theft) (*NJD*: 69). Republicans must therefore aim to prevent crime, and to punish those who commit it, in order to promote dominion by minimizing its invasion. That is why Braithwaite and Pettit insist that republicans must be consequentialists.

What is it about dominion, though, that will enable Braithwaite and Pettit's republican consequentialism to withstand the objections brought against other consequentialist theories? Is it not likely that the desire to maximize dominion will lead to the punishment of an innocent person or some other injustice? Braithwaite and Pettit's confidence that their theory overcomes such objections seems to rest on three requirements that are built into the concept of dominion: the "comparative," "assurance," and "common knowledge" requirements (*NJD*: 65).

Dominion is a *comparative* concept because everyone who has full dominion stands on an equal footing, under the law, with every other citizen, enjoying "no less a prospect of liberty than is available to other citizens" (*NJD*: 64). Unlike utility, say, which may be accumulated and enjoyed without reference to other persons, Braithwaite and Pettit's dominion is an essentially comparative concept that requires formal equality. If your "prospect of liberty" or dominion grows while mine does not, then my dominion is effectively diminished. In this respect dominion resembles power as Hobbes depicts it in chapter XI of *Leviathan*: I might think that I have enough power to satisfy my needs, but I also know that the amount I have effectively dwindles when others acquire more and I do not. The resemblance, though, between Hobbesian power and Braithwaite and Pettit's dominion does not extend from comparison to competition. In Hobbes's analysis, the comparative nature of power leads inexorably to a "restlesse desire for power after power that ceaseth only in death" because no one can be satisfied, in the state of nature, with the amount of power he or she has. In Braithwaite and Pettit's analysis, however, someone who has "no less a prospect of liberty than is available to other citizens" has no compelling reason to seek more. Equality of dominion is what matters, not superiority.

Dominion also requires assurance and common knowledge. Dominion is subject to invasion and loss, and those who must fend off attacks, or take precautions to avoid them, will find their dominion diminished. *Assurance* that one's prospect of liberty will not be destroyed or diminished, however, enables one to be secure in his or her dominion, much as the sovereign's assurance of one's safety should bring a halt, in Hobbes's theory, to the deadly competition for power. The requirement that one's equal standing, with "no less a prospect of liberty than is available to other citizens," be a matter of *common knowledge* also contributes to this security. "Common knowledge" in this case entails recognition of one's status and rights as a citizen. The language that Braithwaite and Pettit use in this context appears to be straightforwardly descriptive – "she enjoys no less a prospect of liberty than is available to other citizens"; "it is common knowledge among citizens that this condition obtains" – but the prescriptive element is not far below the surface. As a citizen, one is *entitled* to no less a prospect of liberty than that available to other citizens. If this is a matter of common knowledge – if I know that I am so entitled, and if others know it, and if I know that others know it – then I will be even more sure of my ability to go about my life without fear of assault or invasion, and thus more secure in my dominion.

To say that crime constitutes an invasion of dominion, then, is to say that the republican must consider crime an assault on one's equal standing as a citizen – as someone who is entitled, as much as any other, to be free from such assaults and threats of assault in going about one's life. That is why Braithwaite and Pettit state that "promoting dominion involves three [lexically] ordered tasks," the first of which is "to create as much equality as possible in liberty prospects" (*NJD*: 68).[4] One way to do this is to fight crime, whether by working to eliminate its causes, deter those who would engage in it, or punish those who do. The more successful we are in fighting crime, the more successful we are, presumably, in promoting dominion. Does it then follow that any measure that will reduce criminal invasions of dominion – even framing and punishing an innocent person – is justified if it will promote dominion?

Braithwaite and Pettit's answer is no, and we are now in position to see why. Dominion is different from utility and the goods that other consequentialist theories seek to promote because it combines an aggregative element – promoting dominion – with a distributive concern to assure everyone's equal standing as a citizen. Punishing an innocent person could not truly promote dominion, all things considered, because it would trample on the victim's rights as a citizen. Dominion is a good, therefore, that we can best promote in an indirect manner. As Braithwaite and Pettit say, if the criminal justice authorities are bent on promoting dominion, then their responses must not always be determined by direct consideration of that target. If they pursue the promotion of dominion free of any constraints, then they will not promote it. Such a direct pursuit of the objective means open-mindedness about interfering with innocent individuals in order to promote it. And that means that ordinary people are denied *awareness of the equal assurance* against interference which is required for dominion. (*NJD*: 74; emphasis added)

We can only pursue or promote dominion, it seems, in an indirect way, constrained by the need to provide the equal assurance against interference that dominion itself requires. Dominion is indeed a special kind of good – one that can be promoted or maximized without threat to individual rights or considerations of justice – if Braithwaite and Pettit are right. But are they? Their critics certainly do not think so.

Criticizing dominion

Criticism of Braithwaite and Pettit's theory has ranged from a sub-stantial paragraph in Duff's *Punishment, Communication, and Community* (2001: 10) to a pair of essays by leading proponents of the "just deserts" school of criminal punishment (Von Hirsch & Ashworth 1992; Ashworth & von Hirsch 1993–4). The critics are remarkably similar, however, in the objections they raise. These include the following complaints:

1) Braithwaite and Pettit do not clearly define 'dominion' (Montague 1995: 101–3; Von Hirsch & Ashworth 1992: 85).
2) As a result, their appeal to dominion offers insufficient guidance. "Gauging gains and losses of 'dominion' would be still more elusive than totting up costs and benefits in the usual utilitarian fashion"; "almost any sentencing policy (or for that matter, police or prosecution policy) might be defended on the basis that it promotes 'dominion'" (Von Hirsch & Ashworth 1992: 85, 98).
3) What Braithwaite and Pettit take to be a virtue of their republican approach – that it offers a comprehensive theory of criminal justice – is instead one of its defects: "The conception that purports to answer every question is apt to yield answers that are meager at best and, at worst, plain wrong" (Von Hirsch & Ashworth 1992: 98).

4) Finally, their protestations to the contrary notwithstanding, Braithwaite and Pettit's forward-looking republicanism remains subject to the same crippling defect as all other consequentialist theories of punishment. That is, the attempt to maximize dominion will not do justice to the backward-looking considerations of guilt, innocence, or the severity of the offense. For it is surely possible, among other grievous errors, "that penal measures that efficiently reduced crime by infringing the dominion of some innocents would lead to a maximization of dominion overall" (Duff 2001: 10; also Von Hirsch & Ashworth 1992: 87; Montague 1995: 104–6; and Matravers 2000: 29).

What should we make of these objections? I am inclined to discount the first three. Dominion is a concept that is clear enough to provoke a fresh look at long-standing concerns and controversies, and it would be a mistake to abandon it – whether we call it "dominion," "non-domination," or something else – until we are convinced that it is so unclear as to be useless. It would be a similar mistake to reject the republican theory for being, as the second objection has it, vague and indeterminate. The theory may not be as determinate as Braithwaite and Pettit believe, but it does offer useful guidance, if not a step-by-step instruction manual, for dealing with many problems in the theory and practice of criminal justice (see *NJD*: ch. 7; and Pettit 2000). Nor, finally, should we dismiss Braithwaite and Pettit's theory because of their attempt to put forward a comprehensive account of criminal justice. There may be reasons to doubt that such attempts will succeed, but these are not so powerful as to rule them out *ab initio*. To the contrary, there is much to learn from those who try to bring some order or coherence to our scattered ideas and disparate intuitions about crime, punishment, and other matters, even if we ultimately conclude that their systems fail. We should also be open to the possibility that someone's comprehensive account will not fail. That openness is presumably why Duff, one of Braithwaite and Pettit's critics, has set out his own "unitary theory" of criminal punishment (2001: xvi–xvii).

The fourth criticism remains, however, and on this point I think the critics are right. The key question here is whether Braithwaite and Pettit's use of dominion to do both aggregative and distributive work is a virtue of their theory or an ambiguity that obscures a tension at its heart. They state, in a footnote, that "contrary to common assumptions, . . . there is no incoherence in the notion that an aggregative goal like the maximization of dominion may require a certain distributive pattern. Aggregation and distribution are not necessarily in competition" (*NJD*: 65 n. 4). Hence their conception of dominion as an aggregative goal with a distributive component. Not only that, but the distributive component takes priority. In promoting dominion, according to Braithwaite and Pettit, the "first task must be to create as much equality as possible in liberty-prospects" (*NJD*: 68), and only then may we go on to the aggregative task of maximizing dominion – of ensuring every citizen "no less a prospect of liberty *than the best that is compatible with the same prospect for all citizens*" (*NJD*: 65; emphasis added). In other words, *equality* of liberty-prospects takes priority over their *extent*. So Braithwaite and Pettit say. But they speak so often of "maximizing dominion" or "the maximization of dominion" or "trying to maximize the realization of dominion" that the aggregative aspect of dominion – their desire to increase its extent – threatens to overwhelm the desire for its equal distribution.[5] Whatever Braithwaite and Pettit may hope or intend to achieve, the logic of maximization seems to press them towards a consequentialist theory in which aggregation of some good is once again the prime concern.

In addition to their frequent talk of maximizing, an analogy that Braithwaite and Pettit draw in support of their position also reveals, upon examination, their vulnerability to the critics' fourth objection. As Braithwaite and Pettit see it, "the criminal justice enterprise of promoting dominion" is analogous to "the parental enterprise of conferring a sense of independence on a teenage child . . ." (*NJD*: 72), in that both goals are better pursued in an indirect than a direct manner. To confer independence or autonomy on the teenager, you "must give the child authority to make his own decisions over a designated range of issues and, short of disaster situations, you must not withdraw that authority just because you believe he is making a mistake" (*NJD*: 73). By analogy, promoting the goal of dominion "requires the agents of the system individually and collectively to tie their hands in regard to how individuals should be treated and to make it clear to people that this is what they are doing" (*NJD*: 73). Otherwise, "people generally will become aware that they are likely to have their personal dominion invaded if that is for the best overall; and . . . this means that people generally will find that their dominion is seriously compromised" (*NJD*: 74). In sum:

once it becomes a matter of common suspicion that the authorities use the promotion of overall dominion to justify particular invasions, then the dominion of ordinary people in the society is jeopardized. People will cease to believe that they have redress against all forms of interference with the liberties required for dominion; they will realize that far from enjoying equal assurance against interference they are, at least in some respects, at the mercy of the political authorities. (*NJD*: 74)

As with the independence of teenagers, then, so too with dominion. The best way to promote it is not to aim directly at its maximization – at the "overall dominion" of the population – but at securing everyone's equal prospects of liberty, including the prospect that one will not be framed and punished for a crime he or she did not commit. Only such an indirect method will provide the "equal assurance" necessary to achieving the greatest possible dominion for the society as a whole.

The analogy is an interesting and illuminating one, but it works in two ways against Braithwaite and Pettit's position. One is that it raises the possibility that republicans should want to promote *autonomy* rather than dominion – a point I shall return to later. The other is that the escape clause tucked into Braithwaite and Pettit's account of indirectly promoting the teenager's independence undercuts their argument. "You must give the child authority to make his own decisions over a designated range of issues," they say, "and, *short of disaster situations*, you must not withdraw that authority just because you believe he is making a mistake" (*NJD*: 73; emphasis added). When "disaster situations" occur, the parents presumably should intervene directly – saying, for example, "In this case we can best help you to become an independent, autonomous adult by *not* respecting your decision to drive the car when you are obviously drunk." If the analogy holds, however, then "disaster situations" may also arise where dominion is concerned. Such situations would be the ones so often imagined by critics of consequentialist theories of punishment, such as the case of the official who believes that the best way to calm a nearly hysterical public in the midst of a series of horrible crimes is by pinning the blame on an innocent person. If this can be done in such a way that the public never discovers the innocence of the person charged with and convicted of the crime, then the consequentialist must hold that punishing the innocent is, in this case, the right course of action. As consequentialists who admit that "disaster situations" allow for direct pursuit of autonomy in the teenager's case, Braithwaite and Pettit seem committed to a similar position with regard to dominion. In short, if their analogy is sound, it follows that direct attempts to promote overall dominion are in order when we are faced with "disaster situations." Braithwaite and Pettit's theory is indeed vulnerable to their critics' fourth objection.

To be sure, Pettit has elaborated the republican theory of criminal justice in subsequent articles, including two written with Braithwaite in response to the criticisms of Andrew Ashworth and Andrew von Hirsch (Pettit with Braithwaite 1992–3 and 1993–4; Pettit 1997b). In those articles he maintains that his (and Braithwaite's) consequentialist republicanism is not merely another aggregative theory that fails to do justice to individual rights and desert. For example, "courts are designed to promote dominion, as they ought to be under a republican regime"; but "a guilty verdict does not provide the republican court with a license to optimize, where optimization is taken to be entirely a forward-looking matter. If a guilty verdict provides such a license, it does so only in a sense in which the first element in optimization must be the rectification, so far as possible, of the damage to the victim's dominion" (1992–3: 233). So far as I am aware, however, Pettit never confronts the attempt to use his and Braithwaite's analogy against them, if only because no one else – again, so far as I am aware – has advanced this particular criticism. We will not find a response to this criticism in Pettit's subsequent articles, then, but we will find a promising shift in his thinking about republican criminal justice.

Pettit's rejoinder: Rectification and the three Rs

There are many points worth considering in these articles, especially if one advocates, with Ashworth and von Hirsch, the "just deserts" approach to punishment. Three points, however, are particularly pertinent here.

The first is that Pettit continues to hold that one of the attractive features of republicanism is the basis it provides for a comprehensive theory of criminal justice. Others may think it better to concentrate on one or another aspect of criminal justice, such as sentencing practices, and to forsake the quest for a theory unifying so diverse a field. But they are wrong, Pettit says; for "the trouble with focusing on one area in this way is that any initiative taken in one part of the

criminal justice system is liable to impact on other parts of the system"
(1992–3: 225).

The second point is that Pettit also continues to hold that "the
promotion of dominion is the master aim of a republican criminal
justice system . . ." (1993–4: 319). Republican theory thus remains
consequentialist, even if the goal to be promoted contains a distributive element – securing assurance for everyone's enjoyment of dominion – and even if that distributive element takes priority over "the
maximization of assurance overall; principled restraints are built into the
aim of furthering reassurance . . . by the very conception of what that
aim involves" (1993–4: 319). Pettit does give this goal a different name
in "Republican Theory and Criminal Punishment," where "dominion
gives way to "nondomination"; but he does not explain his reasons
for the change, and he mentions it only in a footnote in which he
seems to regard the two terms as equivalent.[6] In any case, whether it
is dominion or nondomination that is to be promoted, the republican
approach to crime and punishment remains, in Pettit's eyes, a consequentialist theory that is superior to the dominant utilitarian and
retributive alternatives.

Yet there is one significant respect – and this is the third point – in
which Pettit's later articles differ from *Not Just Deserts*. This difference
is the prominent part that *rectification* comes to play in the theory.
'Rectification' is not a term that consequentialists usually invoke to
support their position. Consequentialists look forward, to the promotion or maximization of some good; but anyone who wants to *rectify* –
at least where punishment is concerned – must begin with a backward
glance to the way things were. Nor does Pettit contest this point.
As he says, the "first concern in sentencing is backward-looking in
character: it is a concern for the rectification of the past crime, ideally
by way of recognition [of the victim's dominion] and recompense"
(1992–3: 233). What Pettit does, however, is to try to turn this
backward-looking aspect of rectification to his advantage by using it
to demonstrate, once again, how the republican theory of criminal
punishment is both different from and better than either utilitarianism
or retributivism. As he puts the point, republicanism offers

> a third and different way in which we might conceptualize punishment.
> We might see it as an attempt to rectify the crime committed, not as
> an exercise in exacting retribution or in pursuing utility. If I may play

a little on words, we might focus in our view of punishment on making the offender pay up, not on delivering a suitable pay-back and not on securing a suitable pay-off. (1997b: 72)

This new emphasis on "punishment as rectification" also brings with it the "three Rs" of republican punishment. Punishment is meant to rectify or set right some evil that has been done, and on Pettit's account there are three evils associated with crime, with three corresponding republican remedies. The "first evil is the [offender's] assumption of a position of domination over the victim or, as they may be, victims," to which the remedy is *recognition* (1997b: 75). That is, republican punishment will aim at securing the offender's recognition of the victim's standing as a free person whom the offender cannot attempt to dominate without cost. Ideally, then, punishment will secure the offender's acknowledgement not only that he or she cannot interfere with the victim with impunity but that "the victim is deserving of respect and ought not to be exposed to interference" (1997b: 75).

Beyond its attack on the victim's status, crime also typically does physical, financial, or some other kind of harm to the victim. The remedy for this second evil is *recompense*: "The offender must make up to the victim, and/or the victim's dependants, for the loss incurred" (1997b: 76). Where direct restitution is not possible, recompense may involve community service of some kind, or even compensation to the victim or victims by the state itself, which failed to protect the victim. Crime is not simply a matter between the criminal and the victim, in other words. It involves the community as a whole, and it is the community that will feel the third evil associated with crime. This evil "consists in the more general challenge to people's nondomination that is going to be implicit in almost any criminal offence," and the remedy republican punishment will seek is *reassurance* (1997b: 77). This is "the most tricky" of the three Rs, according to Pettit, for one must be careful not to take reassurance to mean maximizing assurance. As with recognition and recompense – and rectification in general – reassurance is meant to be backward looking: "To require reassurance is to require a return to the *status quo* prior to the crime, not to require the maximum assurance attainable for the community" (1997b: 77).

Pettit uses this last point, in particular, against those who charge that his (and Braithwaite's) theory is simply another form of consequentialism in which maximizing the assurance of the public will lead to punishment out of all proportion to the offense or even to punishment of the innocent. Republican reassurance, and rectification in general, will not allow for such excesses, on Pettit's account. But if that is so, one must wonder how much consequentialism remains in republican punishment. The punishment-as-rectification policy of forcing the offender to "pay up" seems, in the end, to be the same as the retributive policy of forcing the offender to "pay back." After all, what determines what the offender must "pay up" is the need to put right the damage he or she has done to those, including the community as a whole, who have been his or her victims. To be sure, Pettit's republican policies may recommend different sentences in particular cases from those that would be handed down by a proponent of the "just deserts" school of retributivism. Retributivism is a broad church, however, and those who preach "just deserts" are not its only adherents. It is even broad enough, it appears, to accommodate republicans.

Duff's Communicative Retributivism

Retributivism is certainly capacious enough to accommodate another philosopher who talks about punishment in terms of "three Rs." That philosopher is R. A. Duff, the author of many important books and articles on punishment. In those works – most notably in *Punishment, Communication, and Community* – Duff sets out a "communicative theory" of punishment, "according to which punishment should be understood as a species of secular penance that aims not just to communicate censure but thereby to persuade offenders to *repentance, self-reform*, and *reconciliation*" (2001: xviii–xix; emphasis added).[7] Repentance, reform, and reconciliation are not identical to Pettit's recognition, recompense, and reassurance, of course, but the similarity of the two sets of "three Rs" is striking. Duff's set may be broader than Pettit's, for he says that "recognition is subsumed by repentance, and reparation by reconciliation" (*PCC*: 214 n. 37). Taking 'reparation' to be roughly equivalent to 'recompense,' Duff's set thus accounts for two of Pettit's "three Rs," with perhaps a bit of extra content added. As for the remaining "Rs" – Duff's reform and Pettit's reassurance – they are connected terms, if not equivalents. If an offender truly reforms by recognizing and repenting the wrong he has done, and by committing himself not to do it again (*PCC*: 108), the knowledge of his reform will provide reassurance to others in the community. If his repentance and reform lead to genuine reconciliation, moreover, the other members of the community will have reason to believe – will be reassured – that he no longer presents a threat to them.

To note these similarities is not to say that Duff and Pettit are simply using different words to say the same things. The similarities are striking, however, and they indicate that the two theories have much in common. Indeed, the commonalities go well beyond their appeal to "three Rs" of punishment.

How Duff's theory resembles Pettit's

Like Braithwaite and Pettit, Duff aspires to a comprehensive or unitary theory of punishment. He admits that there are reasons to regard such a theory with suspicion, particularly in the face of "the familiar phenomenon of value-conflict," which leaves us with "an untidy collection of indissolubly conflicting values between which we can (because we must) reach a series of uncomfortable compromises but which we cannot securely reconcile" (*PCC*: xvii). Nevertheless, Duff puts forward his own unitary theory: "Criminal punishment . . . should communicate to offenders the censure they deserve for their crimes and should aim through that communicative process to persuade them to repent those crimes, to try to reform themselves, and thus to reconcile themselves with those whom they wronged" (*PCC*: xvii).

Another aspiration that Duff shares with Pettit is the desire to accommodate both forward- and backward-looking considerations in a single theory. They approach this task from different directions, but they both hope to "undercut the traditional opposition between retributivist or backward-looking and consequentialist or forward-looking theories" (*PCC*: 89). Where Pettit (and Braithwaite) appeal to dominion or nondomination as the republican goal that looks to both past and future, however, Duff relies on the idea of punishment as a "communicative enterprise" to accomplish the task. We can justify punishment, he argues, "as a communicative enterprise focused on the past crime, as that for which the censure that punishment communicates is deserved; but also looking to a future aim to which it is related, not merely contingently as an instrumental technique, but internally as an intrinsically appropriate means" (*PCC*: 89).

This passage suggests yet another similarity between Pettit's and Duff's approaches to punishment, as both aim at some kind of restoration of full citizenship or membership in the community. In *Not Just Deserts*, Braithwaite and Pettit stress the importance of "reintegration in the community" as a way of restoring the dominion of both victims and offenders (*NJD*: 91).[8] Pettit does not pursue this point in the subsequent essays, but his appeal to "punishment as rectification" certainly hints at it: "after all, total rectification would mean that it is as if the crime did not take place" (1997b: 73). As for Duff, his third "R," reconciliation, speaks directly to his desire for a restoration of relations between the offender and the rest of the community. In his words, reconciliation "is what the repentant wrongdoer seeks with those she has wronged – and what they must seek with her if they are *still to see her as a fellow citizen*" (*PCC*: 109; emphasis added).

A final similarity is that Pettit shares with Duff a desire to avoid, whenever possible, "hard treatment" of those convicted of crimes. A prison sentence may be necessary to reassure society that it is safe from a dangerous offender, he says, but "prison is unlikely to do much in the way of facilitating either recognition or recompense" (1997b: 77). For his part, Duff clearly favors such tactics as probation and community-service orders, while admitting that incarceration is sometimes necessary (*PCC*: ch. 4). Nor is there any doubt that he would endorse Braithwaite and Pettit's assertion, "it is good when societies feel uncomfortable about punishment, when people see punishment as a necessary evil rather than a good in itself" (*NJD*: 6).

In these and other ways, Pettit's and Duff's theories of punishment appear not only to overlap but to be fundamentally similar. But there are also differences worth noting.

How Duff's theory differs from Pettit's

There are three respects in which Duff's theory seems significantly at odds with Pettit's: (1) Duff claims to be a retributivist; (2) he values autonomy rather than dominion or nondomination; and (3) he regards his theory as "liberal-communitarian," not republican. But these differences are not, I think, as serious as they seem.

With regard to Duff's professed retributivism versus Pettit's consequentialism, I have already indicated that neither philosopher is committed to a one-sided position. Indeed, Pettit's conception of punishment as rectification goes so far toward accommodating backward-looking concerns as to raise the question of whether it truly is a consequentialist theory. In Duff's case, there is a similar blurring of the boundaries between consequentialism and retributivism – a point on which it is best to quote him at length. His account of punishment, he says,

> is retributivist: it justifies punishment as the communication of deserved censure. Unlike other forms of retributivism, however, it also gives punishment the *forward-looking* purpose of persuading offenders to repent their crimes (communicative actions in general typically have a forward-looking purpose). This is not to say, however, that my account is a partly consequentialist one – that it seeks to marry a retributivist concern for desert with a consequentialist concern for future benefits: for the relation between punishment and its aim is not, as it is for consequentialists, contingent and instrumental . . . but internal. The very aim of persuading responsible agents to repent the wrongs they have done makes punishment the appropriate method of pursuing it. (*PCC*: 30)

In other words, Duff's theory is retributive because it does not take punishment to be simply a means to an end but a method internally or intrinsically connected, by the nature of the agents it seeks to correct, to wrongs those agents have committed. Those who have done wrong deserve to be condemned because they are "responsible agents" who, at least ideally, could have done otherwise; but as "responsible agents," they also deserve a chance to restore themselves to the fellowship of the community. Punishment is the method by which these wrong-doers – and those they have wronged – are to receive what they deserve.

As Duff's use of "responsible agents" attests, he is much concerned with autonomy. "To address the offender as an autonomous moral agent, as a member of a normative community with autonomy as one of its central values, is to appeal to him to judge his own conduct for himself in the light of values that he has made his own" (*PCC*: 118). By appealing to autonomy, however, Duff is calling on a conception of free and responsible agency that Braithwaite and Pettit explicitly reject when they declare that "dominion" should be distinguished "from the commonly invoked value of autonomy" (*NJD*: 56). Dominion, on their account, is a form of negative liberty – as is Pettit's later "nondomination," or freedom from domination – whereas they identify autonomy with positive liberty. There is clearly a difference between Pettit and Duff on this point, then, but how significant is it?

This question I cannot hope to answer fully in this essay. Such an answer would require not only a close examination of what Duff means by 'autonomy' and Pettit by 'dominion' and 'nondomination'; it would also require an assessment of the troublesome distinction between positive and negative liberty. Providing such an answer would also lead to the further question of whether republicanism is properly grounded in autonomy rather than in nondomination – a question I have taken up elsewhere (Dagger 2005). For present purposes, it is enough to observe that 'autonomy,' 'dominion,' and 'nondomination' are all terms that denote a certain kind of status or standing – that of the free, responsible agent, subject to no master – and that this status is worthy of both preservation and respect. If nothing else, it is clear that dominion and nondomination are closer to autonomy than they are to such typical consequentialist goals as pleasure, happiness, utility, or welfare. In short, there is no reason to think that the difference in terminology betokens some respect in which Duff's theory and Pettit's are fundamentally at odds.

But what of Duff's allegiance to a liberal-communitarian conception of politics? Can this be squared with Pettit's republicanism? In this case, the advantage is on Pettit's side. That is, not only *can* Duff's theory of punishment be squared with republicanism, it *should* be. Duff's theory relies on republican ideas, as I shall now try to show, and it would be a stronger theory if he were to make this latent republicanism manifest.

Republican Retributivism

As the title indicates, community is a central concept in Duff's *Punishment, Communication, and Community*. Taking the "academic community" as his model, Duff identifies two major features of community: first, "community requires a shared commitment by the community's members to certain defining values . . ."; and second, "the members of the community must have a regard for one another as fellow members that is itself structured by the community's defining values" (*PCC*: 43). If the community is a *political* community, or polity, then its members are *citizens* (*PCC*: 48, 52). And if the political community is a *liberal* political community – the kind that Duff favors – then it is "a polity defined and structured by a shared commitment to such central liberal values as freedom, autonomy, privacy, and pluralism, and by a mutual regard that reflects those values" (*PCC*: 47). Punishment thus enters the picture "as a method of protecting citizens from crime that also shows potential and actual criminals the respect and concern due them as citizens" (*PCC*: 113).

How consistent is this picture with Pettit's republicanism? One might think that the two must be inconsistent, for Duff's political community adheres to four liberal values – freedom, autonomy, privacy, and pluralism – whereas Pettit's fixes on the sole republican value of dominion or nondomination, leaving the two theories to differ on both quantitative and qualitative grounds. There are, however, reasons to resist this conclusion. With regard to the qualitative grounds, it is by no means clear that liberalism and republicanism can be easily or sharply distinguished from each other (see e.g. Larmore 2001; Dagger 2005). Just as Duff can conceive of liberal communitarianism, so is it possible to conceive of liberal republicanism or republican liberalism (e.g., Dagger 1997). Nor do the quantitative considerations show Duff's liberal political community to be incompatible with Pettit's republicanism. Pettit does say in *Republicanism* that "freedom as nondomination" is the "supreme political value" of the republican tradition, but he does not say that it is the only one (1997a: 80). Even if it were, dominion or nondomination would be a remarkably expansive "supreme political value," entailing, as we have seen, that the person who enjoys full dominion "enjoys no less a prospect of liberty than is available to other citizens" (*NJD*: 64). "Prospect of liberty" is a rather elastic phrase, and it need not be stretched far to encompass Duff's four values of freedom, autonomy, privacy, and pluralism.

Neither qualitative nor quantitative considerations force us to conclude, then, that Duff's liberal political community is inconsistent with Pettit's republicanism. For that matter, one might argue that republicans need not agree with Pettit's vision of republicanism as a theory with freedom as nondomination at its center. I shall set that possibility aside, however, as something very much like dominion or nondomination does indeed seem to figure prominently in the republican tradition, even if it is not its "supreme political value." For now, the important question is whether there are reasons to think that Duff's liberal communitarianism is positively consistent with Pettit's theory and with republicanism in general.

There are at least three such reasons, beginning with Duff's attempt to find a firm path between the opposing camps in the debate between liberals and communitarians. To recognize oneself "as a fellow member of a political community," he states, is "not to say that for communitarians we must begin (metaphysically or morally) with communities *rather than* with individuals, as if individuals were subordinate to the communities to which they belong. . . . It is to say that we must begin with *individuals in community*, with individuals who already recognize themselves as living in community with others" (*PCC*: 52; emphasis in original). Such a starting point – with *individuals in community* – is one that Pettit (and Braithwaite) can readily accept. So much is evident in the distinction Pettit resurrects between the "freedom of the city" and the "freedom of the heath" (1989; also 1992–3: 227). It is the former – the freedom enjoyed by the citizen living under the rule of law, not the lawless freedom of the isolated heath dweller – that is the republican ideal. Nor do Braithwaite and Pettit entertain the thought that dominion might best be conceived as the prospect of liberty that an isolated individual would enjoy. Dominion or freedom from domination is certainly something to be enjoyed by individuals, but these are, as in Duff's theory, individuals *in community*.

A second point of consistency is that the kind of community that both Duff and Pettit are concerned with is a community under law. For both philosophers it is the rule of law, secured by punishment, that makes it possible for individuals in community to enjoy autonomy, dominion, or freedom from domination. Duff draws a telling connection to the common law in this regard. In contrast to statute law, which a sovereign may impose on the people, the common law "is the law of the community itself." Not only that, it is "a law fit for citizens rather than subjects" (*PCC*: 59). Distinguishing citizen from subject, of course, is a staple of the republican tradition, and one that Pettit draws on frequently. To be a citizen is to be free, ideally, from the domination of others, even if one must live under law. The law may guide one's conduct and constrain one's actions, but as a citizen one at least has a voice in determining what the laws are. In this connection Pettit is fond of citing James Harrington's retort to Hobbes, in which Harrington distinguishes between freedom *from* the laws – the kind of freedom that one *may* be fortunate to enjoy even under a despotic regime – and freedom *by* the laws (*NJD*: 59; 1992–3: 228; 1997a: 38–9; 1997b: 63). So strong is this sense of freedom through civic self-government in the republican tradition that Braithwaite and Pettit refer to it as the "republican notion of liberty *as* citizenship . . ." (*NJD*: 59; emphasis added).

Duff does not go so far as to define liberty as citizenship, but he certainly does link the two concepts. Without invoking "some mysterious collective good" to which one should subordinate one's autonomy, freedom, or privacy, Duff does say that

> within a liberal polity my autonomy has value as that of an autonomous citizen among other autonomous citizens; and so too with freedom and privacy. If I have the freedom to pursue my own projects, while many of my fellow citizens do not, the very character of my freedom differs from that of the freedom of a free citizen among other free citizens; nor does it have the value that freedom has when it is shared in by all – the value that defines it as the good of citizens in a liberal polity. (*PCC*: 55)

In this and other respects, Duff leans heavily on the idea of citizenship – as, of course, does Pettit.

The appeal to citizenship is thus the third point of positive consistency between Duff's theory and Pettit's. In both cases, moreover, this appeal to citizenship carries much of the burden of an inclusive theory of punishment. One reason to try to reintegrate offenders into society, according to Braithwaite and Pettit, is to "save them from becoming stigmatized, second-class citizens" (*NJD*: 132). This opposition to the tendency to treat punishment as something essentially exclusive – as a way of dividing us, the law-abiding members of society, from them, the evildoers – is at least as powerful in Duff's theory. In a passage reminiscent of Rousseau's argument in the *Social Contract* (bk. I, ch. 7), Duff says that "criminal punishment could and should be inclusionary, as something that we can do, not to a 'them' who are implicitly excluded from the (law-abiding) community of citizens, but to *ourselves* as full, if imperfect, members of that community" (*PCC*: 77; emphasis in original). If the law is truly "common law" – "a law fit for citizens rather than subjects" (*PCC*: 59) – then it is a law to which we all, as citizens, subject ourselves. When we fail to live in accordance with this law, then it is only fitting that we suffer punishment. Punishment, however, should aim not at excluding the offender from the community but at encouraging him or her to return to full citizenship. Hence punishment should be understood to be "a burden imposed on an offender for his crime, through which, it is hoped, he will come to repent his crime, to begin to reform himself, and thus reconcile himself with those he has wronged" (*PCC*: 106). Only when "persistent, serious criminal wrongdoing" makes "reconciliation – the maintenance or restoration of *civic fellowship* – impossible" should we subject an offender to "an extended, indeed if necessary life-long, period of imprisonment . . ." (*PCC*: 172; emphasis added).

Citizenship thus plays a major role in Duff's communicative theory of punishment.[9] In this regard Duff's theory proves to be consistent not only with Pettit's but with republican thinking in general. Indeed, the connections to republicanism are strong enough to warrant the claim that Duff's theory is not so much liberal-communitarian as it is liberal-republican. In other words, it is not just any kind of community that underpins Duff's account of punishment; it is a *republican* community that takes citizenship to be of great value. For Duff, as for Cicero (1999: 18), "the commonwealth [*res publica*] is the concern of a people, but a people is not any group of men assembled in any way, but an assemblage of some size associated with one another through agreement on law and community of interest." Duff is certainly a retributivist, as he professes, but he may well be a republican, too.

Conclusion

This essay began with the question, May a republican be a retributivist? As should be clear by now, the answer is yes, for two reasons. The first is that Pettit's (and Braithwaite's) republican theory of punishment does not succeed in ruling retributivism out of bounds. In part this is a consequence of Braithwaite and Pettit's properly ambitious aim, which is to construct a theory that combines forward- and backward-looking elements. As we have seen, however, Pettit's defense of their theory against the charge that it is subject to all of the problems of other consequentialist theories leads to a conception of "punishment as rectification" that is remarkably similar to Duff's retributive theory. The second reason is that Duff's communicative retributivism sounds so many themes congenial to republicans, including major themes of Pettit's "punishment as rectification," that the compatibility of his theory with republicanism seems beyond doubt. Republicanism may have the advantage of offering a more comprehensive theory of criminal justice than retributivism, in sum, but that is not to say that the two are rival theories where punishment is concerned.

Republicans *may* be retributivists, then, but *should* they be? The arguments of this paper strongly suggest that the answer, again, is yes. Pettit will no doubt resist this conclusion, but the difficulties he and Braithwaite face as consequentialists who aim to promote or maximize dominion leave them with an awkward choice. Either they can cling to their consequentialism, in which case they will have to say that in some instances, such as "disaster situations," individuals should be treated as means to the end of maximizing dominion; or they can embrace retributivism. The latter seems to me the better option, especially when Duff has made available a retributive theory that is so congenial to Braithwaite and Pettit's republican theory of punishment.[10]

This leaves us, finally, with a third question: Should a retributivist be a republican? Republicans may have the benefit of a sounder theory of punishment if they adopt retributivism, as I have suggested, but it does not follow that retributivists will benefit from adopting republicanism. Why, then, might a retributivist think that he or she should look to republicanism as a political theory within which to frame his or her approach to punishment? The answer, which I can only touch on here, is that republicanism provides the firmest grounding for retributivist judgments. In Duff's communicative theory we have a highly sophisticated and powerful form of retributivism; but it is also, as I have indicated, a theory that relies implicitly on republican considerations, notably appeals to citizenship. Hence the reason for retributivists to adopt republicanism.

This conclusion may seem to reach too far. After all, the concept of citizenship is not the exclusive property of republicans. If it is to do the kind of work Duff wants it to do, however, citizenship will have to be understood as something more than a merely legal status. Important as it is, legal citizenship is not by itself up to the task of forging the link with punishment that Duff requires. Holding a US passport may give me both a legal status and something in common with millions of other people, but it has not led me to a feeling of "civic fellowship" with the great community of US-passport holders. Something more than common legal standing is necessary if people are to believe that they form a community bound by shared values and a sense of civic fellowship. The law has an important part to play here, to be sure. People may be more likely to see themselves as parts of a community with shared values when they believe that they are protected by the rule of law; they may be more likely to feel a sense of fellowship when they enjoy equal treatment under the law. But they must also appreciate how the rule of law is a cooperative endeavor, not some remote, impersonal force looming over them. Gaining this appreciation will require them to understand that upholding or even improving the rule of law makes demands on them as *public* persons – that is, as *citizens* according to the republican conception of citizenship.

Citizenship, indeed, is not an exclusively republican concept. But it is *republican* citizenship that provides the underpinnings for Duff's powerful form of communicative retributivism and leads to the conclusion that retributivists should also be republicans. To accept this conclusion is to acknowledge a connection that already, albeit implicitly, exists.

ACKNOWLEDGMENTS

This paper was written while I was a Fellow of the Center for Ethics and Public Affairs, Tulane University, and I owe the Center and its Director, Richard Teichgraeber, a deep debt of gratitude for their support in the aftermath of Hurricane Katrina. I am also grateful to the participants in the University of Virginia's Political Theory Workshop, especially Nitu Bagchi, for a helpful discussion of an earlier draft of this paper, and to Antony Duff, Jeffrie Murphy, Philip Pettit, Mary Sigler, and the editors for valuable comments.

NOTES

1 Braithwaite & Pettit 1990: 2. Further references to this book will appear within parentheses in the text as *NJD*.

2 I refer to "Pettit" here rather than "Braithwaite and Pettit" because Pettit has been either the sole or the lead author of the relevant responses. For "punishment as rectification," see e.g. Pettit 1997b: 59, 72, and 77; for "*maximization* of the dominion" (emphasis added), see *NJD*: 54.

3 Indeed, Braithwaite and Pettit seem unconcerned with the difficulties of defining punishment, and they never, to the best of my knowledge, define it themselves.

4 The other two tasks are "to ensure as far as possible that these become and remain a matter of common knowledge" and "to maximize the liberty prospects available consistently with the degree of equality and common knowledge that has been attained" (p. 68).

5 The quoted passages – from pp. 9, 54, and 65 of *NJD*, respectively – are but a few of such references.

6 "Republican Theory and Criminal Punishment," p. 72 n. 29: "Punishment is an offence against nondomination (i.e. what [Braithwaite and I] earlier called dominion) but not necessarily of exactly the same kind as crime . . ."

7 See also §6.1, pp. 107–12, for Duff's explication of "The Three 'R's of Punishment." Further references to this work will appear within parentheses in the text as *PCC*.

8 Braithwaite has also championed "reintegration" and "restorative justice" in other works, notably his *Crime, Shame and Reintegration* (Cambridge: Cambridge University Press, 1989).

9 The appeal to citizenship is even more explicit in Duff 1996.

10 It is worth noting that *NJD* contains three references to Duff's *Trials and Punishments* – the argument of which Duff extends in *PCC* – and all are favorable.

REFERENCES

Ashworth, A. & von Hirsch, A. (1993–4). "Desert and the Three Rs." *Current Issues in Criminal Justice*, 9, 9–12.

Braithwaite, J. (1989). *Crime, Shame, and Reintegration*. Cambridge: Cambridge University Press.

Braithwaite, J. & Pettit, P. (1990). *Not Just Deserts: A Republican Theory of Criminal Punishment*. Oxford: Clarendon Press.

Cicero (1999). *On the Commonwealth and On the Laws*, ed. J. Zetzel. Cambridge: Cambridge University Press.

Dagger, R. (1997). *Civic Virtues: Rights, Citizenship, and Republican Liberalism*. New York: Oxford University Press.

Dagger, R. (2004). "Communitarianism and Republicanism." In G. Gaus & C. Kukathas (eds.), *Handbook of Political Theory*. London: Sage Publications, pp. 167–79.

Dagger, R. (2005). "Autonomy, Domination, and the Republican Challenge to Liberalism." In J. Christman & J. Anderson (eds.), *Autonomy and the Challenges to Liberalism*. Cambridge: Cambridge University Press, pp. 177–203.

Duff, R. A. (1986). *Trials and Punishments*. Cambridge: Cambridge University Press.

Duff, R. A. (1996). "Punishment, Citizenship, and Responsibility." In H. Tam (ed.), *Punishment, Excuses, and Moral Development*. Aldershot, UK: Avebury Publishers, Aldershot.

Duff, R. A. (2001). *Punishment, Communication, and Community*. Oxford: Oxford University Press.

Hart, H. L. A. (1968). "Prolegomenon to the Principles of Punishment." In Hart, *Punishment and Responsibility: Essays in the Philosophy of Law*. Oxford: Oxford University Press, pp. 1–27.

Larmore, C. (2001). "A Critique of Philip Pettit's Republicanism." *Philosophical Issues 11: Social, Political, and Legal Philosophy* (special edition of *Noûs*), 229–43.

Mackie, J. L. (1985). "Morality and the Retributive Emotions." In J. L. Mackie, *Persons and Values: Selected Papers*, vol. II. Oxford: Clarendon Press.

Matravers, M. (2000). *Justice and Punishment: The Rationale of Coercion.* Oxford: Oxford University Press.

Montague, P. (1995). *Punishment as Societal Defense.* Lanham, MD: Rowman & Littlefield.

Murphy, J. G. (1998). "Repentance, Punishment, and Mercy." In Murphy, *Character, Liberty, and Law: Kantian Essays in Theory and Practice.* New York: Kluwer Academic Publishers.

Pettit, P. (1989). "The Freedom of the City: A Republican Ideal." In A. Hamlin & P. Pettit (eds.), *The Good Polity.* Oxford: Blackwell.

Pettit, P. (1997a). *Republicanism: A Theory of Freedom and Government.* Oxford: Clarendon Press.

Pettit, P. (1997b). "Republican Theory and Criminal Punishment." *Utilitas,* 9, 59–79.

Pettit, P. (2000). "Indigence and Sentencing in Republican Theory." In W. C. Heffernan & J. Kleinig (eds.), *From Social Justice to Criminal Justice: Poverty and the Administration of Criminal Law.* Oxford: Oxford University Press, pp. 230–47.

Pettit, P. with Braithwaite, J. (1992–3). "Not Just Deserts, Not Even in Sentencing." *Current Issues in Criminal Justice,* 4, 225–39.

Pettit, P. and Braithwaite, J. (1993–4). "The Three Rs of Republican Sentencing." *Current Issues in Criminal Justice,* 5, 318–25.

Radin, M. J. (1993). *Reinterpreting Property.* Chicago: University of Chicago Press.

Smart, J. J. C. (1973). "An Outline of a System of Utilitarian Ethics." In J. J. C. Smart & B. Williams, *Utilitarianism: For and Against.* Cambridge: Cambridge University Press.

Von Hirsch, A. & Ashworth, A. (1992). "Not Not Just Deserts: A Response to Braithwaite and Pettit." *Oxford Journal of Legal Studies,* 12, 83–98.

Chapter 10
Pettit's Civic Republicanism and Male Domination

Marilyn Friedman

The civic republican tradition is known for its political ideal of active citizen participation in the affairs of state, an ideal at least as old as Aristotle's *Politics*. The ideal citizen participates in the process of legislating the laws to which he (and now she) is subject and by doing so realizes an important form of freedom.

Philip Pettit's version of civic republicanism is not about this Aristotelian/Athenian ideal of self-government. It is about an alternative ideal that, he argues, lies at the core of the Roman republican tradition. Pettit maintains that the predominant concern of the Roman republican conception of freedom is the absence of domination by others. Domination, on Pettit's account, is essentially the capacity to interfere arbitrarily in someone else's life. Pettit's Roman republican ideal of freedom is to live in a way that is politically secured against domination, that is, against arbitrary interference in one's life, by others (Pettit 1997, *passim*).

Pettit tells us that he wrote *Republicanism* not merely in order to revive a political perspective that had been historically lost, but "out of a wish to explore a new vision of what public life might be" (Pettit 1997: 129). My aim in this paper is to explore some of the conceptual underpinnings of that vision. In the interests of doing so, I will ignore questions about the historical accuracy of Pettit's interpretation of the Roman republican tradition. I will also avoid evaluating Pettit's policy proposals for solving the problem of domination. Instead, my focus will be on Pettit's conception of the nature of domination: whether his conception adequately illuminates that social problem and whether Pettit's ideal of nondomination is ideal enough. I am especially concerned to explore Pettit's account of domination from a feminist perspective and consider how well it applies to male domination in particular (cf. Phillips 2000). In my discussion, male domination is understood both as a type of action or pattern of behavior that individual males can enact toward individual females and as a behavioral pattern that can pervade whole societies. Exactly what domination itself consists in is one of the issues to be addressed below.

Pettit's Republicanism

The core of Pettit's republicanism is a conception of freedom as nondomination. Pettit presents his conception of freedom as a third alternative to the conceptions of negative and positive liberty that Isaiah Berlin made famous in his 1958 paper, "Two Concepts of Liberty" (Berlin 1969: 118–72). Negative liberty involves being able to act without interference by others. One lacks freedom in this sense to the extent that others interfere and prevent one from doing what one wants to do (Berlin 1969: 122). Positive liberty, by contrast, is self-mastery. A person with positive liberty acts and lives in accord with her own will and is moved by her own reasons. Berlin expresses the longing for positive liberty with flare: "I wish to be somebody, not nobody; a doer – deciding, not being decided for, self-directed and not acted upon by external nature or by other men as if I were a thing, an animal, or a slave incapable of playing a human role . . ." (Berlin 1969: 131).

Pettit suggests that Berlin's famous dichotomy has made it hard to recognize a third conception of freedom that falls somewhere between the other two. Pettit's third conception is freedom as nondomination. Freedom as nondomination consists in the absence of domination, or mastery, by others. Nondomination is distinct from Berlin's positive liberty in that it does not necessarily involve self-mastery. Rather, non-domination involves merely the absence of mastery of oneself by others. Nondomination is distinct from Berlin's negative liberty because what is absent in negative liberty differs from what is absent in nondomination. Negative liberty is the absence of mere interference by others. Nondomination is instead, and obviously, the absence of domination by others. In Pettit's view, interference and domination are two different "evils" (Pettit 1997: 22).

Pettit defines domination as: (1) the capacity to interfere, (2) on an arbitrary basis, (3) in certain choices that the other is in a position to make (Pettit 1997: 52). These three constituents are each necessary conditions of domination for Pettit. Interference is arbitrary "if it is subject just to the *arbitrium*, the decision or judgment, of the agent [who interferes]; the agent was in a position to choose it or not choose it, at their pleasure." In particular, interference is arbitrary if "it is chosen or rejected without reference to the interests, or the opinions, of those affected. The choice is not forced to track what the interests of those others require according to their own judgements" (Pettit 1997: 55).

Pettit maintains that interference, unlike domination, can occur in a way that tracks the interests of the person subjected to it. One person, A, can interfere with another person, B, on condition that the interference promises to further B's interests. In such a case, interference occurs but domination does not occur. Conversely, on Pettit's view, domination can occur without interference. Pettit's idea – and this is a crucial part of his account – is that domination does not have to involve actual interference. Domination is defined as the *capacity* to interfere arbitrarily in someone else's choices, not necessarily the actual interference in her choices. Domination exists when someone has the power to interfere with another, even if the one with that power does not exercise it (Pettit 1997: 2–3).

Someone who has the power to dominate others may fail to do so for any number of reasons. A slavemaster may let a slave alone out of a kindly disposition and a vulnerable person may avoid domination by ingratiating herself with those who have power over her. In these sorts of cases, the dominated person does not enjoy a secure situation. Her lack of arbitrary interference by others is not "robust" or "resilient." It occurs at the pleasure or whim of the powerful party. The potentially dominated one still remains vulnerable to the sort of interference by the powerful party that fails to track her interests or her ideas. A married woman, for example, argues Pettit, is dominated to the extent that her husband has the capacity to interfere with her even if he does not actually choose to do so. Unless there are institutional constraints that prevent him from dominating her, her freedom from domination becomes hostage to his volition and dependent on his good will (Pettit 1997: 22, 24, 123).

Being in a condition of nondomination involves more than simply the mere absence of arbitrary interference. It also involves immunity or security against arbitrary interference. Nondomination thus requires a political framework that provides such security against arbitrary interference (Pettit 1997: 69). On Pettit's view, the primary role of the state is to foster and preserve political and social conditions that minimize the domination of citizens by other citizens and that do so without fostering the domination of citizens by government. Pettit claims that state interference is not arbitrary, and thus not domination, so long as it tracks "the welfare and world-view of the public," that is, "the shared interests of those affected under an interpretation of what those interests require that is shared . . . by those affected" (Pettit 1997: 56).

Pettit notes that traditional civic republicans were concerned to achieve what he calls nondomination through the political system only for the elite males who constituted the citizenry. Pettit explicitly breaks with that elitism and advocates nondomination as a political ideal for all persons. He claims that social groups far removed from those for whom it was originally articulated can take up the language of freedom as nondomination. Thus, Pettit regards nondomination as a neutral political ideal (Pettit 1997: 95–7, 133).

Male domination has been a definitive concern of feminists. Pettit's reinterpretation of Roman republicanism as a perspective that opposes domination should therefore be a welcome development for feminists. In many of its details, Pettit's position overlaps with positions that are widespread among feminists. For example, Pettit frequently uses the example of relationships between husbands and wives to illustrate aspects of his theory of nondomination and he calls clearly for an end to male domination of women within heterosexual marriage and family. Pettit would surely also agree that male domination of women should be eliminated in all the nonmarital social contexts in which it arises, for example, in the workplace and in all heterosexual sexual relationships. The ideal of nondomination, as applied to all relationships between women and men, would eliminate all the various forms of arbitrary interference that men exert over women's choices. It would end men's interventions in, and affects on, women's lives that make no reference to either women's interests or their perspectives.

Pettit also shares with most feminists the view that freedom as mere noninterference by others (Berlin's "negative liberty") is far from sufficient to ground a complete political philosophy and may be wrongheaded altogether (cf. Hirschmann 2003). The ideal of negative liberty elevates the importance of occasions when noninterference between persons happens to be valuable and this can distort the understanding of personal relationships by mistakenly making it seem as if the best thing people can do for each other in general is to get out of each other's way.

Pettit's account also coincides with most feminist perspectives in taking account of the social; he conceptualizes domination and nondomination each as a kind of "intersubjective status" that is based on group identities and is a matter of "common knowledge." Nondomination is not something to be achieved in isolation; it means the "absence of domination in the presence of other people" (Pettit 1997: 66, 70, 71, 122). Social practices and the reactions of third persons are important factors in determining whether someone can dominate another, and the extent and degree to which they can do so. Pettit notes, for example, how the domination involved in wife-beating is affected by the "censure of . . . neighbours" (Pettit 1997: 57). Finally, Pettit argues that domination has a group-based character. Although the subjects of domination are always, in Pettit's view, individual persons, they may be subject to domination in virtue of a "collective identity or capacity or aspiration" they share with others (Pettit 1997: 52). Domination tends to occur on the basis of certain "markers" such as gender, race, or class. The domination to which someone is exposed is like that to which others of her group are also exposed. Because domination is group-based, the quest for freedom as nondomination has a social character. Nondomination is a "communitarian" good (Pettit 1997: 12–25).

Thus, Pettit's approach to nondomination is congruent with typical feminist approaches. At the same time, there are several feminist concerns that are missing from Pettit's account. Before turning to those concerns, I will note, in the next section, one problem with Pettit's account that is not specifically about feminist issues. In the four sections that follow, I will respectively raise four feminist concerns that suggest ways to modify Pettit's promising account of freedom as nondomination.

The Ubiquity of Capacities for Arbitrary Interference

Pettit claims that interference and domination are distinct evils and may occur one without the other. At first glance, this may seem incorrect, given Pettit's own terminology. Since he defines domination as arbitrary interference, it seems that domination is merely one type of interference, and, therefore, that where there is domination, there must also be interference (though not vice versa). However, this would be to ignore an important asymmetry in Pettit's handling of the concepts of interference and domination. Pettit treats interference as a certain type of behavior. By contrast, he explicitly defines domination as a *capacity* for a certain type of behavior, rather than as a certain type of behavior. Pettit's requirement of freedom as nondomination is, in at least one formal respect, more demanding than the negative liberty requirement of mere noninterference. Pettit's nondomination principle requires that a person experience not merely the absence of certain behaviors by others (viz., arbitrary interference with her choices); in addition, it requires that others lack certain *capacities* to act in the unwanted ways (viz., capacities to interfere arbitrarily with her choices).

Is Pettit's requirement too demanding? The capacity for arbitrary interference accompanies any excess of power that a person possesses with respect to any other person. Big and strong people can physically overpower weak people; smart people can outwit those with less intelligence, and rich people can find ways to control the poor. When someone actually exercises a capacity for arbitrary interference, it is legitimate to consider subjecting her to political control. The key question however is whether someone should be controlled even when she does not use her capacities for arbitrary interference. One powerful reason to avoid regulating unused capacities is that any state that uses its power to suppress all the various capacities that people have for dominating each other would be acting so pervasively in people's lives that it would amount to a totalitarian police state. It would exemplify the excessive state control of "*imperium*" that Petit seeks to avoid.

Pettit argues that when someone has a power over me they are not exercising, yet the state does not restrain that exercise, then I am vulnerable to this power because the person could effectively exercise it at her own pleasure and I would have no way to stop her arbitrary interference in my life. I am insecure because I lack the power to resist, on my own, the possible arbitrary exercises against me of the other party's power. I have no guarantee that the party with the power will voluntarily hold it in abeyance. This condition of insecurity involves, for Pettit, as much a form of domination by that other party as a condition in which a person does successfully act to interfere with me arbitrarily.

Pettit's position, however, does not seem right. Although a utilized power advantage and one that is not utilized may both be worrisome, there are crucial differences between them. Someone who uses her power advantage over me to interfere arbitrarily with my choices does change the outcomes of my choices. In that case, my life does not go as I would have chosen it to go and a wrong may thereby have been done to me. However, a power advantage that someone possesses over me does not actually harm me if it is unused. Of course, if someone has a mere capacity to interfere arbitrarily with my choices, I am, as Pettit argues, vulnerable to that potential interference. If I know I am vulnerable, I may suffer from fear and anxiety. However this alone does not entail that the state should suppress people's unexercised powers.

First, the fear of someone's interference that fails to occur is usually less injurious than the actual interference would have been. Second, a state often controls behavior by means of punishment or penalties. However, someone who does not exercise her capacity to interfere arbitrarily with others does not deserve to be punished or penalized by the state. Punishment is not appropriate for a mere capacity to act badly that a person does not exercise. Punishment should be inflicted only for actual or, sometimes, attempted wrongful behavior. Pettit's preferred political solution to the problem of power advantages is to create political means by which those with less power can hold the more powerful parties accountable and challenge their capacities for arbitrary interference (Pettit 1997: 63, 67–9, 184–200). Yet if they have not exercised their powers, what are they to account for? Pettit is unclear about how the mechanism of political control would operate on those who have not exercised their capacities for domination. Third, a state that continually regulates relative power advantages among its people would be exercising the *imperium* of a police state, something that Pettit himself seeks to avoid. Fourth, the governmental regulation of unexercised personal power threatens to be so extensive as to swamp the political process.

The best way to amend Pettit's account to eliminate this problem of unwarranted excessive scope is to redefine "domination" so as to narrow its range of application to cases of actual or attempted arbitrary interference. A state that tried to achieve this narrower ideal of nondomination would be less likely to engage in *imperium* than a state that tried also to suppress mere capacities for domination.

Capacities for Arbitrary Interference and Feminism

Eva Kittay distinguishes between domination in a relationship and what she calls (mere) inequality of power in a relationship. Kittay characterizes domination as involving "the exercise of power over another against her best interests and for purposes that have no moral legitimacy." She does not specifically define the term "inequality of power" but the implication of her usage is that this term refers to capacities for domination that may not be exercised. Domination, in Kittay's treatment of it, involves the actual wielding of comparatively greater power over another; an unexercised inequality of power does not constitute domination (Kittay 1999: 33–4).

In the previous section, I argued that a political ideal of nondomination that rules out both used and unused capacities for arbitrary interference is too demanding because it could not be realized by anything short of a totalitarian police state. Feminists recognize a different reason for thinking that this ideal is too demanding. The capacities of people to interfere arbitrarily in the lives of others are often, if not always, also capacities to interfere nonarbitrarily for the benefit and care of those others. A capacity to benefit someone must be diverse and adaptable enough so that the person who possesses the capacity can handle an indeterminate variety of situations that may arise in caretaking. A good caretaker must be able to respond to at least some range of unpredictable contingencies with behavior that benefits the one for whom she cares. Such capacities are essential to interpersonal relationships in which people depend on others for care, nurturance, love, and support. Yet an open, adaptable capacity to help another person in an indeterminate variety of ways is also a capacity to act in ways that harm the other person.

Kittay is particularly concerned with relationships of dependency. She reminds us that dependency relationships are necessary throughout human life. Yet these relationships tend to be neglected by political theory and are therefore not adequately incorporated into our understandings of our most important political norms or values. Someone is dependent on another person when that someone has a need she cannot satisfy by herself and the other person is able to do so. The party who is able to satisfy the need has, in that respect, a power that the dependent person lacks. Thus, whenever there is a relationship of dependency, there is also an inequality of power; otherwise, the needy person could not be genuinely dependent on the other party. Any caretaker, who has some power greater than that of the one for whom she cares and whose needs she meets, also at the same time has a capacity to interfere in that someone's life without regard to the latter's interests or ideas. The capacity to clean someone's wound is also the capacity to infect it. The capacity to help someone climb the stairs is also the capacity to throw her down the stairs. An excess of power relative to another, which almost certainly constitutes domination on Pettit's view, seems nevertheless to be a necessary feature of relationships in which some people care for and meet the needs of others. That caretakers must have greater power in some respects than those for whom they care provides another reason to distinguish the mere capacity to interfere arbitrarily in someone's life from actual acts of arbitrary interference. Arbitrary interference is always *prima facie* problematic; the mere capacity for it not so.

Pettit sometimes refers to the person who could be the subject of arbitrary interference as a "dependent" (Pettit 1997: 63). However, Pettit gives scant attention to the needs of dependent persons for adequate care. Nor does he acknowledge that some capacities for arbitrary interference in the lives of others are also capacities for benefiting those others in ways that are necessary for their survival and flourishing. Pettit sometimes seems scornful of the status of dependency and does not treat it as normal or necessary, as in this passage:

> Domination is generally going to involve the awareness of control on the part of the powerful, the awareness of vulnerability on the part of the *powerless*, and the mutual awareness – indeed, the common awareness among all the parties to the relationship – of this consciousness on each side. The powerless are not going to be able to *look the powerful in the eye*, conscious as each will be – and conscious as each will be of the other's consciousness – of this asymmetry. (Pettit 1997: 60–1, italics mine)

Commenting on how an individual is still dominated even when the one with the capacity to interfere arbitrarily does not actually do so, Pettit writes: "the power-victim acts in the relevant area by the leave, explicit or implicit, of the power-bearer; it means that *they live at the mercy* of that person, that they are in the position of a *dependent or debtor* or something of the kind" (Pettit 1997: 63, italics mine). And Pettit praises the absence of domination in these terms:

> You do not have to live either in fear of that other, then, or in deference to them. The non-interference you enjoy at the hands of others is not enjoyed by their grace and *you do not live at their mercy. You are a*

somebody in relation to them, not a nobody. You are a person in your own legal and social right. (Pettit 1997: 71)

This passage echoes Berlin's first-personal expression of what it is to enjoy positive liberty: "I wish to be somebody, not nobody; a doer . . . not acted upon by . . . other men as if I were a thing, an animal, or a slave . . ." (Berlin 1969: 131).

Thus, Pettit links the condition of being dominated to that of being a dependent, and links dependency, in turn, to that of being a debtor, a nobody, someone who is powerless, lives at the mercy of her caretaker, and cannot "look the powerful in the eye" as if she, the dependent, were in a shameful condition. John Rawls has been criticized for idealizing all citizens as "fully cooperating members of society over a complete life" (Rawls 1995: 3), yet he is not the only political philosopher to neglect the significance of human interdependency for political theory. Pettit's disparaging reference to "dependents" exemplifies the same inadequate grasp of the essential role of dependency relationships in human life. Everyone is dependent on some others for at least some stages of life and few if any human beings are ever completely self-sufficient at any stage of life. Being dependent on others for at least some times or some aspects of survival is the common lot of all human beings. There is nothing to scorn in dependency. What is needed instead is a proper appreciation of how to manage the *inter*-dependencies of human relationships in ways that benefit all participants while minimizing the arbitrary interferences and abuses that dependency may permit to happen.

The crucial issue that Kittay addresses but that Pettit neglects to consider is this: how do we ensure that caretakers have the liberty and power they need to care well for their charges while preventing caretakers from using that power to abuse or otherwise dominate their charges? Could Pettit modify his ideal of freedom as nondomination to accommodate this concern?

Pettit could reply by suggesting that we should find the right balance between, on the one hand, allowing caretakers the liberty they need to exercise their capacities (for domination) in the form of the nonarbitrary care of dependents, and, on the other hand, preventing caretakers (and others) from ignoring the interests or ideas of those being cared for (and anyone else less powerful than they are). Only when a parent, say, abuses her child should the state step in to restrain her; so long as she merely possesses but does not enact a capacity to abuse her child, the state should leave her alone. No one should be accountable to the state or its citizens merely for the possession of *unexercised* capacities to act in improper ways.

This modification would allow for beneficial exercises of the greater powers that some have over others, yet install political and legal means for preventing persons with greater power from abusing those for whom they care or who are comparatively less powerful. However, this change would redefine Pettit's ideal of nondomination and alter his account considerably. His ideal would no longer prohibit the mere capacity to interfere arbitrarily with others. It would prohibit only actual exercises of that capacity. Yet if my various arguments about this point are correct, Pettit should make this adjustment.

The objection could be raised that a policy of punishing men for individual acts of dominating women will be insufficient to bring male domination to an end. Male domination as a social problem is not merely the aggregated result of individual men engaging in acts of domination of individual women. Instead male domination is a structural and institutionalized feature of a whole society. Social structures and institutions enable, encourage, and reward men for dominating women. These structures and institutions are not in any way diminished merely by policies of deterring individual men from dominating women, since law enforcement is inconsistent and may well be ineffective against the force of institutional support for male domination.

The institutional nature of male domination is indeed an important feature of this social problem and should be dealt with. However, the way to deal with it is not to make individual men vulnerable to governmental sanctions for the mere possession of capacities to dominate women that they do not exercise. Indeed, those who do not exercise their capacities may be precisely those persons who are actively trying to combat male domination in their personal lives. The institutions that reward or promote male domination can be reformed by means other than the governmental control of men's unexercised capacities for dominating women; for example, institutions of public education can promote egalitarian treatment of females and males in all educational contexts and thereby provide models of mutually respectful interaction between the genders. Although Pettit does not emphasize these structural social reforms, they are not inconsistent with his account and suggest an additional amendment to his account that would improve its ability to deal with male domination.

Still More About Arbitrariness

I have just maintained that Pettit's definition of arbitrary interference in terms of mere capacities to interfere is too wide in scope. A different part of Pettit's definition of arbitrary interference, however, is too narrow. This is the notion of lacking regard for the interests or ideas of the person who is being interfered with. Sometimes, in practices of male domination, men act as protectors or breadwinners to women and, just to the extent of this protective or breadwinning behavior, men might genuinely be serving those women's interests – and even doing so in accord with the ideas these particular women happen to have about male gallantry or male role responsibilities. Men's protective and breadwinning behaviors, in themselves, have often been genuine. Millions of men have really earned income for households in which their wives had no alternative sources of support and may have genuinely protected their wives against intruders or other threats. Yet these behaviors often occur within a larger pattern of behavior that also includes the subordination of the women who are being protected. Without much conscious thought about it, a man who "brings home the bacon" for his "little woman" may simply assume she will attend to his domestic needs, be sexually available at all times, and do what he says. He may regard his home as his "castle" and assume that he will – and should – "wear the pants" around the house. He may think that this arrangement is "for her own good." Despite the genuine benefits such a man confers on his wife, he still dominates her overall in his relationship with her.

One sort of domination that Pettit's account may miss is that which characterizes a whole relationship in which the dominator does pay some regard to the ideas or interests of the dominated person. Someone who has an ongoing relationship with another person may dominate her even if some of his actions toward her are beneficial and protective. Traditional long-term heterosexual relationships can be complex, featuring many diverse and interwoven strands of interactions. Some of those strands may genuinely serve a woman's interests. Genuine benefits are usually parts of the "bargain" that many women have acquired in traditional marriage. A man's behavior that benefits a woman may not be easy to isolate from an overall relationship with her in which, say, he determines where the family lives, whether his wife works outside the home, whether or not she can have an abortion during a difficult pregnancy in her forties, and so on. The occasional benefits he confers may make a dominator feel entitled to dominate his partner, as if he had earned this privilege in exchange for the good he does her. A man's domination of a woman may be inextricable from the pattern of occasional benefits he confers on her; the latter may seem – to both parties – to justify the former.

Thus a complex and interconnected set of behaviors comprising a whole relationship may still constitute a relationship of domination despite involving a great deal of behavior that does track the interests or ideas – and maybe both – of the one dominated. Pettit himself sees that a whole relationship can be what involves domination. He writes that "Domination . . . is exemplified by the *relationship* of master to slave or master to servant" (Pettit 1997: 22, italics mine), and this, even in cases in which the master is benign and does not actually interfere arbitrarily with the slave. My point is that a whole relationship can be one of domination even though it involves interactions in which the powerful party does *benefit* the weaker party some of the time. Thus interference that is not arbitrary, in that it tracks the interests or ideas of the weaker party, might well be positively present in (relationships of) domination. In order to apply to whole, complex relationships, the concept of domination should not be defined so as to make a complete disregard of the dominated person's interests and ideas a necessary condition of its application.

One way to modify Pettit's account to accommodate this point is to differentiate acts of domination from relationships of domination. Pettit's definition as it stands seems tailored to acts of domination. The conception of a dominating relationship should allow for the possibility of occasions on which the dominating party does track the interests or ideas of the weaker party. To be sure, if a relationship is one of domination, then one party must often and substantially disregard the interests or ideas of the other party. Yet there may be many interactions within a dominating relationship which, if regarded out of context, would appear not to constitute domination at all. Thus, a relationship can constitute domination even if one party sometimes, perhaps often, pays regard to the interests or ideas of the other party. My tentative reformulation of Pettit's criterion to take account of this point is this: a relationship is one of domination when, over the course of time, one party interferes arbitrarily in a substantial way with the other party and the other party does not do the same in return. Whether a relationship is one of domination must be determined by grasping the relationship as a whole.

Arbitrariness: Ignoring Interests, Ideas, or Both?

An act of interference is arbitrary, according to Pettit, if "it is subject just to the *arbitrium*, the decision or judgment, of the agent; the agent was in a position to choose it or not choose it, at their pleasure." The agent ignores something important about the person subjected to the interference. However, what Pettit thinks the agent ignores is not always specified in the same way. Pettit often writes that arbitrary interference "is chosen or rejected without reference to the interests, or the opinions, of those affected." On this formulation, interference is arbitrary if it ignores *two* things about the subjected party: her interests and her opinions. However, following the passage just quoted, Pettit writes, "The choice is not forced to track what the *interests* of those others require *according to* their own *judgements*" (Pettit 1997: 55, italics mine). This second formulation construes acts of interference as domination simply if they disregard certain *ideas* of the subject, namely, her ideas about her own interests.

Finally, a third formulation is suggested in still other passages. For example, Pettit claims, "an act of interference will be *non*arbitrary to the extent that it is forced to track the interests *and* ideas of the person suffering the interference. Or . . . at least forced to track the relevant ones" (Pettit 1997: 55). Pettit does not say whether he is here expressing a necessary or a sufficient condition for interference to count as nonarbitrary. If this formulation expresses a necessary condition, then it would count interference as nonarbitrary (and, thus, as nondomination) only if the interference tracked *both* the interests *and* ideas of the person subjected to it. In that case, interference would constitute domination even if it disregarded only one of the two features about a subject, *either* her interests *or* her ideas.

Since Pettit's characterization of arbitrariness, and therefore of domination, seems to vary, and he does not specify in each case whether he is stating necessary or sufficient conditions, his exact conception in unclear. The key question is: which understanding of acts of arbitrary interference illuminates the nature of domination best? Is it interference that: (1) ignores both her interests and her ideas; (2) ignores either her interests or her ideas (but not necessarily both); or (3) ignores her interests as she judges them to be? The third sort of case may seem to be a mere instance of the second sort of case; it involves ignoring certain ideas that someone has (about her interests) but not necessarily her (actual) interests. However, I single it out for special attention since I believe that, with qualifications, it provides the best account of the nature of domination. More on this below.

Why not the first formulation, namely, that acts of interference are arbitrary (and therefore constitute domination) if they ignore both the subject's interests *and* her ideas? If this formulation is meant to express a necessary or definitive condition of domination, then treatment does not constitute domination if it ignores only the subject's interests or only her ideas. The problem is that this formulation is too narrow. It rules out certain types of cases that do seem to involve something like domination. Suppose I treat someone in a way that promotes her interests but that she rejects because she disagrees that those are her actual interests. I ignore her judgment and impose my treatment on her. Even if my treatment of her does promote her actual interests, there is something wrong with the way I override or ignore her own judgment about how she wants to be treated. From a first-person perspective, such treatment would seem like being dominated. A certain kind of respect for persons calls for taking account of someone's perspective in some way even when she is wrong. The first formulation identifies a type of treatment that is *sufficient* to constitute domination: one party ignores the ideas *and* interests of the other party. I suggest, however, that it does not express a necessary, or *defining*, condition for domination.

What about the second formulation, namely, that an act of interference is arbitrary and amounts to domination in case one party treats another in disregard of either the other's interests or her ideas but not necessarily both? On this approach, domination need not involve ignoring both a person's interests and her perspective. The problem with this formulation is that it is too wide; it counts as domination certain kinds of treatment that seem not to be so. Suppose someone misunderstands her own interests. Her ideas thus run contrary to those interests. If I were to treat her in accord with the way she wants to be treated, I would be harming her in some way that she does not grasp.

My treatment would accord with her judgment about what she wants or what she thinks is best for her. I might be doing her a grave harm but she accepts it or regards it as appropriate. Yet despite her acceptance, this treatment counts as domination under this second formulation. The treatment does seem problematic but, as I shall argue shortly, the problem is not that of domination.

The third formulation on our list counts as domination only those types of treatment that ignore someone's perspective. The third formulation, to reiterate, is that interference is arbitrary, and constitutes domination, in case it ignores the subject's interests as she judges them to be. Notice that this formulation construes interference as domination only when it disregards certain ideas of the subject, namely, her ideas about her own interests. This formulation ignores the subject's actual interests. On what basis should we choose between the second and third formulations? If a person's interests and her perspective are equally relevant to the question of whether she is dominated, then the second formulation is the better of the two. However, if a person's perspective is more important to the nature of domination than are her interests, then the third formulation is the better of the two. The latter alternative is, I believe, the better one. Here is why.

Primary dictionary definitions of "to dominate" include "to rule, to govern, to predominate over" (*Webster's* 1983: 544), and "to bear rule over, control, sway; to have a commanding influence on; to master" (OED 1971: 595). The predominant idea in these definitions is that of ruling. To rule someone is to influence, guide, or direct her, usually in virtue of some authority one exercises over her (*Webster's* 1983: 1,585). Ruling someone is exercising a form of control that ignores or contravenes her own ideas about how she wants or thinks she ought to be treated. This form of control contrasts with that which is imposed on someone who either lacks ideas of her own about how she wants or ought to be treated or who agrees or accepts the treatment. The former sort of control, ruling or dominating someone, is achieved by compelling obedience from the subject or by overcoming her resistance. In the latter sort of case, the subject does not resist. For someone to be dominated, in the sense of being ruled or governed, she must be capable of apprehending what is happening to her and of having a contrary frame of mind. Domination, in the special sense I am isolating, is arbitrary and effective interference in the choices of someone who rejects or resists that treatment.

My proposal is to treat behavior as domination only if it runs contrary to the ideas or judgment of the one who is subjected to it. This contrariness is a necessary condition for behavior to constitute domination. If a dominant party treats a person in ways that merely harm her interests but do not ignore her perspective (or if she does not have any ideas about how she wants to be, or should be, treated), then we should say she is injured rather dominated. It is possible to harm someone's interests without dominating her, that is, without ruling her, without imposing treatment on her that opposes her own ideas about how she wants or thinks she ought to be treated.

This is not to say that injury is a lesser moral problem than domination. Injuring someone, harming her interests, may be just as serious as dominating her or may be even more serious. Many of the most egregious harms, such as torture, rape, and murder, involve injuries to the victim that are far worse than the harm involved in ignoring her perspective. Some forms of treatment, of course, can involve multiple kinds of harm. Yet, in some of these cases the domination may not be the worst part of the wrong done. However, when harms are mixed, the dimension that constitutes the domination is that which involves ignoring or overriding the victim's own perspective about her interests.

If harms to interests can be worse than domination, why bother to differentiate the harm of domination and to isolate it from the rest? One reason for differentiating domination, as I define it, from other harms is that harms that do and harms that do not conflict with a subject's ideas about her own interests need to be remedied differently. If someone is injured in a way that does not conflict with any of her ideas about her interests or how she wants to be treated, then she may not realize that she is injured. She may accept the injurious treatment unquestioningly as legitimate or simply have no ideas about the matter. Dominating someone, on my interpretation, involves treatment that contrasts with what the victim wants or thinks she deserves. The victim rejects the treatment inflicted on her. She believes that she ought to do something to resist that treatment, something that is not true of someone whose interests are harmed but who does not recognize that this is so. A person who views her treatment as unwanted or unacceptable may try to resist it actively, and friends or supportive social services may have an easier time of helping her to succeed in doing so.

I have been arguing that domination is best thought of as treatment that disregards the perspective, judgments, and ideas of the person who is subjected to it, indeed that runs contrary to those ideas. However some types of cases seem like counterexamples to my position. Suppose a woman is being abused by her husband but does not consider his physical assaults on her to be "abuse" because she does not realize that she does not deserve to be treated this way. Suppose also that she has a friend who understands what is happening and who could interfere effectively to stop the abusive treatment inflicted on her. This intervention would go against the abused woman's own ideas about how she wants to be treated or believes she ought to be treated. On my account of domination, the friend's interference would amount to domination while the husband's abusive treatment, because it accords with the abused woman's own ideas about her interests, would not. In this sort of situation, we seem to have two relationships that are both counterexamples to my account, one that suggests my account is too wide and one that suggests my account is too narrow.

The most troublesome cases seem to be ones in which, like that of the acquiescent abused woman, a person is being treated in a seriously harmful way yet does not grasp that treatment as harm, perhaps because she misunderstands her own interests. In those cases, the harm to her interests is still harm even if she does not recognize it to be so. However, because such treatment accords with the way the woman wants or thinks she ought to be treated, I suggest that we do not call that treatment domination. "Domination" is, of course, not the only term available to us for moral criticism. We have a rich set of moral concepts for identifying harms that the recipient may not reject or oppose. There are harms of abuse, exploitation, humiliation, shaming, ridicule, and so on. These are all types of treatment that a recipient may regard as acceptable. The treatment in such cases does not necessarily run contrary to the ideas of the recipient. This does not mean that these forms of treatment are morally benign. However, the moral wrong is something other than domination. If I am right about this, then the abused woman's relationship to her husband in my example does not show that my conception of domination is overly narrow.

Is it overly wide? What about the cases in which one person interferes in another person's life to serve the interests of the recipient, even though the recipient does not recognize that this is what is going on. What about the friend in my earlier example who tries to help an abused woman by putting a stop to the abusive situation, contrary to the wishes of the abused woman? Cases such as these fit the definition of "domination" I have given so far. However, there seems to be something wrong in labeling as "domination" behavior which is intended to help a person who is in trouble.

The solution to this problem is to build exceptions into the idea of domination. The questions is: what, in general, would make interference that disregards a recipient's ideas about her own interests nevertheless not domination? At least two conditions seem relevant. First, the interference must be aimed at the well-being of the recipient in some important respect. It should be undertaken genuinely for the sake of some important interest of hers. Second, the interference should be carried out with expressions of clear concern for the recipient's well-being. The one imposing the treatment should appeal to the recipient's understanding, explain the nature and intent of the treatment, attempt to convince the recipient to change her mind, and, if these attempts fail, still treat the recipient with as much care and restraint as the situation allows. The manner of intervention should convey the agent's concern for the recipient's interests. If I treat you in some way for your own good that you nevertheless reject, but I do not explain what I am doing or attempt to convince you that it really is good for you and I ignore your protests in the process, then this treatment is a type of domination, even if done for your own good. In other words, there are dominating and nondominating ways to intervene in someone's life to protect interests of hers that she resists protecting. The dominating interventions are those that also disregard her perspective. At stake is a kind of respect for the person whose perspective is being overridden for the sake of her own well-being (cf. Friedman 2003: ch. 3).

Thus, we should distinguish between utterly disregarding someone's perspective, treating her with no concern for her own ideas about how she wants to be treated, and treating her in a way that runs contrary to how she wants to be treated but that takes account of her perspective and shows this by trying to convince her to change her mind, expressing concern for her well-being, and so on. These respectful forms of intervention, though they run contrary to the judgment of the recipient, do not constitute domination. Instead, they constitute paternalism – or parentalism (Kultgen 1995, *passim*). This type of treatment may well be warranted in cases in which the recipient's neglected interests are serious enough.

In general, then, domination is arbitrary interference in someone's choices that runs contrary to the perspective, ideas, or judgment of the recipient about how she wants to be treated – except when the interference is (1) for the sake of an important interest of the recipient, contrary to her ideas about it, and is (2) carried out in a manner that pays due regard to her perspective in various ways. In these exceptional cases, the interference amounts to paternalism (parentalism) but not domination.

Women as a Group

Pettit argues that a person is free of domination only "so far as non-domination is ensured for those in the same vulnerability class" as she is, that is, only so far as those of her "ilk" are also free of domination. She is dominated to the extent that others like her "in matters of resistance and exposure to interference" are also dominated. If women are not protected against abusive male behavior by law or culture, then "any woman can be abused on an arbitrary basis by her husband" and "womanhood is a badge of vulnerability in this regard." In such a situation, Pettit claims, even a woman whose husband is unlikely to interfere arbitrarily with her is still dominated by him (Pettit 1997: 122–3).

Pettit's view seems to group all women together in the same vulnerability class. He does not consider the differences among women that not only make them vulnerable in different ways to male domination but that also make some women vulnerable to domination by other women. One of the most far-reaching trends in feminism throughout the past three decades has been the growing recognition of differences among women themselves and the ways in which women are socially positioned with respect to each other (cf. Hackett & Haslanger 2006). Some women are very privileged with respect to other women in virtue of such social categorizations as race, religion, sexuality, class, age, or able-ness. Early in the "second wave" of the feminist movement, lesbian feminists challenged the universalistic claims of oppression made by heterosexual feminists and black feminists challenged the universalistic claims of oppression made by white feminists. These and other complex female identities seem to demarcate significant differences of experience, interest, and perspective. It cannot be presumed that persons who are all women but who differ in other socially salient identities nevertheless share identical interests or ideas "as women."

Given this diversity among women, it is not clear what reference class Pettit could cite when offering specific criteria for determining whether an individual woman is being dominated. Could Pettit reply that the significant group identities in his account should simply be complex identities such as Asian-American middle-class lesbian? This approach does not seem to be workable. These complex categories would be too precise to be the basis of any well-known schemes of social understanding. Yet women with complex identities of these sorts should be as free of domination as anyone else. The solution to this problem, I suggest, is to define the arbitrariness of (dominating) interference in individual terms. A woman experiences male domination, on the face of it, if a man or men treat her in ways that ignore her perspective, judgments, and ideas. What she thinks about her own interests and about the forms of interfering treatment to which she is vulnerable may well differ from the ideas that other women have about themselves. There is no need for uniformity in specifying this part of the account of domination.

An individualistic treatment of arbitrariness does not preclude the institutional response to male domination that I mentioned earlier. Even if we need to understand a particular man's domination of a particular woman in terms of that woman's own judgments and perspective, we can still grasp how social structures and institutions broadly speaking permit, encourage, and reward men in general for intervening in women's lives without reference to whatever particular ideas those women may have about how they want to live. From the standpoint of traditional social institutions, it does not matter much how particular women want to live their lives. Yet the arbitrariness of a dominating male intervention in a woman's life is precisely that her particular perspective is ignored.

Conclusion

I have suggested these modifications to Pettit's ideal of freedom as nondomination:

1. Domination should not be defined as the mere capacity for arbitrary interference in someone's choices because this definition would make domination so ubiquitous that only a totalitarian state could suppress it; instead it should be defined only as the exercise of arbitrary interference in someone's choices.

2. The capacity for arbitrary interference is also a capacity for beneficial nonarbitrary caring for dependents and others; thus this capacity should be regulated to prevent abuses but not suppressed altogether lest we lose the crucial capacity to care for the dependents among us.

3. Actions that seem to be benign because they do pay some regard to the interests or ideas of the person subject to them might nevertheless be integral parts of relationships that amount to domination overall. Thus acts of regard for the interests and ideas of someone are not sufficient to indicate nondomination in a relationship; those acts must be considered in the context of the relationships of which they are integrally a part.

4. Domination should be understood as the treatment of someone that conflicts with her ideas about how she wants to be treated but not necessarily with her interests. This holds except when the treatment aims at the recipient's well-being and is carried out with expressions of concern for her and with some sort of genuine regard for her perspective.

5. Women are members of so many diverse other groups that a single, homogeneous understanding of women's vulnerability to male domination is not feasible. A more individualized understanding of particular cases of male domination may better capture that diversity. Yet this understanding does not preclude recognizing that male domination is a structural and institutional problem.

These changes would help to make Pettit's civic republican ideal of freedom as nondomination even more useful than it already is in helping us to understand and bring an end to male domination.

ACKNOWLEDGMENTS

I am grateful to Larry May, Anne Margaret Baxley, Cécile Laborde, John Maynor, members of the Washington University Workshop on Politics, Ethics, and Society, and the philosophy colloquium audience at Saint Louis University for comments on earlier drafts of this paper.

REFERENCES

Berlin, Isaiah. (1969). *Four Essays on Liberty*. London: Oxford University Press. "Two Concepts of Liberty" was delivered as an Inaugural Lecture at the University of Oxford on October 31, 1958, and published that year by the Clarendon Press.

Friedman, Marilyn. (2003). *Autonomy, Gender, Politics.* New York: Oxford University Press.

Hackett, Elizabeth and Sally Haslanger (eds.) (2006). *Theorizing Feminisms: A Reader.* New York: Oxford University Press.

Hirschmann, Nancy. (2003). *The Subject of Liberty: Toward a Feminist Theory of Freedom.* Princeton: Princeton University Press.

Kittay, Eva Feder. (1999). *Love's Labor: Essays on Women, Equality, and Dependency.* New York: Routledge.

Kittay, Eva Feder and Ellen K. Feder (eds.) (2002). *The Subject of Care: Feminist Perspectives on Dependency.* Lanham, MD: Rowman & Littlefield.

Kultgen, John. (1995). *Autonomy and Intervention: Parentalism in the Caring Life.* New York: Oxford University Press.

Oxford English Dictionary, Compact Edition. (1971). Glasgow: Oxford University Press.

Pettit, Philip. (1997). *Republicanism: A Theory of Freedom and Government.* Oxford: Oxford University Press.

Pettit, Philip. (2002). "Keeping republican freedom simple: on a difference with Quentin Skinner." *Political Theory*, 30, 339–356.

Phillips, Anne. (2000). "Survey Article: Feminism and Republicanism: Is This a Plausible Alliance?" *Journal of Political Theory*, 8, 279–93.

Rawls, John. (1995). *Political Liberalism.* New York: Columbia University Press.

Ruddick, Sara. (1989). *Maternal Thinking.* New York: Beacon Press.

Sevenhuijsen, Selma. (1998). *Citizenship and the Ethics of Care: Feminist Considerations on Justice, Morality and Politics,* tr. Liz Savage. London: Routledge.

Tronto, Joan. (1993). *Moral Boundaries: A Political Argument for an Ethic of Care.* New York: Routledge.

Webster's New Twentieth Century Dictionary of the English Language (1983). Unabridged; 2nd ed. New York: Prentice-Hall.

Index

NOTE: Page numbers in bold indicate a chapter by that author.

269